CONTEMPORARY FICTION IN AMERICA AND ENGLAND, 1950-1970

AMERICAN LITERATURE, ENGLISH LITERATURE, AND WORLD LITERATURES IN ENGLISH: AN INFORMATION GUIDE SERIES

Series Editor: Theodore Grieder, Curator, Division of Special Collections, Fales Library, New York University, New York, New York

Associate Editor: Duane DeVries, Assistant Professor, Polytechnic Institute of New York, Brooklyn, New York

Other books on American and English literature in this series:

AMERICAN FICTION TO 1900—*Edited by David Kirby*

AMERICAN FICTION, 1900-1950—*Edited by James Woodress*

CONTEMPORARY DRAMA IN AMERICA AND ENGLAND, 1950-1970—*Edited by Richard Harris***

CONTEMPORARY POETRY IN AMERICA AND ENGLAND, 1950-1970—*Edited by Calvin Skaggs***

ENGLISH FICTION, 1660-1800—*Edited by Jerry C. Beasley***

ENGLISH FICTION, 1800-1850—*Edited by Duane DeVries***

ENGLISH FICTION, 1900-1950—*Edited by Thomas Rice***

THE ENGLISH LITERARY JOURNAL TO 1900—*Edited by Robert B. White, Jr.*

THE ENGLISH LITERARY JOURNAL, 1900-1950—*Edited by Michael N. Stanton***

THE LITERARY JOURNAL IN AMERICA TO 1900—*Edited by Edward Chielens*

THE LITERARY JOURNAL IN AMERICA, 1900-1950—*Edited by Edward Chielens**

THE LITTLE MAGAZINE IN AMERICA, 1950-1975—*Edited by Robert Bertholf***

*in press
**in preparation

The above series is part of the

GALE INFORMATION GUIDE LIBRARY

The Library consists of a number of separate series of guides covering major areas in the social sciences, humanities, and current affairs.

General Editor: Paul Wasserman, Professor and former Dean, School of Library and Information Services, University of Maryland

CONTEMPORARY FICTION IN AMERICA AND ENGLAND, 1950-1970

A GUIDE TO INFORMATION SOURCES

Volume 10 in the American Literature, English Literature, and World Literatures in English Information Guide Series

Alfred F. Rosa

Associate Professor of English
University of Vermont

Paul A. Eschholz

Associate Professor of English
University of Vermont

Gale Research Company
Book Tower, Detroit, Michigan 48226

Library of Congress Cataloging in Publication Data

Rosa, Alfred F
    Contemporary fiction in America and England, 1950-1970.

    (American literature, English literature, and world literatures in
English; v. 10) (Gale information guide library)
    Includes index.
    1. American fiction--20th century--History and criticism--
Bibliography. 2. English fiction--20th century--History and criticism--
Bibliography. 3. American fiction--20th century--Bibliography.
4. English fiction--20th century--Bibliography. I. Eschholz, Paul A.,
joint author. II. Title.
Z1231.F4R57 [PS379]   016.823'9'1408   73-16990
ISBN 0-8103-1219-0

To our parents

VITAE

Alfred F. Rosa is currently associate professor of English at the University of Vermont. He received his B.A. from the University of Connecticut and his M.A. and Ph.D. from the University of Massachusetts. During 1973-74 he was a Fulbright lecturer on American literature and language in Italy. He is the author of numerous critical articles on language and American and English literature and has edited a collection of essays in honor of Charles Angoff to be published by Fairleigh Dickinson University Press.

Paul A. Eschholz is currently associate professor of English at the University of Vermont. He received his B.A. from Wesleyan University, his M.A. from the University of Vermont, and his Ph.D. from the University of Minnesota. Eschholz has authored articles on nineteenth-century American literature and linguistics. He has edited THE LITERATURE OF VERMONT: A SAMPLER (with A. W. Biddle), CRITICS ON WILLIAM DEAN HOWELLS, and VERMONT: A STUDY OF INDEPENDENCE.

Together Professors Rosa and Eschholz have coauthored critical articles and have edited, with Virginia P. Clark, LANGUAGE: INTRODUCTORY READINGS and LANGUAGE AWARENESS.

CONTENTS

Contents

Contents

Contents

INTRODUCTION

CONTEMPORARY FICTION IN AMERICA AND ENGLAND, 1950-1970 is a bibliography of novels and short stories by important literary figures writing in English today. Not all those writing today have been included; it is inevitable that critical judgments had to be made based on an author's productivity, readership, critical reputation, and general appeal, and the exigencies of space in a volume this size. This bibliography is the only one for this period that lists available primary materials as well as literary criticism. In compiling individual bibliographies for the authors included, our primary concern was comprehensiveness. Rather than be selective and make arbitrary decisions about critical judgments which themselves have not been subjected to the test of time, we thought it preferable to be thorough in our treatment of each author.

Part I, "Studies and Reference Works," is divided into four sections. Each entry in each of these sections is annotated. Section A lists historical studies of the period; we have tried to make this section as relevant as possible by including only those works in which the major emphasis is on the contemporary period. Section B includes American, British, and American and British reference works. Section C lists bibliographies, both American and British, for the period. Section D is a bibliography of individual studies or collections of essays on the contemporary novel. It is important to note that essays included in these collections are not cross-referenced under Critical Articles for each author.

Part II, "Journals Concerned with Contemporary Fiction," contains a listing of some journals devoted primarily to publishing articles on contemporary writers. This listing can be supplemented by the journals included in the Table of Useful Periodicals and Abbreviations.

Part III, "Individual Authors," is devoted to 136 authors, 80 American and 56 British. In selecting authors we have not restricted ourselves to England proper but have also included a small number of authors such as Chinua Achebe, Leonard Cohen, Mordecai Richler, and Samuel Beckett who reside outside of England. In addition to those authors whose initial or major works are clearly within the time period covered by this bibliography, we have also included authors such as Robert Penn Warren, H.E. Bates, C.P. Snow, Graham Greene, and Vladimir Nabokov, who were established authors before 1950 but who also continued to publish in the 1950s and 1960s. These authors, therefore, are not included in other volumes of the Gale Information Guide Series. We have also included authors such as Robert Coover, Paul Theroux, Jerzy Kosinski, Robert Shaw, and Sylvia Ashton-Warner, who did not begin to publish until well into the 1950s and 1960s and who, therefore, have little or no scholarly criticism devoted to them.

For the sake of clarity and accuracy, we have in all cases adhered to the 1970 terminus date for both primary and secondary works. All the authors in Part III are presented in alphabetical order; the format for each author entry is as follows:

A. Novels: These are listed chronologically by date of publication. The first American or English publication dates have been used except in cases where titles have been changed.

B. Short stories: Only collections of short stories are included. These are listed chronologically by date of publication.

C. Bibliographies: This section includes both bibliographical articles and books, listed alphabetically.

D. Critical books: These are listed alphabetically by author. Inevitably, they contain some biographical material.

E. Special issues: Listed alphabetically, these are special issues of a journal devoted to an author. The articles in the special issues are not listed separately in the sections on the critical articles.

F. Critical articles: These are listed alphabetically by the critic and often refer the user by abbreviations, given in the TABLE OF USEFUL PERIODICALS AND ABBREVIATIONS, to the journals in which the articles appear. Multiple critical articles by one author are listed alphabetically by title.

ACKNOWLEDGMENTS

We would like to express our appreciation to Dean William H. Macmillan and the Institutional Grants Committee of the Graduate College of the University of Vermont for a grant in aid for the preparation of the manuscript. We also owe a special note of gratitude to Lori Serratelli for her dauntless assistance in collecting bibliographical data, especially in the early stages of the project, and to Susan Danley for her work on the index. Finally, to Evelyn Kyle, our typist, for whom such acknowledgments have become commonplace, we offer our sincere thanks.

                                                          Alfred F. Rosa
                                                          Paul A. Eschholz

TABLE OF USEFUL PERODICALS AND ABBREVIATIONS

A&S	ARTS AND SCIENCES (New York University)
ABR	AMERICAN BENEDICTINE REVIEW
	ACCENT
	ADAM: INTERNATIONAL REVIEW
AI	AMERICAN IMAGO
AJP	AMERICAN JOURNAL OF PSYCHOANALYSIS
AL	AMERICAN LITERATURE
AlaR	ALABAMA REVIEW
ALitASH	ACTA LITTERARIA ACADEMIAE SCIENTIARUM HUNGARICAE (Budapest)
	ALPHABET
AmD	AMERICAN DIALOG
	AMERICA
	AMERICANA-AUSTRIACA
	AMERICAN HEBREW
	AMERICAN LITERARY REVIEW
	AMISTAD: WRITINGS ON BLACK HISTORY AND CULTURE
AN&Q	AMERICAN NOTES AND QUERIES
AnRev	ANCHOR REVIEW
AntigR	ANTIGONISH REVIEW
	APPROACH
AQ	AMERICAN QUARTERLY
AR	ANTIOCH REVIEW
	ARCADIA
ArlQ	ARLINGTON QUARTERLY

Periodicals and Abbreviations

ArQ	ARIZONA QUARTERLY
AS	AMERICAN SPEECH
ASch	AMERICAN SCHOLAR
ASoc	ARTS IN SOCIETY
	ASPECT
	ATLANTIC MONTHLY
	ATLANTIC REVIEW
AUC	ANALES DE LA UNIVERSIDAD DE CHILE
	AUDIT
AUMLA	JOURNAL OF THE AUSTRALASIAN UNIVERSITIES LANGUAGE AND LITERATURE ASSOCIATION
	AUT AUT
BA	BOOKS ABROAD
BAASB	BRITISH ASSOCIATION FOR AMERICAN STUDIES BULLETIN
	BALCONY
BB	BULLETIN OF BIBLIOGRAPHY
BDEC	BULLETIN OF THE DEPARTMENT OF ENGLISH OF CALCUTTA UNIVERSITY
BFLS	BULLETIN DE LA FACULTE DES LETTRES DE STRASBOURG
BI	BOOKS AT IOWA
BJA	BRITISH JOURNAL OF AESTHETICS
	BLACKFRIARS
BlackW	BLACK WORLD (formerly NEGRO DIGEST)
BLM	BONNIERS LITTERARA MAGASIN
BNYPL	BULLETIN OF THE NEW YORK PUBLIC LIBRARY
	BOOKS AND BOOKMEN
	BOOK WEEK
	BRITAIN TODAY
BRMMLA	BULLETIN OF THE ROCKY MOUNTAIN MODERN LANGUAGE ASSOCIATION
BSUF	BALL STATE UNIVERSITY FORUM (formerly BALL STATE TEACHERS COLLEGE FORUM)
BSTCF	BALL STATE TEACHERS COLLEGE FORUM
BuR	BUCKNELL REVIEW
BYUS	BRIGHAM YOUNG UNIVERSITY STUDIES
	CALIBAN (Toulouse)

CalR	CALCUTTA REVIEW
	CAMBRIDGE JOURNAL
CamQ	CAMBRIDGE QUARTERLY
CamR	CAMBRIDGE REVIEW
	CANADIAN LIBRARY
CanL	CANADIAN LITERATURE
	CARNEGIE MAGAZINE
CarQ	CAROLINA QUARTERLY (Chapel Hill, North Carolina)
CathW	CATHOLIC WORLD
CC	CROSS CURRENTS (West Nyack, New York)
CE	COLLEGE ENGLISH
CEA	CEA CRITIC
CEJ	CALIFORNIA ENGLISH JOURNAL
CentR	THE CENTENNIAL REVIEW (Michigan State University)
CHA	CUADERNOS HISPANOAMERICANOS (Madrid)
ChC	CHRISTIAN CENTURY
	CHELSEA
	CHIMERA
ChiR	CHICAGO REVIEW
ChrPer	CHRISTIAN PERSPECTIVES (Toronto)
ChS	CHRISTIAN SCHOLAR
CimR	CIMARRON REVIEW (Oklahoma State University)
	CITHARA (St. Bonaventure University)
CJF	CHICAGO JEWISH FORUM
CL	COMPARATIVE LITERATURE
CLAJ	COLLEGE LANGUAGE ASSOCIATION JOURNAL (Morgan State College, Baltimore)
ClareQ	CLAREMONT QUARTERLY
CLC	COLUMBIA LIBRARY COLUMNS
CLS	COMPARATIVE LITERATURE STUDIES (University of Illinois)
CM	CARLETON MISCELLANY
ColF	COLUMBIA FORUM (formerly COLUMBIA UNIVERSITY FORUM)
ColQ	COLORADO QUARTERLY
Com	COMMENTARY
	CONGRESS BI-WEEKLY

ConL	CONTEMPORARY LITERATURE (formerly WISCONSIN STUDIES IN CONTEMPORARY LITERATURE)
ContempR	CONTEMPORARY REVIEW (London)
	CONTEMPORA (Atlanta, Georgia)
	CONVIVIUM (Bologna)
CRAS	CANADIAN REVIEW OF AMERICAN STUDIES
	CRESSET (Valparaiso University)
	CRISIS
Crit	CRITIQUE: STUDIES IN MODERN FICTION
	CRITIC
	CRITICAL ESSAYS IN ENGLISH AND AMERICAN LITERATURE
	CRITICISM (Wayne State University)
	CRITIQUE (Paris)
CritQ	CRITICAL QUARTERLY
CritR	CRITICAL REVIEW (University of Melbourne)
CuF	COLUMBIA UNIVERSITY FORUM
	CULTURE
CWCP	CONTEMPORARY WRITERS IN CHRISTIAN PERSPECTIVE
Cweal	COMMONWEAL
	DAEDALUS
Delta	DELTA: THE CAMBRIDGE LITERARY REVIEW (Cambridge, England)
DeltaR	DELTA REVIEW
	DESCANT
	DIPLOMAT
	DISCOURSE
	DISSENT
DM	THE DUBLIN MAGAZINE (formerly THE DUBLINER)
DR	DALHOUSIE REVIEW
DU	DER DEUTSCHUNTERRICHT
DubR	DUBLIN REVIEW (London, now called WISEMAN REVIEW)
DUJ	DURHAM UNIVERSITY JOURNAL
DWB	DIETSCHE WARANDE EN BELFORT
EA	ETUDE ANGLAISES
E&S	ESSAYS AND STUDIES BY MEMBERS OF THE ENGLISH ASSOCIATION

ECr	L'ESPRIT CREATEUR (Lawrence, Kansas)
	ECRITS DU CANADA FRANCAISE
EDH	ESSAYS BY DIVERS HANDS
EIC	ESSAYS IN CRITICISM (Oxford)
EigoS	EIGO SEINEN [THE RISING GENERATION] (Tokyo)
Eire	IRELAND: A JOURNAL OF IRISH STUDIES
EJ	ENGLISH JOURNAL
Elem Eng	ELEMENTARY ENGLISH
ELH	JOURNAL OF ENGLISH LITERARY HISTORY
ELN	ENGLISH LANGUAGE NOTES
EM	ENGLISH MISCELLANY
	ENCOUNTER (London)
	ENGLISH (London)
EngR	ENGLISH RECORD
	ENVOY
	EPOCH
ES	ENGLISH STUDIES
ESA	ENGLISH STUDIES IN AFRICA (Johannesburg)
	ESPRIT
ESPSL	O ESTADO DE SAO PAULO, SUPPLEMENTO LITERARIO
	ESQUIRE
ESRS	EMPORIA STATE RESEARCH STUDIES
	EUROPE
	EVERGREEN REVIEW
Expl	EXPLICATOR
	EXPLORATIONS (Department of English, Government College, Lahore)
	EXPRESSION
	EXTRAPOLATION
	FACT
FaS	FAULKNER STUDIES
FH	FRANKFURTER HEFTE
	FILM SOCIETY REVIEW
	FITZGERALD NEWSLETTER
FL	FIGARO LITTERAIRE

FLe	LA FIERA LETTERARIA
FMod	FILOLOGIA MODERNA
	FOLIO
	FOLKLORE (London)
ForumH	FORUM (Houston)
	FOUR QUARTERS
FQ	FLORIDA QUARTERLY
FR	FRENCH REVIEW
	FREEDOMWAYS
FurmS	FURMAN STUDIES
	GALLERIA
GaR	GEORGIA REVIEW
	GENRE
	THE GRIFFIN
GRM	GERMANISCH-ROMANISCHE MONATSSCHRIFT, NEUE FOLGE
	GUARDIAN (Rangoon)
Harper's	HARPER'S MAGAZINE
HarvardA	HARVARD ADVOCATE
HC	THE HOLLINS CRITIC
HJ	HIBBERT JOURNAL (London)
	HOLIDAY
HoR	HOPKINS REVIEW
	HORISONT (Vasa)
	HORIZON
HPR	THE HOMILETIC AND PASTORAL REVIEW
HudR	HUDSON REVIEW
	HUMANIST
IEY	IOWA ENGLISH YEARBOOK
IJAS	INDIAN JOURNAL OF AMERICAN STUDIES
IJES	INDIAN JOURNAL OF ENGLISH STUDIES
ILA	INTERNATIONAL LITERARY ANNUAL (London)
	INDICE (Madrid)
	INFORMATIONS ET DOCUMENTS
	INOSTRANNAJA LITERATURA
	INSULA

	INVENTARIO
	IRISH DIGEST
IrEccRec	IRISH ECCLESIASTICAL RECORD
IrM	IRISH MONTHLY
	IZRAZ (Sarajevo)
JA	JAHRBUCH FUR AMERIKASTUDIEN
JAAC	JOURNAL OF AESTHETICS AND ART CRITICISM
JAF	JOURNAL OF AMERICAN FOLKLORE
JAMS	JOURNAL OF AMERICAN STUDIES
	JAMMU AND KASHMIR UNIVERSITY REVIEW
JeuneA	JEUNE AFRIQUE (Paris)
JGE	JOURNAL OF GENERAL EDUCATION
	JIMBUN KENKYU
	JOURNAL OF EXISTENTIAL PSYCHOLOGY
JML	JOURNAL OF MODERN LITERATURE
JPC	JOURNAL OF POPULAR CULTURE
	JUBILEE
	JUDAISM
KAL	KYUSHA AMERICAN LITERATURE (Fukuoka, Japan)
KanQ	KANSAS QUARTERLY (formerly KANSAS MAGAZINE)
KFQ	KEYSTONE FOLKLORE QUARTERLY
KM	KANSAS MAGAZINE
KN	KWARTALNIK NEOFILOLOGICZNY (Warsaw)
KQ	KORFANA QUARTERLY (Seoul)
KR	KENYON REVIEW
KyR	KENTUCKY REVIEW
	LANDFALL
L&I	LITERATURE AND IDEOLOGY (Montreal)
L&P	LITERATURE AND PSYCHOLOGY (University of Hartford)
LanM	LES LANGUES MODERNES
LCrit	LITERARY CRITERION (University of Mysore, India)
LCUT	LIBRARY CHRONICLE OF THE UNIVERSITY OF TEXAS
LetN	LETTRES NOUVELLES
	LETTURE
LHR	LOCK HAVEN REVIEW (Lock Haven State College, Pa.)

LHY	LITERARY HALF-YEARLY (Mysore, India)
	LIFE
	LINGUISTICS
	LISTENER
LitR	LITERARY REVIEW (Fairleigh Dickinson University)
	LITTERAIR PASPOORT
LonM	LONDON MAGAZINE
LS	LE LINGUE STRANIERE (Roma)
Luc	LUCEAFARUL (Bucharest)
	LUGANO REVIEW
LWU	LITERATUR IN WISSENSCHAFT UND UNTERRICHT (Kiel)
	MAG LITTERAIRE
Mahfil	MAHFIL: A QUARTERLY OF SOUTH ASIAN LITERATURE (Michigan State University)
	MAINSTREAM
	MALAHAT REVIEW
	MAPOCHO (Santiago)
MASJ	MIDCONTINENT AMERICAN STUDIES JOURNAL
	MASSES AND MAINSTREAM
MCR	CRITICAL REVIEW: MELBOURNE
MdF	MERCURE DE FRANCE
Meanjin	MEANJIN QUARTERLY (University of Melbourne)
	MELBOURNE CRITICAL QUARTERLY
	MERKUR
MFS	MODERN FICTION STUDIES
	MIDSTREAM
MinnR	MINNESOTA REVIEW
MissQ	MISSISSIPPI QUARTERLY
MLN	MODERN LANGUAGE NOTES
MLQ	MODERN LANGUAGE QUARTERLY
ModA	MODERN AGE (Chicago)
ModSp	MODERN SPRACHEN: ORGAN DES VERBANDES DES OSTER-REICHISCHEN NEUPHILOLOGEN FUR MODERNE SPRACHEN, LITTERATUR, UND PADAGOGIK
Monat	DER MONAT
	MONATSHEFTE

	LE MONDE
	MONTH
Mosaic	MOSAIC: A JOURNAL FOR THE COMPARATIVE STUDY OF LITERATURE AND IDEAS
	MOTIVE
MP	MODERN PHILOLOGY
MQ	MIDWEST QUARTERLY (Pittsburgh, Kansas)
MQR	MICHIGAN QUARTERLY REVIEW
MR	MASSACHUSETTS REVIEW
MRR	MAD RIVER REVIEW (Dayton, Ohio)
MSE	MASSACHUSETTS STUDIES IN ENGLISH
MSpr	MODERNA SPRAK (Stockholm)
	MYTHLORE (Maywood, California)
NALF	NEGRO AMERICAN LITERATURE FORUM
N&Q	NOTES AND QUERIES
	NATION
NatR	NATIONAL REVIEW
NegroD	NEGRO DIGEST
	NEW DURHAM
NewL	NEW LEADER
	NEW LEFT REVIEW
	NEW VOICES
	NEW WORLDS
	NEW YORK HERALD TRIBUNE
	NIEKAS
NL	NOUVELLES LITTERAIRES
NMQ	NEW MEXICO QUARTERLY
NMW	NOTES ON MISSISSIPPI WRITERS (University of Southern Mississippi)
	NORSEMAN
	NORTH AMERICAN REVIEW
NOVEL	NOVEL: A FORUM ON FICTION
NRep	NEW REPUBLIC
NRF	NOUVELLE REVUE FRANCAISE
NS	DIE NEUEREN SPRACHEN
NStat	NEW STATESMAN

NWR	NORTHWEST REVIEW
NY	NEW YORKER
NyA	NYA ARGUS
NYRB	NEW YORK REVIEW OF BOOKS
NYTBR	NEW YORK TIMES BOOK REVIEW
NYTMag	NEW YORK TIMES MAGAZINE
NZSJ	NEW ZEALAND SLAVONIA JOURNAL
OB	ORD OCH BILD
Orcrist	ORCRIST: BULLETIN OF THE UNIVERSITY OF WISCONSIN J.R.R. TOLKIEN SOCIETY
	ORION
OUR	OHIO UNIVERSITY REVIEW
	OVERLAND
	PARAGONE
ParisR	PARIS REVIEW
PBSA	PAPERS OF THE BIBLIOGRAPHICAL SOCIETY OF AMERICA
PCP	PACIFIC COAST PHILOLOGY
PELL	PAPERS ON ENGLISH LANGUAGE AND LITERATURE
Per	PERSPECTIVE
	PER/SE
Person	THE PERSONALIST
	PERSPECTIVE ON IDEAS AND THE ARTS
	PERSPECTIVES USA
	PHOENIX (College of Charleston, South Carolina)
	PHYLON
	PLAYBOY
PLL	PAPERS ON LANGUAGE AND LITERATURE (formerly PAPERS ON ENGLISH LANGUAGE AND LITERATURE) (Southern Illinois University)
PMASAL	PAPERS OF THE MICHIGAN ACADEMY OF SCIENCE, ARTS, AND LETTERS
PMLA	PMLA: PUBLICATIONS OF THE MODERN LANGUAGE ASSOCIATION OF AMERICA
Ponte	IL PONTE
PQ	PHILOLOGICAL QUARTERLY
PR	PARTISAN REVIEW

	PREUVES
PrS	PRAIRIE SCHOONER
	PSYCHOTHERAPY
PW	PUBLISHER'S WEEKLY
QJS	QUARTERLY JOURNAL OF SPEECH
QQ	QUEENS QUARTERLY
Quadrant	QUADRANT: AN AUSTRALIAN BI-MONTHLY
	QUEST (Bombay)
	QUINZAINE LITTERAIRE
	RAMPARTS
RdP	REVUE DE PARIS
REL	REVIEW OF ENGLISH LITERATURE (Leeds)
Ren	RENASCENCE
	REPORTER
RevN	LA REVUE NOUVELLE (Paris)
RGB	REVUE GENERAL BELGE
RLM	LA REVUE DES LETTRES MODERNES
RLMC	RIVISTA DI LETTERATURE MODERNE E COMPARATE (Firenze)
RLV	REVUE DES LANGUES VIVANTES (Bruxelles)
RMS	RENAISSANCE AND MODERN STUDIES (University of Nottingham)
RomN	ROMANCE NOTES (University of North Carolina)
RoLit	ROMANIA LITERARA
RP	LA REVUE DE PARIS
RQ	RIVERSIDE QUARTERLY (University of Saskatchewan)
RS	RESEARCH STUDIES
RusR	RUSSIAN REVIEW
	RUSSAKAJA LETTATURA
SA	STUDI AMERICANI (Roma)
	SAMTIDEN
SAQ	SOUTH ATLANTIC QUARTERLY
SatR	SATURDAY REVIEW
SB	STUDIES IN BIBLIOGRAPHY: PAPERS OF THE BIBLIOGRAPHICAL SOCIETY OF THE UNIVERSITY OF VIRGINIA
	THE SCHOOL LIBRARIAN
	SCRUTINY

SDR	SOUTH DAKOTA REVIEW
SEL	STUDIES IN ENGLISH LITERATURE, 1500-1900
SELit	STUDIES IN ENGLISH LITERATURE (English Literary Society of Japan)
Serif	THE SERIF (Kent, Ohio)
SFQ	SOUTHERN FOLKLORE QUARTERLY
SG	STUDIUM GENERALE
SGG	STUDIA GERMANICA GANDENSIA
	SHENANDOAH
	SHIPPENSBURG STATE COLLEGE REVIEW
SHR	SOUTHERN HUMANITIES REVIEW
SLitI	STUDIES IN THE LITERARY IMAGINATION (Georgia State College)
SLJ	SOUTHERN LITERARY JOURNAL
SNL	SATIRE NEWSLETTER (State University College, Oneonta, New York)
SNNTS	STUDIES IN THE NOVEL (North Texas State University)
SoR	SOUTHERN REVIEW (Louisiana State University)
SoRA	SOUTHERN REVIEW: AN AUSTRALIAN JOURNAL OF LITERARY STUDIES (University of Adelaide)
SovL	SOVIET LITERATURE
	SPECTATOR
	SPECTRUM
	SPIEGHEL HISTORIAEL VAN DE BOND VAN GENTSTE GERMAN-ISTEN
SR	SEWANEE REVIEW
SSF	STUDIES IN SHORT FICTION (Newberry College, South Carolina)
SSI	SOCIAL SCIENCE INFORMATION
SSI	SCANDO-SLAVICA (Copenhagen)
StL	STUDIES ON THE LEFT
	STUDIES (Dublin)
	STUDIES IN ENGLISH LITERATURE AND LANGUAGE
	STUDIES IN HUMANITIES
	SUMMARY (London)
	SUR
SWR	SOUTHWEST REVIEW
Sym	SYMPOSIUM
	SYNTHESES

SZ	STIMMEN DER ZEIT
TamR	TAMARACK REVIEW (Toronto)
T&T	TIME AND TIDE (London)
TC	TWENTIETH CENTURY
TCL	TWENTIETH CENTURY LITERATURE
	THEOLOGY
	THEORIA
	THOTH (Department of English, Syracuse University)
	THOUGHT
	TIRADE (Antwerp)
TJ	TOLKIEN JOURNAL (Belknap College, New Hampshire)
TLS	[London] TIMES LITERARY SUPPLEMENT
TM	TEMPS MODERNES
	TOMORROW
	TOWN AND COUNTRY PLANNING
TP	TERZO PROGRAMMA (Roma)
TQ	TEXAS QUARTERLY (University of Texas)
	TRACE
Tradition	TRADITION: A JOURNAL OF ORTHODOX JEWISH THOUGHT
	TRANSATLANTIC REVIEW
TriQ	TRI-QUARTERLY (Evanston, Illinois)
TSL	TENNESSEE STUDIES IN LITERATURE
TSLL	TEXAS STUDIES IN LITERATURE AND LANGUAGE
TVUB	TIJDSCHRIFT VAN DE VRIJE UNIVERSITEIT VAN BRUSSEL
TWA	TRANSACTIONS OF THE WISCONSIN ACADEMY OF SCIENCES, ARTS, AND LETTERS
	UCLAN
UCQ	UNIVERSITY COLLEGE QUARTERLY (Michigan State University)
UDQ	UNIVERSITY OF DENVER QUARTERLY
UDR	UNIVERSITY OF DAYTON REVIEW
UKCR	UNIVERSITY OF KANSAS CITY REVIEW
	UMANESIMO (University of Maryland)
UMSE	UNIVERSITY OF MISSISSIPPI STUDIES IN ENGLISH
	UPSTREAM
UR	UNIVERSITY REVIEW (Kansas City, Missouri)

Periodicals and Abbreviations

UTQ	UNIVERSITY OF TORONTO QUARTERLY
UWR	UNIVERSITY OF WINDSOR REVIEW (Windsor, Ontario)
	VAR LOSEN
	VENTURE (University of Karachi)
VeP	VITA E PENSEIRO
VIG	DE VLAAMSE GIDS
	VOLUSIA REVIEW
VQR	VIRGINIA QUARTERLY REVIEW
WAL	WESTERN AMERICAN LITERATURE
WascanaR	WASCANA REVIEW (Regina, Saskatchewan)
	WATERLOO REVIEW
WF	WESTERN FOLKLORE
WHR	WESTERN HUMANITIES REVIEW
WiseR	WISEMAN REVIEW
WisSL	WISCONSIN STUDIES IN LITERATURE
WoR	WORLD REVIEW (University of Queensland, Australia)
WR	WESTERN REVIEW: A JOURNAL OF THE HUMANITIES
WSCL	WISCONSIN STUDIES IN CONTEMPORARY LITERATURE
WuW	WELT UND WORT
	WUWAHR
WVUPP	WEST VIRGINIA UNIVERSITY PHILOLOGICAL PAPERS
WWR	WALT WHITMAN REVIEW
WZUR	WISSENSCHAFTLICHE ZEITSCHRIFT DER U. ROSTOCK
XR	X, A QUARTERLY REVIEW
XUS	XAVIER UNIVERSITY STUDIES
YFS	YALE FRENCH STUDIES
YLM	YALE LITERARY MAGAZINE
YR	YALE REVIEW
ZAA	ZEITSCHRIFT FUR ANGLISTIK UND AMERIKANISTIK (East Berlin)
	ZAGAGLIA

Part I

STUDIES AND REFERENCE WORKS

Part I

STUDIES AND REFERENCE WORKS

A. LITERARY HISTORIES

Allen, Walter. THE MODERN NOVEL IN BRITAIN AND THE UNITED STATES. New York: E.P. Dutton & Co., 1964.

> Covers the period from 1920-60. This is a sequel to the author's THE ENGLISH NOVEL. No authors included whose first work appeared after 1955.

Allsop, Kenneth. THE ANGRY DECADE: A SURVEY OF THE CULTURAL REVOLT OF THE NINETEEN-FIFTIES. London: Owen, 1964.

> A careful study of the "Angry Young Men" movement.

Bradbury, John M. RENAISSANCE IN THE SOUTH: A CRITICAL HISTORY OF THE LITERATURE, 1920-1960. Chapel Hill: University of North Carolina Press, 1963.

> Useful discussions of lesser-known southern novelists.

Klein, Marcus, ed. THE AMERICAN NOVEL SINCE WORLD WAR II. Greenwich, Conn.: Fawcett, 1969.

> A collection of essays by leading critics and novelists which provides an overview of the period.

O'Connor, William Van. THE NEW UNIVERSITY WITS AND THE END OF MODERNISM. Carbondale: Southern Illinois University Press, 1963.

> Concerns the British novelists of the fifties who had university connections and who represented and reflected the social and cultural shifts in the welfare state.

Sampson, George. THE CONCISE CAMBRIDGE HISTORY OF ENGLISH LITERATURE. New York: Macmillan, 1941. 3rd ed. rev. by R.C. Churchill. New York: Cambridge University Press, 1970.

3

Standard reference work which is stronger on earlier periods.

WRITERS AT WORK: THE PARIS REVIEW INTERVIEWS. FIRST SERIES. Introduction by Malcolm Cowley. SECOND SERIES. Introduction by Van Wyck Brooks. THIRD SERIES. Introduction by Alfred Kazin. New York: Viking Press, 1959-67.

Invaluable interviews with Warren, Styron, Capote, Durrell, McCarthy, Ellison, Updike, and others.

B. REFERENCE WORKS

1. American

Hart, James D., ed. THE OXFORD COMPANION TO AMERICAN LITERATURE. 4th ed. New York: Oxford University Press, 1965.

Brief descriptions of authors and works. Better on writers well established before 1950.

Herzberg, Max, Jr., ed. THE READER'S ENCYCLOPEDIA OF AMERICAN LITERATURE. New York: Crowell, 1962.

Dictionary of authors, works, topics.

Kunitz, Stanley J., ed. TWENTIETH CENTURY AUTHORS: FIRST SUPPLEMENT. New York: H.W. Wilson, 1955.

Brief biographies, listings of primary works, and short bibliographies.

2. British

Harvey, Paul, ed. THE OXFORD COMPANION TO ENGLISH LITERATURE. 4th ed., rev. Oxford: Clarendon Press, 1967.

Brief descriptions of authors and works. Better on writers well established before 1950.

3. American and British

BOOK REVIEW DIGEST. New York: H.W. Wilson, 1905- . Monthly except February and July, annual cumulations.

Gives excerpts of book reviews. Each excerpt represents the major thrust of the review; lengths of reviews are also indicated.

BOOK REVIEW INDEX. Detroit: Gale Research Co., 1965- . Bimonthly, annual cumulations.

Indexes many more reviews than BOOK REVIEW DIGEST; no excerpts included.

Burgess, Anthony. THE NOVEL NOW: A GUIDE TO CONTEMPORARY FICTION. New York: W.W. Norton, 1967.

A far-ranging survey with lists of primary works.

CONTEMPORARY AUTHORS. Detroit: Gale Research Co., 1962– . Twice yearly.

An extremely useful guide to biographical and primary materials. Revised periodically.

Fleischman, Wolfgang Bernard, ed. ENCYCLOPEDIA OF WORLD LITERATURE IN THE TWENTIETH CENTURY. 3 vols. New York: Ungar, 1967.

Biographies and bibliographies for major writers of the twentieth century.

C. BIBLIOGRAPHIES

1. American

AMERICAN LITERARY SCHOLARSHIP: AN ANNUAL. Durham, N.C.: Duke University Press, 1963– . Quarterly.

Each volume includes a bibliographical essay on recent American fiction.

AMERICAN LITERATURE. Durham, N.C.. Duke University Press, 1929–

Bibliography of "Articles on American Literature Appearing in Current Periodicals" published in each issue.

Chapman, Abraham. THE NEGRO IN AMERICAN LITERATURE AND A BIBLIOGRAPHY OF LITERATURE BY AND ABOUT NEGRO AMERICANS. Oshkosh: Wisconsin Council of Teachers of English, 1960.

Coan, Otis, and Richard G. Lillard. AMERICA IN FICTION: AN ANNOTATED LIST OF NOVELS THAT INTERPRET ASPECTS OF LIFE IN THE UNITED STATES, CANADA, AND MEXICO. 5th ed. Palo Alto, Calif.: Pacific Books, 1967.

Deodene, Frank, and William P. French. BLACK AMERICAN FICTION SINCE 1952. Chatham, N.J.: Chatham Bookseller, 1970.

Continues the work of Maxwell Whiteman, A CENTURY OF FICTION BY AMERICAN NEGROES 1853–1952 (Philadelphia: Jacobs,

1955).

Gerstenberger, Donna, and George Hendrick. THE AMERICAN NOVEL: A CHECKLIST OF TWENTIETH-CENTURY CRITICISM ON NOVELS WRITTEN SINCE 1789. 2 vols. Denver: Swallow, 1961, 1970.

Volume 1 contains criticism written between 1900 and 1959, and Volume 2 contains criticism written between 1960 and 1968.

Jones, Howard Mumford, and Richard M. Ludwig. GUIDE TO AMERICAN LITERATURE AND ITS BACKGROUND SINCE 1890. 3rd ed. Cambridge, Mass.: Harvard University Press, 1964.

Suggestive and rather definitive reading list introduced by short essays. Emphasis is on literary background.

Leary, Lewis G., ed. ARTICLES ON AMERICAN LITERATURE 1950-1967. Durham, N.C.: Duke University Press, 1970.

Comprehensive listing of critical articles on American writers.

MLA INTERNATIONAL BIBLIOGRAPHY OF BOOKS AND ARTICLES ON THE MODERN LANGUAGES AND LITERATURES. New York: Modern Language Association of America, 1972- .

This important compilation began as "American Bibliography for 1921" in PMLA, 37 (1922). Since 1972 the bibliographies for twentieth-century American literature and for twentieth-century British literature have appeared in the first volume of a multi-volume work.

Nevius, Blake. THE AMERICAN NOVEL: SINCLAIR LEWIS TO THE PRESENT. New York: Appleton-Century-Crofts, 1970.

Includes brief bibliographies of twenty-three of the writers in this Guide.

Nilon, Charles H. BIBLIOGRAPHY OF BIBLIOGRAPHIES IN AMERICAN LITERATURE. New York: Bowker, 1970.

Arranged by individual author and by subject.

Rubin, Louis D., ed. A BIBLIOGRAPHICAL GUIDE TO THE STUDY OF SOUTHERN LITERATURE. Baton Rouge: Louisiana State University Press, 1969.

The most extensive bibliography of its kind, divided into general topics and checklists of 134 writers from all periods.

Woodress, James, ed. DISSERTATIONS IN AMERICAN LITERATURE, 1891-1966. Durham, N.C.: Duke University Press, 1968.

Broad coverage of dissertations in American literature; includes all theses from foreign countries and theses done in departments other than English.

2. British

ANNUAL BIBLIOGRAPHY OF ENGLISH LANGUAGE AND LITERATURE. Cambridge: Modern Humanities Research Association, 1921- .

Each annual volume contains a section on the twentieth century.

Bell, Inglis F., and Donald Baird. THE ENGLISH NOVEL 1578-1956: A CHECKLIST OF TWENTIETH-CENTURY CRITICISM. Denver: Alan Swallow, 1958.

Most valuable for writers well established before 1950.

Bufkin, E.C. THE TWENTIETH CENTURY NOVEL IN ENGLISH: A CHECK-LIST. Athens: University of Georgia Press, 1967.

Most valuable for writers established before 1950.

Daiches, David. THE PRESENT AGE IN BRITISH LITERATURE. Bloomington: Indiana University Press, 1958.

Excellent bibliography of the novel.

Temple, Ruth Z., and Martin Tucker. TWENTIETH CENTURY BRITISH LITER-ATURE: A REFERENCE GUIDE AND BIBLIOGRAPHY. New York: Frederick Ungar Publishing Co., 1968.

A tri-genre bibliography; includes sections on "Novel: Histories, Theory and Special Studies" and on "Author Bibliographies" (pri mary works).

THE YEAR'S WORK IN ENGLISH STUDIES. London: English Association of London, 1921- . Annual.

A bibliography of books and articles.

3. American and British

McNamee, Lawrence F. DISSERTATIONS IN ENGLISH AND AMERICAN LIT-ERATURE. New York: Bowker, 1968.

Coverage is from 1865 to 1964 of British, American, and German theses. A supplement covering 1964-68 appeared in 1969.

D. STUDIES AND COLLECTIONS

1. American

Aldridge, John W. IN SEARCH OF HERESY: AMERICAN LITERATURE IN AN AGE OF CONFORMITY. New York: McGraw-Hill Book Co., 1956.

A collection of essays on modern and contemporary writers who either reinforce traditional moral values or "assert the need to oppose conformism even though the culture presents no alternative to it."

_____. TIME TO MURDER AND CREATE: THE CONTEMPORARY NOVEL IN CRISIS. New York: McKay, 1966.

Essays concerning the need for real experimentation in novelistic form. Includes discussions of O'Hara, Styron, Bellow, McCarthy, Mailer, Updike, Cheever, and Sillitoe.

Alter, Robert. AFTER THE TRADITION: ESSAYS ON MODERN JEWISH WRITING. New York: E.P. Dutton & Co., 1969.

Several introductory chapters on "Varieties of Jewish Experience" are used to introduce four Jewish writers, including Bellow and Malamud.

Auchincloss, Louis. PIONEERS AND CARETAKERS: A STUDY OF NINE AMERICAN WOMEN NOVELISTS. Minneapolis: University of Minnesota Press, 1965.

Includes essays on McCarthy and McCullers.

Axthelm, Peter M. THE MODERN CONFESSIONAL NOVEL. New Haven, Conn.: Yale University Press, 1967.

A good introduction to the history of the modern confessional novel with a long chapter on Bellow.

Balakian, Nona, and Charles Simmons, eds. THE CREATIVE PRESENT: NOTES ON CONTEMPORARY AMERICAN FICTION. Garden City, N.Y.: Doubleday, 1963.

Essays by various hands on Baldwin, Salinger, Nabokov, McCullers, Capote, Bellow, Styron, Mailer, Welty, Jones, Kerouac, Malamud, Gold, Updike, and McCarthy.

Baumbach, Jonathan. THE LANDSCAPE OF NIGHTMARE: STUDIES IN THE CONTEMPORARY AMERICAN NOVEL. New York: New York University Press, 1965.

Chapters on Warren, Bellow, Salinger, Ellison, O'Connor, Malamud, Styron, and Morris.

Bigsby, C.W.E. THE BLACK AMERICAN WRITER. Vol. I: FICTION

DeLand, Fla.: Everett Edwards, 1969.

A collection of essays by various hands on Black writers; special emphasis is given to Ralph Ellison and James Baldwin.

Blotner, Joseph L. THE MODERN AMERICAN POLITICAL NOVEL, 1900–1960. Austin: University of Texas Press, 1966.

A thorough study of the twentieth-century American political novel. Includes an excellent bibliography of primary and secondary sources.

Bone, Robert A. THE NEGRO NOVEL IN AMERICA. Rev. ed. New Haven, Conn.: Yale University Press, 1965.

A standard work in the field.

Core, George, ed. SOUTHERN FICTION TODAY: RENASCENCE AND BEYOND. Athens: University of Georgia Press, 1969.

Five symposium papers on the state of southern fiction.

Feied, Frederick. NO PIE IN THE SKY: THE HOBO AS AMERICAN CULTURAL HERO IN THE WORKS OF JACK LONDON, JOHN DOS PASSOS, AND JACK KEROUAC. New York: Citadel, 1964.

Finklestein, Sidney. EXISTENTIALISM AND ALIENATION IN AMERICAN LITERATURE. New York: International Publishers, 1965.

Introductory chapters on continental origins of existentialism followed by discussions of Styron, Salinger, Updike, Mailer, Bellow, and Baldwin.

French, Warren, ed. THE FIFTIES: FICTION, POETRY, DRAMA. DeLand, Fla.: Everett/Edwards, 1970.

A collection of essays by various hands. Includes essays on Salinger, Mailer, Bellow, McCarthy, O'Connor, Agee, and Malamud.

Fuller, Edmund. MAN IN MODERN FICTION: SOME MINORITY OPINIONS ON CONTEMPORARY AMERICAN WRITING. New York: Random House, 1958.

A provocative work on the view of man as seen in contemporary American literature.

Galloway, David D. THE ABSURD HERO IN AMERICAN FICTION. Austin: University of Texas Press, 1966.

Concerned with various theories of the absurd. Checklists on Styron, Bellow, and Salinger.

9

Gossett, Louise Y. VIOLENCE IN SOUTHERN FICTION. Durham, N.C.: Duke University Press, 1965.

>A study of the violent elements in the fiction of Warren, O'Connor, Welty, Styron, Capote, and McCullers.

Green, Martin. RE-APPRAISALS: SOME COMMONSENSE READINGS IN AMERICAN LITERATURE. London: Hugh Evelyn, 1963.

>Includes chapters on Salinger and Nabokov.

Harper, Howard M., Jr. DESPERATE FAITH: A STUDY OF BELLOW, SALINGER, MAILER, BALDWIN, AND UPDIKE. Chapel Hill: University of North Carolina Press, 1967.

>Essays concerning the response of these five novelists to universal problems.

Hassan, Ihab. RADICAL INNOCENCE: STUDIES IN THE CONTEMPORARY AMERICAN NOVEL. Princeton, N.J.: Princeton University Press, 1961.

>An existential reading of the contemporary novel that touches almost all major figures.

Hemenway, Robert, ed. THE BLACK NOVELIST. Columbus, Ohio: Merrill, 1970.

>Essays about Black novelists and essays by Black writers.

Hicks, Granville, ed. THE LIVING NOVEL: A SYMPOSIUM. New York: Macmillan, 1957.

>Essays by Bellow, Ellison, Morris and O'Connor.

Hill, Herbert, ed. ANGER AND BEYOND: THE NEGRO WRITER IN THE UNITED STATES. New York: Harper & Row, 1966.

>A collection of essays, some by leading Black critics, on the Black literary tradition in America.

Hoffman, Frederick J. THE ART OF SOUTHERN FICTION: A STUDY OF SOME MODERN NOVELISTS. Carbondale: Southern Illinois University Press, 1967.

>Includes chapters on Agee, Price, Capote, McCullers, O'Connor, Styron, Warren, and Welty.

Klein, Marcus. AFTER ALIENATION: AMERICAN NOVELS IN MID-CENTURY. Cleveland: World, 1964.

>Chapters on Bellow, Ellison, Baldwin, Morris, and Malamud.

Kostelanetz, Richard, ed. ON CONTEMPORARY LITERATURE. New York: Avon, 1965.

Short essays on many leading writers of the contemporary period.

Lesser, Simon O. FICTION AND THE UNCONSCIOUS. Boston: Beacon Press, 1957.

Standard work on the relationship between literature and psychology.

Littlejohn, David. BLACK ON WHITE. New York: Viking Press, 1966.

After several introductory chapters on the Black literary scene before and after NATIVE SON, there are two substantial chapters on twentieth-century black novelists.

Malin, Irving. JEWS AND AMERICANS. Carbondale: Southern Illinois University Press, 1965.

Includes essays on Bellow, Roth, and Malamud.

_____. NEW AMERICAN GOTHIC. Carbondale: Southern Illinois University Press, 1962.

Treats the gothic elements in the writings of Capote, Purdy, O'Connor, Hawkes, McCullers, and Salinger.

Margolies, Edward. NATIVE SONS: A CRITICAL STUDY OF TWENTIETH-CENTURY NEGRO AMERICAN AUTHORS. Philadelphia: Lippincott, 1968.

From W.E.B. DuBois to LeRoi Jones.

Miller, Wayne Charles. AN ARMED AMERICA: A HISTORY OF THE AMERICAN MILITARY NOVEL. New York: New York University Press, 1970.

Includes a chapter entitled "The Military Novel in the Nuclear Age" that is largely devoted to Heller.

Milne, Gordon. THE AMERICAN POLITICAL NOVEL. Norman: University of Oklahoma Press, 1966.

An historical look at the American political novel, with a section on Warren.

Mizener, Arthur. THE SENSE OF LIFE IN THE MODERN NOVEL. Boston: Houghton Mifflin, 1964.

Includes essays on Salinger and Updike.

Moore, Harry T., ed. CONTEMPORARY AMERICAN NOVELISTS. Carbondale: Southern Illinois University Press, 1964.

11

> Essays by various hands on McCullers, Mailer, Welty, Kerouac, Salinger, McCarthy, Bellow, Heller, Hawkes, Updike, Styron, Baldwin, Donleavy, and others.

Noble, David W. THE ETERNAL ADAM AND THE NEW WORLD GARDEN: THE CENTRAL MYTH IN THE AMERICAN NOVEL SINCE 1830. New York: Braziller, 1968.

> An intellectual historian's look at the American novel. Includes discussions of Warren, Mailer, Baldwin, and Bellow.

Parkinson, Thomas, ed. A CASE BOOK ON THE BEAT. New York: Crowell, 1961.

> Includes primary material, critical comments, and a bibliography of beat-generation authors.

Podhoretz, Norman. DOINGS AND UNDOINGS: THE FIFTIES AND AFTER IN AMERICAN WRITING. New York: Farrar, Straus, 1964.

> Includes sections on O'Hara, McCarthy, Mailer, Bellow, Baldwin, and Updike.

Rubin, Louis D. THE FARAWAY COUNTRY: WRITERS OF THE MODERN SOUTH. Seattle: University of Washington Press, 1963.

> Includes chapters on Warren, Styron, and Welty.

Rubin, Louis D., and Robert D. Jacobs. SOUTH: MODERN SOUTHERN LITERATURE IN ITS CULTURAL SETTING. Garden City, N.Y.: Doubleday, 1961.

> Essays by various hands on Warren, Welty, Caldwell, and McCullers. Also includes a chapter on the "Renascence in the Fifties."

_____. SOUTHERN RENASCENCE: THE LITERATURE OF THE MODERN SOUTH. Baltimore: Johns Hopkins Press, 1953.

> Interesting sections on "The Mind of the South" and "Themes of Southern Literature." Includes discussions of Warren and Welty.

Rupp, Richard H. CELEBRATION IN POSTWAR AMERICAN FICTION: 1945–1967. Coral Gables, Fla.: University of Miami Press, 1970.

> A study of "celebration" in Cheever, Updike, Welty, O'Connor, Agee, Salinger, Baldwin, Ellison, Malamud, and Bellow.

Scholes, Robert. THE FABULATORS. New York: Oxford University Press, 1967.

> A thesis book which discusses the relationship between novel and fabulation and possible trends for the future of the novel. Includes

discussions of Durrell, Vonnegut, Hawkes, Murdoch, and Barth.

Simonini, Rinaldo C., Jr., ed. SOUTHERN WRITERS: APPRAISALS IN OUR TIME. Charlottesville: University Press of Virginia, 1964.

> A collection of essays by various hands that aims at an historical perspective of Southern literature; a chapter on "The Youngest Generation of Southern Fiction Writers" treats prominent contemporaries.

Sutherland, William O.S., ed. SIX CONTEMPORARY NOVELS: SIX INTRODUCTORY ESSAYS IN MODERN FICTION. Austin: University of Texas Department of English, 1962.

> Includes essays on Durrell, Snow, and Beckett. Sutherland states that "each takes a significant critical fact about a work of fiction and develops from it a critical statement."

Tischler, Mary M. BLACK MASKS: NEGRO CHARACTERS IN MODERN SOUTHERN FICTION. University Park: Pennsylvania State University Press, 1969.

> Investigates character types, archetypes, stereotypes, and motifs.

Weinberg, Helen. THE NEW NOVEL IN AMERICA: THE KAFKAN MODE IN CONTEMPORARY FICTION. Ithaca, N.Y.: Cornell University Press, 1970.

> Chapters on Bellow, Mailer, and Salinger.

2. British

Bergonzi, Bernard. THE SITUATION OF THE NOVEL. London: Macmillan, 1970.

> Primarily on British novelists from 1950 to 1970 with one chapter on American novelists.

Gindin, James. POSTWAR BRITISH FICTION: NEW ACCENTS AND ATTITUDES. Berkeley and Los Angeles: University of California Press, 1962.

> Includes chapters on Sillitoe, Amis, Lessing, Wain, Murdoch, and Golding.

Hall, James. THE TRAGIC COMEDIANS: SEVEN MODERN BRITISH NOVELISTS. Bloomington: Indiana University Press, 1963.

> Includes discussions of L.P. Hartley and Anthony Powell.

Karl, Frederick R. THE CONTEMPORARY ENGLISH NOVEL. New York: Farrar, Straus and Giroux, 1962.

Major emphasis is on earlier writers. Some mention is made of Golding, Murdoch, Beckett, Durrell, Greene, and the "Angry Young Men."

Mooney, Harry J., and Thomas F. Staley, eds. THE SHAPELESS GOD: ES-SAYS ON MODERN FICTION. Pittsburgh: University of Pittsburgh Press, 1969.

Essays which attempt "to analyze specific components of what might be regarded as the religious awareness" of such writers as Greene and O'Connor.

Rabinovitz, Rubin. THE REACTION AGAINST EXPERIMENT IN THE ENGLISH NOVEL, 1950-1960. New York: Columbia University Press, 1967.

Includes a chapter on "The Novelists of the 1950's," special treatments of Amis, Angus Wilson, and Snow, and a good general bibliography.

Shapiro, Charles, ed. CONTEMPORARY BRITISH NOVELISTS. Carbondale: Southern Illinois University Press, 1965.

Essays by various hands on Amis, Durrell, Golding, Lessing, Mur-doch, Sillitoe, Snow, Spark, and Wilson.

3. American and British

Glicksberg, Charles I. THE IRONIC VISION IN MODERN LITERATURE. The Hague: Martinus Nijhoff, 1969.

An extensive study of irony in British, Continental, and American literature with a section on the absurd which includes Beckett.

Hall, James. THE LUNATIC GIANT IN THE DRAWING ROOM: THE BRIT-ISH AND AMERICAN NOVEL SINCE 1930. Bloomington: Indiana University Press, 1968.

Examines Bowen, Warren, Greene, Bellow, and Murdoch.

Kazin, Alfred. CONTEMPORARIES. Boston: Little, Brown, 1962.

Mostly reprinted essays, introductions, and reviews; includes dis-cussions of Algren, Malamud, Salinger, Durrell, Capote, Roth, Baldwin, and others.

Kermode, Frank. PUZZLES AND EPIPHANIES: ESSAYS AND REVIEWS 1958-1961. London: Routledge and Paul, 1962.

Includes pieces on Snow, Salinger, Greene, Beckett, Durrell, Angus Wilson, Golding, and Nabokov.

Whitbread, Thomas B. SEVEN CONTEMPORARY AUTHORS: ESSAYS ON COZZENS, MILLER, WEST, GOLDING, HELLER, ALBEE, AND POWERS. Austin: University of Texas Press, 1968.

Essays by various hands.

JOURNALS CONCERNED

WITH

CONTEMPORARY FICTION

Part II

JOURNALS CONCERNED
WITH
CONTEMPORARY FICTION

AMERICAN LITERATURE. Durham, N.C.: Duke University Press, 1929- .
Quarterly.

> Historical, critical, and bibliographic articles on American litera-
> ture; book reviews.

CHICAGO REVIEW. Chicago: University of Chicago, 1946- . Quarterly.

> Critical articles on all aspects of contemporary literature.

CONTEMPORARY LITERATURE. Madison: University of Wisconsin, 1960- .
Quarterly.

> Critical and scholarly articles on literature since 1940.

CRITICAL QUARTERLY. Manchester: Manchester University, 1959- . Quarterly.

> Literary criticism of twentieth-century British, American and Euro-
> pean writers.

CRITIQUE: STUDIES IN MODERN FICTION. Minneapolis: University of
Minnesota, 1956- . 3/year.

> Literary criticism of contemporary novels and collections of short
> fiction.

DENVER QUARTERLY. Denver: University of Denver, 1966- . Quarterly.

> Critical articles on modern literature.

ENGLISH LANGUAGE NOTES. Boulder: University of Colorado, 1963- .
Quarterly.

> Scholarly articles on all areas of English and American literature.

ENGLISH STUDIES. Ghent, Belgium: Swets & Zeitlinger, 1919- . 6/year.

Critical articles on all areas of English language and literature, including American.

EXPLICATOR. Richmond: Virginia Commonwealth University, 1942- . Monthly September–June.

Contains explications de texte.

GEORGIA REVIEW. Athens: University of Georgia, 1947- . Quarterly.

Critical, biographical, and explicative articles on American literature, especially southern.

HOLLINS CRITIC. Hollins College, Va.: Hollins College, 1964- . 5/year.

Critical essays on current writers.

HUDSON REVIEW. New York: Hudson Review, 1948- . Quarterly.

Fiction by eminent contemporaries as well as young writers; literary criticism; book reviews.

IOWA ENGLISH YEARBOOK. Ames: Iowa State University, 1956- . Annual

Critical and scholarly articles on English and American language and literature.

IOWA REVIEW. Iowa City: University of Iowa, 1969- . Quarterly.

Critical articles on modern and contemporary literature.

LITERATURE AND PSYCHOLOGY. Teaneck, N.J.: Fairleigh Dickinson University, 1951- . Quarterly.

Literary criticism reflecting the various schools of psychology.

MINNESOTA REVIEW. St. Paul, Minn.: Macalester College, 1960- . Quarterly.

Emphasis on creative material; also, essays on younger writers.

MISSISSIPPI QUARTERLY; A JOURNAL OF SOUTHERN CULTURE. State College: Mississippi State University, 1947- . Quarterly.

Essays on southern writers and southern culture.

MODERN FICTION STUDIES. Lafayette, Ind.: Purdue University, 1955- . Quarterly.

Criticism, scholarship, and bibliography of American and English fiction of the past 100 years.

NEGRO AMERICAN LITERATURE FORUM. Terre Haute: Indiana State University, 1967- . Quarterly.

Critical articles on Black American literature.

NEW ENGLAND QUARTERLY. Brunswick, Me.: Colonial Society of Massachusetts, 1928- . Quarterly.

Scholarly articles on the culture of New England, especially literature.

NOTES ON CONTEMPORARY LITERATURE. Carrollton: West Georgia College, 1970- . 5/year.

Notes on fiction written since 1940.

NOVEL: A FORUM ON FICTION. Providence, R.I.: Brown University, 1967- . 3/year.

Critical articles on the novel in all ages.

OCCIDENT. Berkeley: University of California, 1881- . Annual, plus special issues.

Creative criticism and articles on contemporary matters.

PMLA: PUBLICATIONS OF THE MODERN LANGUAGE ASSOCIATION. New York: Modern Language Association of America, 1885- . Quarterly.

Scholarly articles on the modern languages and literatures.

RESEARCH STUDIES. Pullman: Washington State University, 1929- . Quarterly.

Articles on contemporary literature with an emphasis on speculative analysis and cultural commentary.

SOUTH DAKOTA REVIEW. Vermillion: University of South Dakota, 1963- . Quarterly.

Critical articles on American literature with an emphasis on western American literature, history, and culture.

SOUTHERN LITERARY JOURNAL. Chapel Hill: University of North Carolina, 1968- .

Essays on the literature of the South.

SOUTHERN REVIEW. Baton Rouge: Louisiana State University, 1935-42, 1965- . Quarterly.

Critical articles on modern literature, especially southern.

SOUTHWEST REVIEW. Dallas, Tex.: Southern Methodist University, 1915- . Quarterly.

Critical articles on contemporary American literature.

STUDIES IN BLACK LITERATURE. Fredericksburg, Va.: Mary Washington College, 1970- . 3/year.

Critical, analytical, interpretive, bibliographic, and source-study articles on Afro-American and African literature.

STUDIES IN SHORT FICTION. Newberry, S.C.: Newberry College, 1963- . Quarterly.

Major critical articles and notes, such as explications de texte, on short fiction from all periods.

STUDIES IN THE NOVEL. Denton: North Texas State University, 1969- . Quarterly.

Scholarly and critical articles on all aspects of the novel.

TEXAS STUDIES IN LITERATURE AND LANGUAGE. Austin: University of Texas, 1959- . Quarterly.

Critical, textual, bibliographical, or explicative articles on the humanities.

TWENTIETH CENTURY LITERATURE: A SCHOLARLY AND CRITICAL JOURNAL. Los Angeles: Immaculate Heart College, 1955- . Quarterly.

Scholarly and critical articles on twentieth-century literature; bibliographies.

WESTERN AMERICAN LITERATURE. Ft. Collins: Colorado State University, 1965- . Quarterly.

Articles on American literature in and about the American West.

YALE REVIEW. New Haven, Conn.: Yale University, 1911- . Quarterly.

Interdisciplinary journal, often containing articles on contemporary writers.

PART III

INDIVIDUAL AUTHORS

CHINUA ACHEBE (1930-), NIGERIAN

NOVELS

THINGS FALL APART. London: Heinemann, 1958.

NO LONGER AT EASE. London: Heinemann, 1960.

ARROW OF GOD. London: Heinemann, 1964.

A MAN OF THE PEOPLE. London: Heinemann, 1966.

SHORT STORIES

THE SACRIFICIAL EGG AND OTHER STORIES. Onitsha, Nigeria: Etudo, 1962.

CRITICAL BOOKS

Carroll, David. CHINUA ACHEBE. New York: Twayne, 1970.

Killam, G.D. THE NOVELS OF CHINUA ACHEBE. London: Heinemann; New York: Africana Publishing Corp., 1969.

Ravenscroft, Arthur. CHINUA ACHEBE. London: Longman, 1969.

CRITICAL ARTICLES

Meyers, Jeffrey. "Culture and History in THINGS FALL APART." Crit, 11 (1969), 25-32.

Weinstock, Donald, and Cathy Ramadan. "Symbolic Structure in THINGS FALL APART." Crit, 11 (1969), 33-41.

JAMES AGEE (1909-55), AMERICAN

NOVELS

THE MORNING WATCH. Boston: Houghton Mifflin, 1951.

A DEATH IN THE FAMILY. New York: McDowell, Obolensky, 1957.

SHORT STORIES

THE COLLECTED SHORT PROSE OF JAMES AGEE. Edited and with a Memoir by Robert Fitzgerald. Boston: Houghton Mifflin, 1968.

BIBLIOGRAPHY

Fabre, Genevieve. "A Bibliography of the Works of James Agee." BB, 24 (1965), 145-48, 163-66.

CRITICAL BOOKS

MacDonald, Dwight. AGAINST THE AMERICAN GRAIN. New York: Random House, 1962.

Ohlin, Peter H. AGEE. New York: Ivan Obolensky, 1966.

Seib, Kenneth. JAMES AGEE: PROMISE AND FULFILLMENT. Pittsburgh: University of Pittsburgh Press, 1968.

CRITICAL ARTICLES

[Agee, James.] "James Agee, by Himself." ESQUIRE, 60 (June 1963), 149,

289-90.

Barker, George. "Three Tenant Families." NATION, 153 (27 September 1941), 282.

Breit, Harvey. "Cotton Tenantry." NRep., 105 (15 September 1941), 348.

Broughton, George, and Panthea R. Broughton. "Agee and Autonomy." SHR, 4 (1970), 101-11.

Burger, Nash K. "A Story to Tell: Agee, Wolfe, Faulkner." SAQ, 63 (1964), 32-43.

Croce, Arlene. "Hollywood the Monolith." Cweal, 69 (23 January 1959), 430.

Curry, Kenneth. "Notes on the Text of James Agee's A DEATH IN THE FAMILY." PBSA, 64 (1970), 84-99.

da Ponte, Durant. "James Agee: The Quest for Identity." TSL, 8 (1963), 25-37.

DeJong, David Cornel. "Money and Rue." CM, 6 (Winter 1965), 50.

Evans, Walker. "James Agee in 1936." ATLANTIC MONTHLY, 206 (July 1960), 74.

Fitzgerald, Robert. "James Agee: A Memoir." KR, 30 (1968), 587-624.

Frohock, W.M. "James Agee: The Question of Unkept Promise." SWR, 62 (1957), 221-29.

Grossman, James. "Mr. Agee and the NEW YORKER." PR, 12 (1945), 112.

Hayes, Richard. "Rhetoric of Splendor." Cweal, 68 (12 September 1958), 591-92.

Holder, Alan. "Encounter in Alabama." VQR, 42 (1966), 189.

Kramer, Victor A. "Agee in the Forties: The Struggle To Be a Writer." TQ, II, i (1968), 9-17.

_____. "James Agee Papers at the University of Texas." LCUT, 8, ii (1966), 33-36.

Larsen, Erling. "Let Us Not Now Praise Ourselves." CM, 2 (Winter 1961), 86.

MacDonald, Dwight. "Death of a Poet." NY, 33 (16 November 1957), 224–41.

_____. "James Agee." ENCOUNTER, 19 (December 1962), 73–84.

Oulahan, Richard. "A Cult Grew around a Many-Sided Writer." LIFE, 55 (1 November 1963), 69–72.

Phillipson, John S. "Character, Theme, and Symbol in THE MORNING WATCH." WHR, 15 (1961), 359–67.

Roe, Michael Morris, Jr. "A Point of Focus in James Agee's A DEATH IN THE FAMILY." TCL, 12 (1966), 149–53.

Shepherd, Allen. "'A Sort of Monstrous Grinding Beauty': Reflections on Character and Theme in James Agee's A DEATH IN THE FAMILY." IEY, 14 (1969), 17–24.

Sosnoski, James J. "Craft and Intention in James Agee's A DEATH IN THE FAMILY." JGE, 20 (1968), 170–83.

Trilling, Lionel. "The Story and the Novel." THE GRIFFIN, 7 (January 1958), 4–12.

Updike, John. "No Use Talking." NRep, 147 (13 August 1962), 23.

NELSON ALGREN (1909-   ), AMERICAN

NOVELS

SOMEBODY IN BOOTS. New York: Vanguard Press, 1935.

NEVER COME MORNING. New York: Harper, 1942.

THE MAN WITH THE GOLDEN ARM. Garden City, N.Y.: Doubleday, 1949.

A WALK ON THE WILD SIDE. New York: Farrar Straus, 1956.

SHORT STORIES

THE NEON WILDERNESS. New York: Doubleday, 1947.

NELSON ALGREN'S OWN BOOK OF LONESOME MONSTERS. (Includes THE HOUSE OF THE HUNDRED GRASSFIRES). New York: Lancer Books, 1962.

CRITICAL ARTICLES

Algren, Nelson. "The Emblems and the Proofs of Power." CRITIC, 25 (February-March 1967), 20-26.

Beauvoir, Simone de. "An American Rendezvous: The Question of Fidelity." Harper's, 229 (December 1964), 111-22.

Bluestone, George. "Nelson Algren." WR, 22 (Autumn 1957), 27-44.

Donohue, H.E.F. "Nelson Algren Interviewed." CM, 4 (February 1963), 3-36.

Geismar, Maxwell. "Nelson Algren: The Iron Sanctuary." CE, 14 (1953), 311-15.

Hinchliffe, Arnold P. "The End of a Dream." SA, 5 (1959), 315-23.

Holmes, J.C. "Existentialism and the Novel." ChiR, 18 (Summer 1959), 144-51.

Lipton, Lawrence. "A Voyeur's View of the Wild Side: Nelson Algren and His Critics." ChiR, 10 (Winter 1957), 4-14.

Miyamoto, Youkichi. "Chicago Naturalism--Nelson Algren." SEL, 36 (1959), 177-78.

Perlongo, Robert A. "Interview with Nelson Algren." ChiR, 11 (Autumn 1958), 92-98.

Pourtois, Anne. "Conversation avec Nelson Algren." EUROPE, 52 (October 1964), 72-77.

Ray, David. "A Talk on the Wild Side: A Bowl of Coffee with Nelson Algren." REPORTER, 20 (11 June 1959), 31-33.

KINGSLEY AMIS (1922-), ENGLISH

NOVELS

LUCKY JIM. London: Gollancz, 1954.

THAT UNCERTAIN FEELING. London: Gollancz, 1955.

I LIKE IT HERE. London: Gollancz, 1958.

TAKE A GIRL LIKE YOU. London: Gollancz, 1960.

ONE FAT ENGLISHMAN. London: Gollancz, 1963.

THE EGYPTOLOGISTS (with Robert Conquest). London: Cape, 1965.

THE ANTI-DEATH LEAGUE. London. Gollancz, 1966.

COLONEL SUN: A JAMES BOND ADVENTURE (as Robert Markham). London: Cape, 1968.

I WANT IT NOW. London: Cape, 1968.

THE GREEN MAN. London: Cape, 1969.

SHORT STORIES

MY ENEMY'S ENEMY. London: Gollancz, 1962.

BIBLIOGRAPHY

Vann, J. Donn, and James T.F. Tanner. "Kingsley Amis: A Checklist of Recent Criticism." BB, 26 (1969), 105, 111, 115–17.

CRITICAL ARTICLES

Amis, Kingsley. "My Kind of Comedy." TC, 170 (1961), 46–50.

Boyle, Ted E., and Terence Brown. "The Serious Side of Kingsley Amis's LUCKY JIM." Crit, 9 (1967), 100–107.

Bergonzi, Bernard. "Kingsley Amis." LonM, n.s. 3 (January 1964), 50–65.

Chase, Richard. "Middlebrow England: The Novels of Kingsley Amis." Com, 22 (September 1956), 263–69.

Colville, Derek. "The Sane New World of Kingsley Amis." BuR, 9 (March 1960), 46–57.

Conquest, Robert. "Christian Symbolism in LUCKY JIM." CritQ, 7 (1965), 87–92.

Genthe, Charles V. "What Price Academe? Or, Kingsley Amis Revisited." SNL, 1 (1964), 44.

Gindin, James. "The Reassertion of the Personal." TQ, 1, iv (1958), 126–34.

Green, Martin. "Amis and Salinger: The Latitude of Private Conscience." ChiR, 11 (Winter 1958), 20–25.

Hamilton, Kenneth. "Kingsley Amis, Moralist." DR, 44 (Autumn 1964), 339–47.

Hopkins, Robert. "The Satire of Kingsley Amis's I LIKE IT HERE." Crit, 8 (1966), 62–70.

Hurrell, John D. "Class and Conscience in John Braine and Kingsley Amis." Crit, 2 (1958), 39–53.

Lebowitz, Naomi. "Kingsley Amis: The Penitent Hero." Per, 10 (1958), 129–36.

Lodge, David. "The Modern, the Contemporary, and the Importance of Being Amis." CritQ, 5 (1963), 335-54.

Moberg, George. "Structure and Theme in Amis's Novels." CEA, 25 (March 1963), 7, 10.

Parker, R.B. "Farce and Society: The Range of Kingsley Amis." WSCL, 2 (Fall 1961), 27-38.

Soule, George. "The High Cost of Plunging." CM, 5 (Fall 1964), 106-11.

CHARLES ANGOFF (1902-), AMERICAN

NOVELS

JOURNEY TO THE DAWN. New York: Beechhurst Press, 1951.

IN THE MORNING LIGHT. New York: Beechhurst Press, 1952.

THE SUN AT NOON. New York: Beechhurst Press, 1955.

BETWEEN DAY AND DARK. New York and London: Thomas Yoseloff, 1959.

THE BITTER SPRING. New York and London: Thomas Yoseloff, 1961.

SUMMER STORM. New York and London: Thomas Yoseloff, 1963.

MEMORY OF AUTUMN. South Brunswick, New York, and London: Thomas Yoseloff, 1968.

WINTER TWILIGHT. South Brunswick, New York, and London: Thomas Yoseloff, 1970.

SHORT STORIES

ADVENTURES IN HEAVEN. New York: Bernard Ackerman, 1945.

WHEN I WAS A BOY IN BOSTON. New York: Beechhurst Press, 1947.

SOMETHING ABOUT MY FATHER AND OTHER PEOPLE. New York: Thomas Yoseloff, 1956.

CRITICAL ARTICLES

Angoff, Charles. "The Origins and Aims of the Polonsky Saga." CJF, 25 (1966), 32-41.

Greenfield, Louis. "Charles Angoff." UKCR, 17 (Spring 1951), 205-12.

Ribalow, Harold U. "Charles Angoff: A Literary Profile." CJF, 20 (1961), 21-23.

Yoseloff, Thomas, and Harold U. Ribalow. "The Importance of Charles Angoff." LitR, 4 (Autumn 1960), 37-48.

SYLVIA ASHTON-WARNER (1908-), ENGLISH

NOVELS

SPINSTER. London: Secker and Warburg, 1958.

INCENSE TO IDOLS. London: Secker and Warburg, 1960.

TEACHER. London: Secker and Warburg, 1963.

BELL CALL. New York: Simon and Schuster, 1964.

GREENSTONE. London: Secker and Warburg, 1967.

THREE. New York: Knopf, 1970.

LOUIS AUCHINCLOSS (1910-), AMERICAN

NOVELS

THE INDIFFERENT CHILDREN (as Andrew Lee). New York: Prentice-Hall, 1947.

SYBIL. Boston: Houghton Mifflin, 1952.

A LAW FOR THE LION. Boston: Houghton Mifflin, 1953.

THE GREAT WORLD AND TIMOTHY COLT. Boston: Houghton Mifflin, 1956.

VENUS IN SPARTA. Boston: Houghton Mifflin, 1958.

PURSUIT OF THE PRODIGAL. Boston: Houghton Mifflin, 1959.

THE HOUSE OF FIVE TALENTS. Boston: Houghton Mifflin, 1960.

PORTRAIT IN BROWNSTONE. Boston: Houghton Mifflin, 1962.

THE RECTOR OF JUSTIN. Boston: Houghton Mifflin, 1964.

THE EMBEZZLER. Boston: Houghton Mifflin, 1966.

A WORLD OF PROFIT. Boston: Houghton Mifflin, 1968.

SHORT STORIES

THE INJUSTICE COLLECTORS. Boston: Houghton Mifflin, 1950.

THE ROMANTIC EGOISTS: A REFLECTION IN EIGHT MINUTES. Boston:

Houghton Mifflin, 1954.

POWERS OF ATTORNEY. Boston: Houghton Mifflin, 1963.

TALES OF MANHATTAN. Boston: Houghton Mifflin, 1967.

SECOND CHANCE. Boston: Houghton Mifflin, 1970.

CRITICAL ARTICLES

Kane, Patricia. "Lawyers at the Top: The Fiction of Louis Auchincloss." Crit, 7 (1965), 36–46.

Milne, Gordon. "Auchincloss and the Novel of Manners." UKCR, 29 (March 1963), 177–85.

ELLIOTT BAKER (1922-), AMERICAN

NOVELS

A FINE MADNESS. New York: Putnam, 1964.

THE PENNY WARS. New York: Putnam, 1968.

CRITICAL ARTICLES

Noland, Richard W. "Lunacy and Poetry: Elliott Baker's A FINE MADNESS." Crit, 8 (1966), 71-78.

NIGEL BALCHIN (1908-70), ENGLISH

NOVELS

NO SKY. London: H. Hamilton, 1934.

SIMPLE LIFE. London: H. Hamilton, 1935.

LIGHTBODY ON LIBERTY. London: Collins, 1936.

DARKNESS FALLS FROM THE AIR. London: Collins, 1942.

THE SMALL BACK ROOM. London: Collins, 1943.

MINE OWN EXECUTIONER. London: Collins, 1945.

THE BORGIA TESTAMENT. London: Collins, 1948.

A SORT OF TRAITORS. London: Collins, 1949.

THE ANATOMY OF VILLAINY. London: Collins, 1950.

A WAY THROUGH THE WOOD. London: Collins, 1951.

SUNDRY CREDITORS. London: Collins, 1953.

THE FALL OF THE SPARROW. London: Collins, 1955.

SEEN DIMLY BEFORE DAWN. London: Collins, 1962.

IN THE ABSENCE OF MRS. PETERSEN. London: Collins, 1966.

KINGS OF INFINITE SPACE. London: Collins, 1967.

SHORT STORIES

LAST RECOLLECTIONS OF MY UNCLE CHARLES. London: Collins, 1954.

JAMES BALDWIN (1924-), AMERICAN

NOVELS

GO TELL IT ON THE MOUNTAIN. New York: Knopf, 1953.

GIOVANNI'S ROOM. New York: Dial Press, 1956.

ANOTHER COUNTRY. New York: Dial Press, 1962.

TELL ME HOW LONG THE TRAIN'S BEEN GONE. New York: Dial Press, 1968.

SHORT STORIES

GOING TO MEET THE MAN. New York: Dial Press, 1965.

BIBLIOGRAPHY

Fisher, Russell G. "James Baldwin: A Bibliography, 1947-1962." BB, 24 (1965), 127-30.

Kindt, Kathleen A. "James Baldwin: A Checklist, 1947-1962." BB, 24 (1965), 123-26.

Standley, Fred L. "James Baldwin: A Checklist, 1963-1967." BB, 25 (1968), 135-37, 160.

CRITICAL BOOKS

Eckman, Fern Marja. THE FURIOUS PASSAGE OF JAMES BALDWIN. New York: Evans, 1966.

James Baldwin

CRITICAL ARTICLES

Alexander, Charlotte. "The 'Stink' of Reality: Mothers and Whores in James Baldwin's Fiction." L&P, 18 (1968), 9-26.

Baldwin, James. "The Discovery of What It Means to Be an American." NYTBR, 25 January 1959, pp. 4, 22.

_____. "Letters from a Journey." Harper's, 226 (May 1963), 48-52.

_____. "'Pour liberer les Blancs...' (PROPOS RECUEILLIS PAR FRANCOIS BONDY)." PREUVES, no. 152 (1963), 3-17.

Baldwin, James, and Francois Bondy. "Die Weissen zu befreien: Ein Gesprach." MONATSHEFTE, 16 (October 1963), 9-20.

Beja, Morris. "It Must Be Important: Negroes in Contemporary American Fiction." AR, 24 (1964), 333-36.

Berry, B.M. "Another Man Done Gone: Self-Pity in Baldwin's ANOTHER COUNTRY." MQR, 5 (February 1966), 285-90.

Blount, Trevor. "A Slight Error in Continuity in James Baldwin's ANOTHER COUNTRY." N&Q, 13 (1966), 102-3.

Bluefarb, Sam. "James Baldwin's 'Previous Condition': A Problem of Identification." NALF, 3 (1969), 26-29.

Bone, Robert A. "The Novels of James Baldwin." TriQ, no. 2 (1965), 3-20.

Bonosky, Philip. "The Negro Writer and Commitment." MAINSTREAM, 15, ii (1962), 16-22.

Bradford, M.E. "Faulkner, James Baldwin, and the South." GaR, 20 (1966), 431-43.

Cartey, Wilfred. "The Realities of Four Negro Writers." ColF, 9 (1966), 34-42.

Charney, Maurice. "James Baldwin's Quarrel with Richard Wright." AQ, 15 (1963), 65-75.

Clark, K.B. "A Conversation with James Baldwin." FREEDOMWAYS, 3 (Summer 1963), 361-68.

Coles, Robert. "Baldwin's Burden." PR, 31 (1964), 409-16.

Collier, Eugenia W. "The Phrase Unbearably Repeated." PHYLON, 25 (1964), 288-96.

Cox, C.B., and A.R. Jones. "After the Tranquilized Fifties: Notes on Sylvia Plath and James Baldwin." CritQ, 6 (1964), 107-21.

Elkoff, Marvin. "Everybody Knows His Name." ESQUIRE, 62, ii (1964), 59-64, 120-23.

Evanier, David. "The Identity of James Baldwin." Cweal, 77 (28 December 1962), 365-66.

Fabre, Michel. "Peres et fils dans GO TELL IT ON THE MOUNTAIN, de James Baldwin." EA, 23 (1970), 47-61.

Fares, Nabile. "James Baldwin: Une interview exclusive." JeuneA, 1 September 1970, pp. 20-24.

Finn, James. "The Identity of James Baldwin." Cweal, 77 (26 October 1962), 113-16.

_____. "James Baldwin's Vision." Cweal, 78 (26 July 1963), 447-49.

Foote, Dorothy N. "James Baldwin's 'Holler Books.'" CEA, 25, viii (1963), 8, 11.

Foote, F.G. "Therapeutique de la haine." PREUVES, no. 167 (1965), 70-73.

Friedman, Neil. "James Baldwin and Psychotherapy." PSYCHOTHERAPY, 3 (1966), 177-83.

Gayle, Addison, Jr. "A Defense of James Baldwin." CLAJ, 10 (1967), 201-8.

Georgakas, Dan. "James Baldwin...in Conversation." ASoc, 3 (1966), 550-57.

Gerard, Albert. "James Baldwin et la religiosite noire." RevN, 33 (February 1961), 177-86.

Graves, Wallace. "The Question of Moral Energy in James Baldwin's GO TELL IT ON THE MOUNTAIN." CLAJ, 7 (1964), 215-23.

Gross, Theodore. "The World of James Baldwin." Crit, 7 (1965), 139-49.

Hagopian, John V. "James Baldwin: The Black and the Red-White-and-Blue." CLAJ, 7 (1963), 133-40.

Heiberg, Inger. "James Baldwin--negerforfatter og dikter." SAMTIDEN, 74 (1965), 280-87.

Hernton, Calvin C. "Blood of the Lamb and a Fiery Baptism: The Ordeal of James Baldwin." AMISTAD, 1 (1970), 183-225.

Howard, Jane. "Doom and Glory of Knowing Who You Are." LIFE, 54 (24 May 1963), 86, 88-90.

Howe, Irving. "James Baldwin: At Ease in Apocalypse." Harper's, 237 (September 1968), 92-100.

Isaacs, Harold R. "Five Writers and Their African Ancestors." PHYLON, 21 (1960), 243-65, 317-36.

Jacobson, Dan. "James Baldwin as Spokesman." Com, 32 (December 1961), 497-502.

Kattan, Naim. "Deux ecrivains americains." ECRITS DU CANADA FRANCAIS, 17 (1964), 87-135.

Kazin, Alfred. "Close to Us." REPORTER, 25 (17 August 1961), 58-60.

Kent, George E. "Baldwin and the Problem of Being." CLAJ, 7 (1964), 202-14.

Lash, J.S. "Baldwin Beside Himself: A Study in Modern Phallicism." CLAJ, 8 (1964), 132-40.

Leaks, Sylvester. "James Baldwin--I Know His Name." FREEDOMWAYS, 3 (Winter 1963), 102-5.

Le Clec'h, Guy. "James Baldwin." FL, 19, iv (1964), 23-30.

Levin, David. "Baldwin's Autobiographical Essays: The Problem of Negro Identity." MR, 5 (1964), 239-47.

Long, Robert E. "Love and Wrath in the Fiction of James Baldwin." EngR, 19 (1969), 50-57.

Luce, P.A., and Eugene Gordon. "Communications on James Baldwin." MAINSTREAM, 15 (May 1960), 45-48.

MacInnes, Colin. "Dark Angel: The Writings of James Baldwin." ENCOUNTER, 21, ii (1963), 22-33.

Mayfield, Julian. "And Then Came Baldwin." FREEDOMWAYS, 3 (Spring 1963), 143-55.

Mergen, Bernard. "James Baldwin and the American Conundrum." MSpr, 57 (December 1963), 397-406.

Mohrt, Michel. "James Baldwin, ce combattant noir." FL, 19, iii (1964), 3.

Moore, John R. "An Embarrassment of Riches: Baldwin's GOING TO MEET THE MAN." HC, 2, (1965), 1-12.

Newman, Charles. "The Lesson of the Master: Henry James and James Baldwin." YR, 56 (1966), 45-59.

O'Daniel, Therman B. "James Baldwin: An Interpretive Study." CLAJ, 7 (1963), 37-47.

Petersen, Fred. "James Baldwin and Eduardo Mallea: Two Essayists' Search for Identity." DISCOURSE, 10 (1967), 97-107.

Plessner, Monika. "James Baldwin und das Land der Verheissung: Zwischen Farbsymbolik und Farbindifferenz." MERKUR, 20 (1966), 515-33.

Potter, Vilma. "Baldwin and Odets: The High Cost of 'Crossing.'" CEJ, I, iii (1965), 37-41.

Raddatz, Fritz. "Schwarz ist die Farbe der Einsamkeit: Skisse zu einer Portrat James Baldwin." FH, 20 (1965), 44-52.

Reilly, John M. "'Sonny's Blues'": James Baldwin's Image of Black Community." NALF, 4 (1970), 56-60.

Schroth, Raymond A., S.J. "James Baldwin's Search." CathW, 198 (February 1964), 288-94.

Silvera, Frank. "Towards a Theater of Understanding." NegroD, 18 (1969), 33-35.

Spender, Stephen. "James Baldwin: Voice of a Revolution." PR, 30 (1963), 256-60.

Standley, Fred L. "James Baldwin: The Artist as Incorrigible Distruber of the Peace." SHR, 4 (1970), 18-30.

_____. "James Baldwin: The Crucial Situation." SAQ, 65 (1966), 371-81.

Watson, Edward A. "The Novels of James Baldwin: Casebook of a 'Lover's War' with the United States." MR, 6 (1965), 385-402.

Wustenhagen, Heinz. "James Baldwin's Essays und Romane: Versuch einer ersten Einschatzung." ZAA, 13 (1965), 117-57.

J[AMES]. G[RAHAM]. BALLARD (1930-   ), ENGLISH

NOVELS

THE WIND FROM NOWHERE. New York: Berkley, 1962.

THE DROWNED WORLD. London: Gollancz, 1963.

THE DROUGHT. London: Cape, 1965.

THE CRYSTAL WORLD. London: Cape, 1966.

THE ATROCITY EXHIBITION. London: Cape, 1970.

SHORT STORIES

THE VOICES OF TIME AND OTHER STORIES. New York: Berkley, 1962.

BILLENIUM AND OTHER STORIES. New York: Berkley, 1962.

THE FOUR-DIMENSIONAL NIGHTMARE. London: Gollancz, 1963.

PASSPORT TO ETERNITY AND OTHER STORIES. New York: Berkley, 1963.

THE TERMINAL BEACH. London: Gollancz, 1964.

THE DISASTER AREA. London: Cape, 1967.

THE DAY OF FOREVER. London: Panther, 1968.

THE OVERLOADED MAN. London: Panther, 1968.

JOHN BARTH (1930-), AMERICAN

NOVELS

THE FLOATING OPERA. New York: Appleton-Century-Crofts, 1956.

THE END OF THE ROAD. Garden City, N.Y.: Doubleday, 1958.

THE SOT-WEED FACTOR. Garden City, N.Y.: Doubleday, 1960.

GILES GOAT-BOY; OR, THE REVISED NEW SYLLABUS. Garden City, N.Y.: Doubleday, 1966.

SHORT STORIES

LOST IN THE FUNHOUSE: FICTION FOR PRINT, TAPE, LIVE VOICE. Garden City, N.Y.: Doubleday, 1968.

BIBLIOGRAPHY

Bryer, Jackson R. "John Barth." Crit, 6 (1963), 86 89.

SPECIAL ISSUES

CRITIQUE: STUDIES IN MODERN FICTION, 6 (1963), "John Hawkes and John Barth Issue."

CRITICAL ARTICLES

Barth, John. "The Literature of Exhaustion." ATLANTIC MONTHLY, 220 (August 1967), 29-34.

Binni, Francesco. "John Barth e il romanzo di societa." SA, 12 (1966), 277-300.

Bluestone, George. "John Wain and John Barth: The Angry and the Accurate." MR, 1 (1960), 582-89.

Byrd, Scott. "GILES GOAT-BOY Visited." Crit, 9 (1967), 108-12.

Dippie, Brian W. "'His Visage Wild, His Form Exotick': Indian Themes and Cultural Guilt in John Barth's THE SOT-WEED FACTOR." AQ, 21 (1969), 113-21.

Diser, Philip E. "The Historical Ebenezer Cooke." Crit, 10 (1968), 48-59.

Enck, John. "John Barth: An Interview." WSCL, 6 (Winter-Spring 1965), 3-14.

Garis, Robert. "What Happened to John Barth?" Com, 47 (October 1966), 89-95.

Gross, Beverly. "The Anti-Novels of John Barth." ChiR, 20 (November 1968), 95-109.

Holder, Alan. "'What Marvelous Plot...Was Afoot?' History in Barth's THE SOT-WEED FACTOR." AQ, 20 (1968), 596-604.

Kennard, Jean E. "John Barth: Imitations of Imitations." Mosaic, 3 (Winter 1970), 116-31.

Kerner, David. "Psychodrama in Eden." ChiR, 13 (Winter-Spring 1959), 59-67.

Kiely, Benedict. "Ripeness Was Not All: John Barth's GILES GOAT-BOY." HC, 3, iv (1966), 1-12.

Knapp, Edgar H. "Found in the Barthhouse: Novelist as Savior." MFS, 14 (1968-69), 446-51.

Majdiak, Daniel. "Barth and the Representation of Life." CRITICISM, 12 (1970), 51-67.

Miller, Russell H. "THE SOT-WEED FACTOR: A Contemporary Mock-Epic." Crit, 8 (1966), 88-100.

Noland, Richard W. "John Barth and the Novel of Comic Nihilism." WSCL, 7 (Autumn 1966), 239-57.

Samuels, Charles T. "John Barth: A Buoyant Denial of Relevance." Cweal, 85 (21 October 1966), 80-81.

Sommavilla, Guido. "Il cinismo cosmico di John Barth." LETTURE, 24 (1969), 98-110.

Stubbs, John C. "John Barth as a Novelist of Ideas: The Themes of Value and Identity." Crit, 8 (1966), 101-16.

Sugiura, Ginsaku. "Imitations-of-Novels--John Barth no Shosetsu." EigoS, 115 (1969), 612-13.

Sutcliffe, Denham. "Worth a Guilty Conscience." KR, 23 (1961), 181-86.

Tanner, Tony. "The Hoax That Joke Bilked." PR, 34 (1967), 102-9.

Tilton, John W. "GILES GOAT-BOY: An Interpretation." BuR, 18, i (1970), 93-119.

DONALD BARTHELME (1931-), AMERICAN

NOVELS

SNOW WHITE. New York: Atheneum, 1967.

SHORT STORIES

COME BACK, DR. CALIGARI. Boston: Little, Brown, 1964.

UNSPEAKABLE PRACTICES, UNNATURAL ACTS. New York: Farrar, Straus, 1968.

CRITICAL ARTICLES

Longleigh, Peter J., Jr. "Donald Barthelme's SNOW WHITE." Crit, 11 (1969), 30-34.

H[ERBERT]. E[RNEST]. BATES (1905-74), ENGLISH

NOVELS

THE TWO SISTERS. London: Cape, 1926.

CATHERINE FOSTER. London: Cape, 1929.

THE HESSIAN PRISONER. London: Jackson, 1930.

MR. ESMOND'S LIFE. London: [privately printed], 1930.

CHARLOTTE'S ROW. London: Cape, 1931.

THE FALLOW LAND. London: Cape, 1932.

A GERMAN IDYLL. London: Golden Cockerel, 1932.

THE POACHER. London: Cape, 1935.

A HOUSE OF WOMEN. London: Cape, 1936.

SPELLA HO. London: Cape, 1938.

FAIR STOOD THE WIND FOR FRANCE. London: Joseph, 1944.

THE CRUISE OF "THE BREADWINNER." London: Joseph, 1946.

THE PURPLE PLAIN. London: Joseph, 1947.

THE JACARANDA TREE. London: Joseph, 1949.

DEAR LIFE. London: Joseph, 1950.

THE SCARLET SWORD. London: Joseph, 1950.

LOVE FOR LYDIA. London: Joseph, 1952.

THE FEAST OF JULY. London: Joseph, 1954.

THE SLEEPLESS MOON. London: Joseph, 1956.

THE DARLING BUDS OF MAY. London: Joseph, 1958.

A BREATH OF FRENCH AIR. London: Joseph, 1959.

WHEN THE GREEN WOODS LAUGH. London: Joseph, 1960. As HARK, HARK, THE LARK! Boston: Little, Brown, 1961.

THE DAY OF THE TORTOISE. London: Joseph, 1961.

A CROWN OF WILD MYRTLE. London: Joseph, 1962.

OH! TO BE IN ENGLAND. London: Joseph, 1963.

A MOMENT IN TIME. London: Joseph, 1964.

THE WEDDING PARTY. London: Joseph, 1965.

THE DISTANT HOURS IN SUMMER. London: Joseph, 1967.

THE WILD CHERRY TREE. London: Joseph, 1968.

A LITTLE OF WHAT YOU FANCY. London: Joseph, 1970.

SHORT STORIES

THE SPRING SONG AND IN VIEW OF THE FACT THAT. London: Archer, 1927.

DAY'S END AND OTHER STORIES. London: Cape, 1928.

SEVEN TALES AND ALEXANDER. London: Scholartis Press, 1929.

A THRESHING DAY. London: Foyle, 1931.

THE STORY WITHOUT AN END AND THE COUNTRY DOCTOR. London:
White Owl Press, 1932.

THE BLACK BOXER: TALES. London: Cape, 1932.

SALLY GO ROUND THE MOON. London: White Owl Press, 1932.

THE HOUSE WITH THE APRICOT AND TWO OTHER TALES. London: Golden
Cockerel Press, 1933.

THE WOMAN WHO HAD IMAGINATION AND OTHER STORIES. London:
Cape, 1934.

THIRTY TALES. London: Cape, 1934.

THE DUET. London: Grayson, 1935.

CUT AND COME AGAIN: FOURTEEN STORIES. London: Cape, 1935.

SOMETHING SHORT AND SWEET: STORIES. London: Cape, 1937.

COUNTRY TALES. London: Readers' union, 1938.

I AM NOT MYSELF. London: Corvinus Press, 1939.

MY UNCLE SILAS: STORIES. London: Cape, 1939.

THE BEAUTY OF THE DEAD AND OTHER STORIES. London: Cape, 1940.

THE GREATEST PEOPLE IN THE WORLD. London: Cape, 1942.

THE BRIDE COMES TO EVENSFORD. London: Cape, 1943.

HOW SLEEP THE BRAVE. London: Cape, 1943.

THIRTY-ONE SELECTED TALES. London: Cape, 1947.

COLONEL JULIAN AND OTHER STORIES. London: Joseph, 1951.

THE NATURE OF LOVE: THREE SHORT NOVELS. London: Joseph, 1953.

THE DAFFODIL SKY. London: Joseph, 1955.

DEATH OF A HUNTSMAN: FOUR SHORT NOVELS. London: Joseph, 1957.
As SUMMER IN SALANDER. Boston: Little, Brown, 1957.

SUGAR FOR THE HORSE. London: Joseph, 1957.

THE WATERCRESS GIRL AND OTHER STORIES. London: Joseph, 1959.

AN ASPIDISTRA IN BABYLON: FOUR NOVELLAS. London: Joseph, 1960.
As THE GRAPES OF PARADISE: FOUR SHORT NOVELS. Boston: Little,
Brown, 1960.

NOW SLEEPS THE CRIMSON PETAL AND OTHER STORIES. London: Joseph,
1961. As THE ENCHANTRESS AND OTHER STORIES. Boston: Little, Brown,
1961.

THE GOLDEN ORIOLE: FIVE NOVELLAS. London: Joseph, 1962.

SEVEN BY FIVE: STORIES 1926–1961. London: Joseph, 1963. As THE
BEST OF H.E. BATES. Boston: Little, Brown, 1963.

THE FABULOUS MRS. V. London: Joseph, 1964.

THE FOUR BEAUTIES. London: Joseph, 1968.

BIBLIOGRAPHY

Gawsworth, John. TEN CONTEMPORARIES. 2nd series. London: Joiner
and Steele, 1933.

SAMUEL BECKETT (1906-), IRISH

NOVELS

MURPHY. London: Routledge, 1938.

MOLLOY. Paris: Editions de Minuit, 1951. Translated by the author and Patrick Bowles as MOLLOY. New York: Grove Press, 1955; London: John Calder, 1959.

MALONE MEURT. Paris: Editions de Minuit, 1951. Translated by the author as MALONE DIES. New York: Grove Press, 1958; London: John Calder, 1959.

L'INNOMABLE. Paris: Editions de Minuit, 1953. Translated by the author as THE UNNAMABLE. New York: Grove Press, 1958; London: John Calder, 1959.

WATT (written in English). Paris: Olympia Press, 1953; New York: Grove Press, 1959; London: John Calder, 1963.

COMMENT C'EST. Paris: Editions de Minuit, 1961. Translated by the author as HOW IT IS. New York: Grove Press, 1964; London: John Calder, 1964.

MERCIER ET CAMIER. Paris: Editions de Minuit, 1970.

COLLECTED WORKS. 16 vols. New York: Grove Press, 1970.
   Includes the novels and short stories.

SHORT STORIES

MORE PRICKS THAN KICKS. London: Chatto and Windus, 1934.

NOUVELLES ET TEXTES POUR RIEN. Paris: Editions de Minuit, 1955.
Translated by the author as STORIES AND TEXTS FOR NOTHING. New York:
Grove Press, 1967; included in NO'S KNIFE: SELECTED SHORTER PROSE,
1945-1966. London: Calder and Boyars, 1967.

BIBLIOGRAPHY

Bryer, J[ackson]. R. "Critique de Samuel Beckett: Selection bibliographique."
RLM, 100 (1964), 169-84.

Cohn, Ruby. "A Checklist of Beckett Criticism." Per, 11 (1959), 193-96.

Tanner, James T.F., and J. Don Vann. SAMUEL BECKETT: A CHECKLIST
OF CRITICISM. Kent, Ohio: Kent State University Press, 1969.

CRITICAL BOOKS

Calder, John, ed. BECKETT AT SIXTY: A FESTSCHRIFT. London: Calder,
1967.

Coe, Richard N. SAMUEL BECKETT. Edinburgh: Oliver, 1964.

Cohn, Ruby. SAMUEL BECKETT: THE COMIC GAMUT. New Brunswick,
N.J.: Rutgers University Press, 1962.

Delye, Huguette. SAMUEL BECKETT OU LA PHILOSOPHIE DE L'ABSURDE.
Aix en Provence: la pensee universitaire, 1960.

Esslin, Martin, ed. SAMUEL BECKETT: A COLLECTION OF CRITICAL ES-
SAYS. Englewood Cliffs, N.J.: Prentice-Hall, 1965.

Federman, Raymond. JOURNEY TO CHAOS: SAMUEL BECKETT'S EARLY
FICTION. Berkeley: University of California Press, 1965.

Fletcher, John. THE NOVELS OF SAMUEL BECKETT. London: Chatto and
Windus, 1964.

Friedman, Melvin J., ed. SAMUEL BECKETT NOW: CRITICAL APPROACHES
TO HIS NOVELS, POETRY, AND PLAYS. Chicago: University of Chicago
Press, 1970.

Harrison, Robert. SAMUEL BECKETT'S "MURPHY": A CRITICAL EXCURSION.
University of Georgia Monographs, no. 15. Athens: University of Georgia
Press, 1968.

Hassan, Ihab. THE LITERATURE OF SILENCE: HENRY MILLER AND SAMUEL BECKETT. New York: Knopf, 1968.

Hoffman, Frederick J. SAMUEL BECKETT: THE LANGUAGE OF SELF. Carbondale: Southern Illinois University Press, 1962.

Jacobsen, Josephine, and William R. Mueller. THE TESTAMENT OF SAMUEL BECKETT: A STUDY. New York: Hill and Wang, 1964.

Kenner, Hugh. FLAUBERT, JOYCE, AND BECKETT: THE STOIC COMEDIANS. London: W.H. Allen, 1964.

_____. SAMUEL BECKETT: A CRITICAL STUDY. New York: Grove Press, 1962.

Maerli, Terje. SAMUEL BECKETT. Oslo: Universitetsforlaget, 1967.

Scott, Nathan A., Jr. SAMUEL BECKETT. London: Bowes, 1965.

Tindall, William York. SAMUEL BECKETT. New York: Columbia University Press, 1964.

SPECIAL ISSUES

PERSPECTIVE, 11 (1959), "Special Beckett Issue."

CRITICAL ARTICLES

Barrett, William. "How I Understand Less and Less Every Year." CuF, 2 (1959), 44–48.

Bataille, Georges. "Le Silence de Molloy." CRITIQUE, 7 (1951), 387–96.

Bersani, Leo. "No Exit for Beckett." PR, 33 (1966), 261–67.

Blanchot, Maurice. "Where Now? Who Now?" EVERGREEN REVIEW, 2 (Winter 1959), 222–29.

Blanzat, Jean. "Les Romans de Samuel Beckett." FL, 13 May 1961, p. 2.

Bowles, Patrick. "How Samuel Beckett Sees the Universe." LISTENER, 59 (19 June 1958), 1011–12.

Bree, Germaine. "Beckett's Abstractors of Quintessence." FR, 36 (1963), 567-76.

Brick, Allan. "The Madman in His Cell: Joyce, Beckett, Nabokov and the Stereotypes." MR, 1 (1959), 40-55.

Brooke-Rose, Christine. "Samuel Beckett and the Anti-Novel." LonM, 5 (December 1958), 38-46.

Chambers, Ross. "Beckett's Brinkmanship." AUMLA, 19 (1963), 57-75.

_____. "Samuel Beckett and the Padded Cell." Meanjin, 21 (1962), 451-62.

Cmarada, Geraldine. "MALONE DIES: A Round on Consciousness." Sym, 14 (1960), 199-212.

Coe, Richard N. "God and Samuel Beckett." Meanjin, 24 (1965), 66-85.

Cohn, Ruby. "Comedy of Samuel Beckett: Something Old, Something New..." YFS, no. 23 (1959), 11-17.

_____. "Philosophical Fragments in the Works of Samuel Beckett." CRITI-CISM, 6 (1964), 33-43.

_____. "Samuel Beckett, Self-Translator." PMLA, 76 (1961), 613-21.

_____. "Still Novel." YFS, no. 24 (1959), 48-53.

_____. "WATT in the Light of THE CASTLE." CL, 13 (Spring 1961), 154-66.

Cooney, Seamus. "Beckett's MURPHY." Expl, 25 (1966), Item 3.

Erickson, John D. "Objects and Systems in the Novels of Samuel Beckett." ECr, 7 (1967), 113-22.

Evers, Francis. "Samuel Beckett: The Incurious Seeker." DM, 7 (Spring 1968), 84-88.

Federman, Raymond. "'How It Is' with Beckett's Fiction." FR, 38 (1965), 459-68.

Finch, Roy. "The Reality of the Nothing: The Importance of Samuel Beckett."

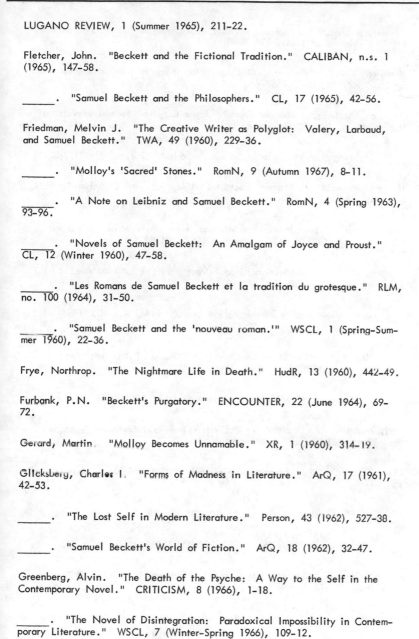

LUGANO REVIEW, 1 (Summer 1965), 211-22.

Fletcher, John. "Beckett and the Fictional Tradition." CALIBAN, n.s. 1 (1965), 147-58.

_____. "Samuel Beckett and the Philosophers." CL, 17 (1965), 42-56.

Friedman, Melvin J. "The Creative Writer as Polyglot: Valery, Larbaud, and Samuel Beckett." TWA, 49 (1960), 229-36.

_____. "Molloy's 'Sacred' Stones." RomN, 9 (Autumn 1967), 8-11.

_____. "A Note on Leibniz and Samuel Beckett." RomN, 4 (Spring 1963), 93-96.

_____. "Novels of Samuel Beckett: An Amalgam of Joyce and Proust." CL, 12 (Winter 1960), 47-58.

_____. "Les Romans de Samuel Beckett et la tradition du grotesque." RLM, no. 100 (1964), 31-50.

_____. "Samuel Beckett and the 'nouveau roman.'" WSCL, 1 (Spring-Summer 1960), 22-36.

Frye, Northrop. "The Nightmare Life in Death." HudR, 13 (1960), 442-49.

Furbank, P.N. "Beckett's Purgatory." ENCOUNTER, 22 (June 1964), 69-72.

Gerard, Martin. "Molloy Becomes Unnamable." XR, 1 (1960), 314-19.

Glicksberg, Charles I. "Forms of Madness in Literature." ArQ, 17 (1961), 42-53.

_____. "The Lost Self in Modern Literature." Person, 43 (1962), 527-38.

_____. "Samuel Beckett's World of Fiction." ArQ, 18 (1962), 32-47.

Greenberg, Alvin. "The Death of the Psyche: A Way to the Self in the Contemporary Novel." CRITICISM, 8 (1966), 1-18.

_____. "The Novel of Disintegration: Paradoxical Impossibility in Contemporary Literature." WSCL, 7 (Winter-Spring 1966), 109-12.

Gresset, Michel. "Le 'parce que' chez Faulkner et le 'donc' chez Beckett." LetN, 9 (November 1961), 124-38.

Hamilton, Carol. "Portrait in Old Age: The Image of Man in Beckett's Trilogy." WHR, 16 (1962), 157-65.

Hamilton, Kenneth. "Boon or Thorn? Joyce Cary and Samuel Beckett on Human Life." DR, 38 (1959), 433-42.

_____. "Negative Salvation in Samuel Beckett." QQ, 69 (1962), 102-11.

Harvey, Lawrence E. "Samuel Beckett on Life, Art, and Criticism." MLN, 80 (1965), 545-62.

Hassan, Ihab. "The Literature of Silence: From Henry Miller to Beckett and Burroughs." ENCOUNTER, 28 (January 1967), 74-82.

Hayman, David. "Introduction to an Extract from THE UNNAMABLE." TQ, 1 (Spring 1958), 127-28.

_____. "Molloy a la recherche de l'absurde." RLM, no. 100 (1964), 131-51.

Hesla, David H. "The Shape of Chaos: A Reading of Beckett's WATT." Crit, 6 (1963), 85-105.

Hughes, Daniel J. "Reality and the Hero." MFS, 6 (1960-61), 345-64.

Karl, Frederick R. "Waiting for Beckett: Quest and Re-Quest." SR, 69 (Fall 1961), 661-76.

Kenner, Hugh. "The Absurdity of Fiction." THE GRIFFIN, November 1959, pp. 13-16.

_____. "The Beckett Landscape." SPECTRUM, 2 (Winter 1958), 8-24.

_____. "Voices in the Night." SPECTRUM, 5 (Spring 1961), 3-20.

Kermode, Frank. "Beckett, Snow, and Pure Poverty." ENCOUNTER, 15 (July 1960), 73-77.

Lancelotti, Mario A. "Observaciones sobre MOLLOY." SUR, 273 (1961), 50-52.

Lee, Warren. "The Bitter Pill of Samuel Beckett." ChiR, 10 (Winter 1957), 77-87.

Leventhal, A.J. "The Beckett Hero." CRITIQUE, 7 (1965), 18-35.

Morse, J. Mitchell. "The Choreography of the New Novel." HudR, 16 (1963), 396-419.

_____. "Contemplative Life According to Samuel Beckett." HudR, 15 (1962-63), 512-24.

Noon, William T. "God and Man in Twentieth Century Fiction." THOUGHT, 37 (1962), 35-36.

_____. "Modern Literature and the Sense of Time." THOUGHT, 33 (1958-59), 571-603.

Oates, J.C. "The Trilogy of Samuel Beckett." Ren, 14 (1962), 160-65.

O'Neill, Joseph P. "The Absurd in Samuel Beckett." Person, 48 (1967), 56-76.

Pingaud, Bernard. "MOLLOY." ESPRIT, 9 (1951), 423-25.

_____. "MOLLOY douze ans apres." TM, 18 (1963), 1283-1300.

Popkin, Henry. "Williams, Osborne, or Beckett?" NYTMag, 13 November 1960, pp. 32-33, 119-21.

Pouillon, Jean. "MOLLOY." TM, 6 (1951), 184-86.

Pritchett, V.S. "Irish Oblomov." NStnt, 59 (2 April 1960), 489.

Rexroth, Kenneth. "The Point Is Irrelevance." NATION, 182 (14 April 1956), 325-28.

Rickels, Milton. "Existential Themes in Beckett's UNNAMABLE." CRITICISM, 4 (1962), 134-47.

Ricks, Christopher. "The Roots of Samuel Beckett." LISTENER, 72 (17 December 1964), 963-64, 980.

Scott, Nathan A., Jr. "The Recent Journey into the Zero Zone." CentR, 4 (1962), 144-81.

Senneff, Susan Field. "Song and Music in Samuel Beckett's WATT." MFS, 10 (1964), 137–49.

Solomon, Philip H. "Samuel Beckett's MOLLOY: A Dog's Life." FR, 41 (1967), 84–91.

Stamirowska, Krystyna. "The Conception of a Character in the Works of Joyce and Beckett." KN, 14 (1967), 443–47.

Steiner, George. "Books: Of Nuance and Scruple." NY, 44 (27 April 1968), 164, 167–70, 173–74.

Strauss, Walter A. "Dante's Belacqua and Beckett's Tramps." CL, 11 (Summer 1959), 250–61.

Thiebaut, Marcel. "Le 'Nouveau roman.'" RP, 65 (1958), 140–55.

Tindall, William York. "Beckett's Bums." CRITIQUE, 2 (1959), 3–15.

Unterecker, John. "Samuel Beckett's No-Man's Land." NewL, 42 (1959), 24–25.

Warhaft, Sidney. "Threne and Theme in WATT." WSCL, 4 (Autumn 1963), 261–78.

Wellwarth, G.E. "Life in the Void: Samuel Beckett." UKCR, 28 (1961), 25–33.

Wendler, Herbert W. "Graveyard Humanism." SWR, 49 (1964), 44–52.

SAUL BELLOW (1915-), AMERICAN

NOVELS

DANGLING MAN. New York: Vanguard Press, 1944.

THE VICTIM. New York: Vanguard Press, 1947.

THE ADVENTURES OF AUGIE MARCH. New York: Viking Press, 1953.

HENDERSON THE RAIN KING. New York: Viking Press, 1959.

HERZOG. New York: Viking Press, 1964.

MR. SAMMLER'S PLANET. New York: Viking Press, 1970.

SHORT STORIES

SEIZE THE DAY: WITH THREE SHORT STORIES AND A ONE-ACT PLAY.
New York: Viking Press, 1956.

MOSBY'S MEMOIRS AND OTHER STORIES. New York: Viking Press, 1968.

BIBLIOGRAPHY

Schneider, Harold W. "Two Bibliographies: Saul Bellow, William Styron."
Crit, 3 (1960), 71-86.

CRITICAL BOOKS

Clayton, John J. SAUL BELLOW: IN DEFENSE OF MAN. Bloomington:

Indiana University Press, 1968.

Detweiler, Robert. SAUL BELLOW: A CRITICAL ESSAY. Grand Rapids, Mich.: Eerdmans, 1967.

Malin, Irving, ed. SAUL BELLOW AND THE CRITICS. New York: New York University Press, 1967.

_____. SAUL BELLOW'S FICTION. Carbondale: Southern Illinois University Press, 1967.

Opdahl, Keith M. THE NOVELS OF SAUL BELLOW: AN INTRODUCTION. University Park: Pennsylvania State University Press, 1967.

Rovit, Earl. SAUL BELLOW. Minneapolis: University of Minnesota Press, 1967.

Tanner, Tony. SAUL BELLOW. Edinburgh: Oliver & Boyd, 1965.

SPECIAL ISSUES

CRITIQUE: STUDIES IN MODERN FICTION, 7 (1965), "Saul Bellow Issue."

CRITICAL ARTICLES

Allen, Michael. "Idiomatic Language in Two Novels by Saul Bellow." JAMS, 1 (1967), 275-80.

Alter, Robert. "The Stature of Saul Bellow." MIDSTREAM, 10 (December 1964), 3-15.

Arnovon, Cyrille. "Le roman africain de Saul Bellow: HENDERSON THE RAIN KING." EA, 14 (1961), 25-35.

Atkins, Anselm. "The Moderate Optimism of Saul Bellow's HERZOG." Person, 50 (1969), 117-29.

Baim, Joseph. "Escape From Intellection: Saul Bellow's DANGLING MAN." UR, 37 (1970), 28-34.

Baker, Sheridan. "Saul Bellow's Bout with Chivalry." CRITICISM, 8 (1966), 109-22.

Baruch, Franklin R. "Bellow and Milton: Professor Herzog in His Garden." Crit, 9 (1967), 74–83.

Bellow, Saul. "Deep Readers of the World, Beware!" NYTBR, 15 February 1959, pp. 1, 34.

———. "Distractions of a Fiction Writer." In NEW WORLD WRITING, pp. 229–43. 12th Mentor Selection. New York: New American Library, 1957.

———. "How I Wrote Augie March's Story." NYTBR, 31 January 1954, pp. 3, 17.

———. "Where Do I Go from Here: The Future of Fiction." MQR, 1 (Winter 1962), 27–33.

Bergler, Edmund. "Writers of Half-Talent." AI, 14 (1957), 155–64.

Bezanker, Abraham. "The Odyssey of Saul Bellow." YR, 58 (1969), 359–71.

Binni, Francesco. "Percorso narrativo di Saul Bellow." Ponte, 22 (1966), 831–42.

Bradbury, Malcolm. "Saul Bellow and the Naturalist Tradition." REL, 4, iv (1963), 80–92.

———. "Saul Bellow's HERZOG." CritQ, 7 (1965), 269–78.

———. "Saul Bellow's THE VICTIM." CritQ, 5 (1963), 119–28.

Cambon, Glauco. "Il nuovo romanzo di Saul Bellow." AUT AUT, 53 (1959), 318–20.

Campbell, Jeff H. "Bellow's Intimations of Immorality: HENDERSON THE RAIN KING." SNNTS, 1 (1969), 323–33.

Chapman, Abraham. "The Image of Man as Portrayed by Saul Bellow." CLAJ, 10 (1967), 285–98.

Chase, Richard. "The Adventures of Saul Bellow: The Progress of a Novelist." Com, 27 (April 1959), 323–30.

Cixous-Berger, Helene. "Situation de Saul Bellow." LetN, March–April 1967, pp. 130–45.

Cook, Bruce. "Saul Bellow: A Mood of Protest." PERSPECTIVES ON IDEAS AND THE ARTS, 12 (1963), 46–50.

Cordesse, Gerard. "L'unite de HERZOG." CALIBAN, 7 (1970), 99-113.

Crozier, Robert D. "Theme in AUGIE MARCH." Crit, 7 (1965), 18-32.

Davis, William V. "Bellow's HERZOG." ORION, 118 (1969), 73.

Demarest, David P., Jr. "The Theme of Discontinuity in Saul Bellow's Fiction: 'Looking for Mr. Green' and 'A Father-to-Be.'" SSF, 6 (1969), 175-86.

Detweiler, Robert. "Patterns of Rebirth in HENDERSON THE RAIN KING." MFS, 12 (1966), 405-14.

Dickstein, Morris. "For Art's Sake." PR, 33 (1966), 617-21.

Dommergues, Pierre. "Rencontre avec Saul Bellow." PREUVES, 191 (1967), 38-47.

Donoghue, Denis. "Commitment and the Dangling Man." STUDIES, 53 (1964), 174-87.

Duesberg, Jacques. "Un jeune romancier americain: Saul Bellow." SYN-THESES, 10 (May-June 1955), 149-51.

Eisinger, Chester E. "Saul Bellow: Love and Identity." ACCENT, 18 (1958), 179-203.

Enck, John. "Saul Bellow: An Interview." WSCL, 6 (Winter-Spring 1965), 156-60.

Fiedler, Leslie A. "No, In Thunder." ESQUIRE, 54 (September 1960), 76-79.

_____. "Saul Bellow." PrS, 31 (1957), 103-10.

Fisch, Harold. "The Hero as Jew: Reflections on HERZOG." JUDAISM, 17 (1968), 42-54.

Flamm, Dudley. "Herzog--Victim and Hero." ZAA, 17 (1969), 174-88.

Fossum, Robert H. "The Devil and Saul Bellow." CLS, 3 (1966), 197-206.

_____. "Inflationary Trends in the Criticism of Fiction: Four Studies of Saul Bellow." SNNTS, 2, i (1970), 99-104.

Frank, Reuben. "Saul Bellow: The Evolution of a Contemporary Novelist."

WR, 18 (1954), 101-12.

Freedman, Ralph. "Saul Bellow: The Illusion of Environment." WSCL, 1 (Winter 1960), 50-65.

Frohock, W.M. "Saul Bellow and His Penitent Picaro." SWR, 53 (1968), 36-44.

Galloway, David D. "The Absurd Man as Picaro: The Novels of Saul Bellow." TSLL, 6 (1964), 226-54.

_____. "An Interview with Saul Bellow." AUDIT, 3 (1963), 19-23.

_____. "Moses-Bloom-Herzog: Bellow's Everyman." SoR, 2 (1966), 61-76.

Garrett, George. "To Do Right in a Bad World: Saul Bellow's HERZOG." HC, 2, ii (1965), 2-12.

Goldberg, Gerald J. "Life's Customer: Augie March." Crit, 3 (1960), 15-27.

Goldfinch, Michael A. "A Journey to the Interior." ES, 48 (1962), 439-43.

Greenberg, Alvin. "The Death of the Psyche: A Way to the Self in the Contemporary Novel." CRITICISM, 8 (1966), 1-18.

Gross, Beverly. "Bellow's Herzog." ChiR, 27, ii-iii (1964-65), 217-21.

Guerard, Albert J. "Saul Bellow and the Activists: On THE ADVENTURES OF AUGIE MARCH." SoR, 3 (1967), 582-96.

Guttmann, Allen. "Bellow's HENDERSON." Crit, 7 (1965), 33-42.

Gutwillig, Robert. "Talk with Saul Bellow." NYTBR, 20 September 1964, pp. 40-41.

Handy, William J. "Saul Bellow and the Naturalistic Hero." TSLL, 5 (1964), 538-45.

Harper, Gordon L. "Saul Bellow--The Art of Fiction XXXVII." ParisR, 36 (Winter 1966), 48-73.

Hasenclever, Walter. "Grosse Menschen und kleine Wirklichkeit." Monat, 13 (1961), 71-75.

Hassan, Ihab H. "Saul Bellow: Five Faces of a Hero." Crit, 3 (1960), 28-36.

Howard, Jane. "Mr. Bellow Considers His Planet." LIFE, 3 April 1970, pp. 57-60.

Hughes, Daniel J. "Reality and the Hero: LOLITA and HENDERSON THE RAIN KING." MFS, 6 (1960-61), 345-64.

Kazin, Alfred. "My Friend Saul Bellow." ATLANTIC MONTHLY, 215 (January 1965), 51-54.

Klein, Marcus. "A Discipline of Nobility: Saul Bellow's Fiction." KR, 24 (1962), 203-26.

Knipp, Thomas R. "The Cost of Henderson's Quest." BSUF, 10 (1969), 37-39.

Lamont, Rosette. "The Confessions of Moses Herzog." LanM, 60 (1966), 116-20.

Leach, Elsie. "From Ritual to Romance Again: HENDERSON THE RAIN KING." WHR, 14 (1960), 223-24.

Lehan, Richard. "Existentialism in Recent American Fiction: The Demonic Quest." TSLL, 1 (1960), 181-202.

Levenson, J.C. "Bellow's Dangling Men." Crit, 3 (1960), 3-14.

Levine, Paul. "Saul Bellow: The Affirmation of the Philosophical Fool." Per, 10 (1959), 163-76.

Lombardo, Agostino. "La narrative di Saul Bellow." SA, 11 (1965), 309-44.

Lucko, Peter. "Herzog--Modell der ACCEPTANCE: Eine Erwiderung." ZAA, 17 (1969), 189-95.

Malin, Irving. "Reputations--XIV: Saul Bellow." LonM, 4 (January 1965), 43-54.

Morrow, Patrick. "Threat and Accommodation: The Novels of Saul Bellow." MQ, 8 (1967), 389-411.

Moss, Judith P. "The Body as Symbol in Saul Bellow's HENDERSON THE

RAIN KING." L&P, 20 (1970), 51-61.

Mudrick, Marvin. "Who Killed Herzog? or Three American Novelists." UDQ, 1 (1966), 61-97.

Nathan, Monique. "Saul Bellow." ESPRIT, 34 (1966), 363-70.

Normand, J. "L'homme mystifie: Les heros de Bellow, Albee, Styron et Mailer." EA, 22 (1969), 370-85.

Overbeck, Pat T. "The Women in AUGIE MARCH." TSLL, 10 (1968), 471-84.

Petillon, Pierre-Yves. "Le heros americain a pris de l'age." CRITIQUE, 23 (January 1967), 159-76.

Poirier, Richard. "Bellow to Herzog." PR, 32 (1965), 264-71.

Porter, M. Gilbert. "HERZOG: A Transcendental Solution to an Existential Problem." ForumH, 7 (1969), 32-36.

Quinton, Anthony. "The Adventures of Saul Bellow." LonM, 6, xii (1959), 55-59.

Raider, Ruth. "Saul Bellow." CamQ, 2 (1967), 172-83.

Rans, Geoffrey. "The Novels of Saul Bellow." REL, 4, iv (1963), 18-30.

Read, Forrest. "HERZOG: A Review." EPOCH, 14 (1964), 81-96.

Ross, Theodore J. "Notes on Saul Bellow." CJF, 18 (Fall 1959), 21-27.

Rovit, Earl. "Bellow in Occupancy." ASch, 34 (1965), 292-98.

Samuel, Maurice. "My Friend, the Late Moses Herzog." MIDSTREAM, 12 (April 1966), 3-25.

Sanavio, Piero. "Il romanzo di Saul Bellow." SA, 2 (1956), 261-84.

Saporta, Marc. "Un roman d'anti-amour: HERZOG de Saul Bellow." PREUVES, 15 (1965), 88-89.

Schorer, Mark. "A Book of Yes and No." HudR, 7 (1954), 134-41.

Shaw, Peter. "The Tough Guy Intellectual." CritQ, 8 (1966), 23-27.

Shulman, Robert. "Myth, Mr. Eliot, and the Comic Novel." MFS, 12 (1966), 395-403.

_____. "The Style of Bellow's Comedy." PMLA, 83 (1968), 109-17.

Stern, Richard G. "Henderson's Bellow." KR, 21 (1959), 655-61.

Stevenson, D.I. "The Activists." DAEDALUS, 92 (Spring 1963), 238-49.

Stock, Irvin. "The Novels of Saul Bellow." SoR, 3 (1967), 13-42.

Tanner, Tony. "Saul Bellow: The Flight from Monologue." ENCOUNTER, 24 (February 1965), 58-70.

Trachtenberg, Stanley. "Saul Bellow's LUFTMENSCHEN: The Compromise with Reality." Crit, 9 (1967), 37-61.

Trowbridge, Clinton W. "Water Imagery in SEIZE THE DAY." Crit, 9 (1967), 62-73.

Uphaus, Suzanne Henning. "From Innocence to Experience: A Study of HERZOG." DR, 46 (Spring 1966), 67-78.

Van Egmond, Peter. "Herzog's Quotation of Walt Whitman." WWR, 13 (1967), 54-56.

Vogel, Dan. "Saul Bellow's Vision Beyond Absurdity: Jewishness in HER-ZOG." Tradition, 9 (Spring 1968), 65-79.

Way, Brian. "Character and Society in THE ADVENTURES OF AUGIE MARCH." BAASB, 8 (1964), 36-44.

Weber, Ronald. "Bellow's Thinkers." WHR, 22 (1968), 305-13.

Weiss, Daniel. "Caliban on Prospero: A Psychoanalytic Study of the Novel SEIZE THE DAY." AI, 19 (1962), 277-306.

Young, James D. "Bellow's View of the Heart." Crit, 7 (1965), 5-17.

PHYLLIS BENTLEY (1894-   ), ENGLISH

NOVELS

ENVIRONMENT. London: Sidgwick and Jackson, 1922.

CAT-IN-THE-MANGER. London: Sidgwick and Jackson, 1923.

THE SPINNER OF THE YEARS. London: Benn, 1928.

THE PARTNERSHIP. London: Benn, 1928.

CARR. London: Benn, 1929.

TRIO. London: Gollancz, 1930.

INHERITANCE. London: Gollancz, 1932.

A MODERN TRAGEDY. London: Gollancz, 1934.

FREEDOM FAREWELL. London: Gollancz, 1936.

SLEEP IN PEACE. London: Gollancz, 1938.

TAKE COURAGE. London: Gollancz, 1940.

MANHOLD. London: Gollancz, 1941.

THE RISE OF HENRY MORCAR. London: Gollancz, 1946.

LIFE STORY. London: Gollancz, 1948.

QUORUM. London: Gollancz, 1950.

THE HOUSE OF MOREYS. London: Gollancz, 1953.

NOBLE IN REASON. London: Gollancz, 1955.

CRESCENDO. London: Gollancz, 1958.

A MAN OF HIS TIME. London: Gollancz, 1966.

RING IN THE NEW. London: Gollancz, 1969.

SHORT STORIES

THE WORLD'S BANE. London: Unwin, 1918.

THE WHOLE OF THE STORY. London: Gollancz, 1935.

PANORAMA. London: Gollancz, 1952.

LOVE AND MONEY. London: Gollancz, 1957.

KITH AND KIN. London: Gollancz, 1960.

TALES OF THE WEST RIDING. London: Gollancz, 1965.

THOMAS BERGER (1924-), AMERICAN

NOVELS

CRAZY IN BERLIN. New York: Scribner, 1958.

REINHART IN LOVE. New York: Scribner, 1962.

LITTLE BIG MAN. New York: Dial Press, 1964.

KILLING TIME. New York: Dial Press, 1967.

VITAL PARTS. New York: Baron, 1970.

CRITICAL ARTICLES

Dipple, Brian W. "Jack Crabb and the Sole Survivors of Custer's Last Stand." WAL, 4 (1969), 189-202.

Gurian, Jay. "Style in the Literary Desert: LITTLE BIG MAN." WAL, 3 (1969), 285-96.

Hassan, Ihab. "Conscience and Incongruity: The Fiction of Thomas Berger." Crit, 5 (1962), 4-15.

Lee, L.L. "American, Western, Picaresque: Thomas Berger's LITTLE BIG MAN." SDR, 4 (1966), 35-42.

Schickel, Richard. "Bitter Comedy." Com, 50 (July 1970), 76-80.

Wylder, Delbert E. "Thomas Berger's LITTLE BIG MAN as Literature." WAL, 3 (1969), 273-84.

VANCE BOURJAILY (1922-), AMERICAN

NOVELS

THE END OF MY LIFE. New York: Scribner, 1947.

THE HOUND OF EARTH. New York: Scribner, 1955.

THE VIOLATED. New York: Dial Press, 1958.

CONFESSIONS OF A SPENT YOUTH. New York: Dial Press, 1960.

THE MAN WHO KNEW KENNEDY. New York: Dial Press, 1967.

BRILL AMONG THE RUINS. New York: Dial Press, 1970.

CRITICAL ARTICLES

DeLancey, Robert W. "Man and Mankind in the Novels of Vance Bourjaily." EngR, 10 (Winter 1959), 3-4.

Dienstfrey, Harris. "The Novels of Vance Bourjaily." Com, 31 (April 1961), 360-63.

Galligan, Edward L. "Hemingway's Staying Power." MR, 8 (1967), 435-37.

JOHN BOWEN (1924-), ENGLISH

NOVELS

THE TRUTH WILL NOT HELP US: EMBROIDERY ON AN HISTORICAL THEME.
London: Chatto and Windus, 1956.

AFTER THE RAIN. London: Faber, 1958.

THE CENTRE OF THE GREEN. London: Faber, 1959.

STORYBOARD. London: Faber, 1960.

THE BIRDCAGE. London: Faber, 1962.

A WORLD ELSEWHERE. London: Faber, 1965.

CRITICAL ARTICLES

Gindin, James. "The Fable Begins to Break Down." WSCL, 8 (1967), 1-18.

PAUL BOWLES (1910-), AMERICAN

NOVELS

THE SHELTERING SKY. New York: New Directions, 1949.

LET IT COME DOWN. New York: Random House, 1952.

THE SPIDER'S HOUSE. New York: Random House, 1955.

UP ABOVE THE WORLD. New York: Simon and Schuster, 1966.

SHORT STORIES

THE DELICATE PREY AND OTHER STORIES. New York: Random House, 1950.

A LITTLE STONE: STORIES. London: Lehmann, 1950.

THE HOURS AFTER NOON. London: Heinemann, 1959.

A HUNDRED CAMELS IN THE COURTYARD. San Francisco: City Lights, 1962.

THE TIME OF FRIENDSHIP. New York: Holt Rinehart, 1967.

PAGES FROM COLD POINT AND OTHER STORIES. London: Peter Owen, 1968.

CRITICAL ARTICLES

Antonini, Giacomo. "Un Americano Vuole evadere." FLe, 8 (15 November 1953), 1-2.

Evans, Oliver. "Paul Bowles and the 'Natural Man.'" Crit, 3 (1959), 43–59.

Fytton, Francis. "The Pipe Dreams of Paul Bowles." LonM, n.s. 6 (February 1967), 102–9.

Glicksberg, Charles I. "The Literary Struggle for Selfhood." Person, 42 (1961), 52–65.

Hassan, Ihab. "The Pilgrim as Prey: A Note on Paul Bowles." WR, 19 (Autumn 1954), 23–36.

Lehan, Richard. "Existentialism in Recent American Fiction: The Demonic Quest." TSLL, 1 (1959), 181–202.

Paetel, K.O. "Gibt es einen amerikanischen Existentialismus." WuW, 15 (1960), 103–5.

KAY BOYLE (1903-   ), AMERICAN

NOVELS

PLAGUED BY THE NIGHTINGALE. New York: Smith, 1931.

YEAR BEFORE LAST. New York: Smith, 1932.

GENTLEMEN, I ADDRESS YOU PRIVATELY. New York: Smith, 1933.

MY NEXT BRIDE. New York: Harcourt, Brace, 1934.

DEATH OF A MAN. New York: Harcourt, Brace, 1936.

MONDAY NIGHT. New York: Harcourt, Brace, 1938.

PRIMER FOR COMBAT. New York: Simon and Schuster, 1942.

AVALANCHE. New York: Simon and Schuster, 1944.

A FRENCHMAN MUST DIE. New York: Simon and Schuster, 1946.

1939. New York: Simon and Schuster, 1948.

HIS HUMAN MAJESTY. New York: Whittlesey House, 1949.

THE SEAGULL ON THE STEP. New York: Knopf, 1955.

GENERATION WITHOUT FAREWELL. New York: Knopf, 1960.

SHORT STORIES

SHORT STORIES. Paris: Black Sun Press, 1929.

WEDDING DAY AND OTHER STORIES. New York: Smith, 1930.

THE FIRST LOVER AND OTHER STORIES. New York: Random House, 1933.

THE WHITE HORSES OF VIENNA AND OTHER STORIES. New York: Harcourt, Brace, 1936.

THE CRAZY HUNTER: THREE SHORT NOVELS. New York: Harcourt, Brace, 1940.

THIRTY STORIES. New York: Simon and Schuster, 1946.

THE SMOKING MOUNTAIN: STORIES OF POST-WAR GERMANY. New York: McGraw-Hill, 1951.

THREE SHORT NOVELS. Boston: Beacon Press, 1958.

NOTHING EVER BREAKS EXCEPT THE HEART. Garden City, N.Y. Doubleday, 1966.

CRITICAL ARTICLES

Carpenter, Richard C. "Kay Boyle." CE, 15 (1953), 81-87.

_____. "Kay Boyle: The Figure in the Carpet." Crit, 7 (1965), 65-78.

JOHN BRAINE (1922-), ENGLISH

NOVELS

ROOM AT THE TOP. London: Eyre and Spottiswoode, 1957.

THE VODI. London: Eyre and Spottiswoode, 1959. As FROM THE HAND OF THE HUNTER. Boston: Houghton Mifflin, 1960.

LIFE AT THE TOP. London: Eyre and Spottiswoode, 1962.

THE JEALOUS GOD. London: Eyre and Spottiswoode, 1964.

THE CRYING GAME. London: Eyre and Spottiswoode, 1968.

STAY WITH ME TILL MORNING. London: Eyre and Spottiswoode, 1970.

CRITICAL BOOKS

Lee, James W. JOHN BRAINE. New York: Twayne, 1968.

CRITICAL ARTICLES

Hurrell, John D. "Class and Conscience in John Braine and Kingsley Amis." Crit, 2 (1958), 39-53.

Jelly, Oliver. "Fiction and Illness." REL, 3 (January 1962), 80-89.

O'Connor, William Van. "Two Types of 'Heroes' in Post-War British Fiction." PMLA, 77 (1962), 168-74.

Shestakov, Dmitri. "John Braine Facing His Fourth Novel." SovL, 8 (1964), 178-81.

Taylor, Archer. "John Braine's Proverbs." WF, 23 (1964), 42-43.

CHRISTINE BROOKE-ROSE (1923-), ENGLISH

NOVELS

THE LANGUAGES OF LOVE. London: Secker and Warburg, 1957.

THE SYCAMORE TREE. London: Secker and Warburg, 1958.

THE DEAR DECEIT. London: Secker and Warburg, 1960.

THE MIDDLEMEN: A SATIRE. London: Secker and Warburg, 1961.

OUT. London: Joseph, 1964.

SUCH. London: Joseph, 1966.

BETWEEN. London: Joseph, 1968.

SHORT STORIES

GO WHEN YOU SEE THE GREEN MAN WALKING. London: Joseph, 1970.

BRIGID BROPHY (1929-), ENGLISH

NOVELS

HACKENFELLER'S APE. London: Hart-Davis, 1953.

THE KING OF A RAINY COUNTRY. London: Secker and Warburg, 1956.

FLESH. London: Secker and Warburg, 1962.

THE FINISHING TOUCH. London: Secker and Warburg, 1963.

THE SNOW BALL. London: Secker and Warburg, 1964.

IN TRANSIT. London: Macdonald, 1969.

SHORT STORIES

THE CROWN PRINCESS AND OTHER STORIES. London: Collins, 1953.

FREDERICK BUECHNER (1926-), AMERICAN

NOVELS

A LONG DAY'S DYING. New York: Knopf, 1950.

THE SEASONS' DIFFERENCE. New York: Knopf, 1952.

THE RETURN OF ANSEL GIBBS. New York: Knopf, 1958.

THE FINAL BEAST. New York: Atheneum, 1965.

THE ENTRANCE TO PORLOCK. New York: Atheneum, 1970.

CRITICAL ARTICLES

Antonini, Giacomo. "Raffinatezza di Buechner." FLe, 8 (20 December 1953), 5.

_____. "Il ritorno di Buechner." FLe, 13 (3 August 1958), 7.

ANTHONY BURGESS (1917-), ENGLISH

NOVELS

TIME FOR A TIGER. London: Heinemann, 1956.

THE ENEMY IN THE BLANKET. London: Heinemann, 1958.

BEDS IN THE EAST. London: Heinemann, 1959.

THE RIGHT TO AN ANSWER. London: Heinemann, 1960.

THE DOCTOR IS SICK. London: Heinemann, 1960.

DEVIL OF A STATE. London: Heinemann, 1961.

ONE HAND CLAPPING (as Joseph Kell). London: Peter Davies, 1961.

THE WORM AND THE RING. London: Heinemann, 1961.

THE WANTING SEED. London: Heinemann, 1962.

A CLOCKWORK ORANGE. London: Heinemann, 1962.

INSIDE MR. ENDERBY (as Joseph Kell). London: Heinemann, 1963.

HONEY FOR THE BEARS. London: Heinemann, 1963.

MALAYAN TRILOGY. London: Heinemann, 1963. As THE LONG DAY
WANES. New York: Norton, 1965.
> Includes TIME FOR A TIGER, THE ENEMY IN THE BLANKET,
> BEDS IN THE EAST.

THE EVE OF ST. VENUS. London: Sidgwick, 1964.

NOTHING LIKE THE SUN: A STORY OF SHAKESPEARE'S LOVE-LIFE. London: Heinemann, 1964.

A VISION OF BATTLEMENTS. London: Sidgwick, 1965.

TREMOR OF INTENT. London: Heinemann, 1966.

ENDERBY OUTSIDE. London: Heinemann, 1968. As ENDERBY. New York: Norton, 1968.
  Includes INSIDE MR. ENDERBY and ENDERBY OUTSIDE.

CRITICAL ARTICLES

Adler, Dick. "Inside Mr. Burgess." NYTMag, 2 April 1967, pp. 47-50.

Aggeler, Geoffrey. "The Comic Art of Anthony Burgess." ArQ, 25 (1969), 234-51.

_____. "Mr. Enderby and Mr. Burgess." MALAHAT REVIEW, 10 (1969), 104-10.

Clemens, Walter. "Anthony Burgess: Pushing On." NYTBR, 29 November 1970, p. 2.

Davis, Earle. "'Laugh Now--Think Later!': The Genius of Anthony Burgess." KM, 1968, pp. 7-12.

Hicks, Granville. "The Fertile World of Anthony Burgess." SatR, 50 (15 July 1967), 27-29.

Horder, John. "Art that Pays." GUARDIAN, 10 October 1964, p. 5.

Mitchell, Julian. "Reputations--X: Anthony Burgess." LonM, n.s. 3 (February 1964), 48-54.

Nichols, Lewis. "Mr. Burgess." NYTBR, 10 April 1966, p. 8.

Pritchard, William H. "The Novels of Anthony Burgess." MR 7 (1966), 525-39.

Ricks, Christopher. "The Epicene." NSat, 5 April 1963, p. 496.

Sullivan, Walter. "Death Without Tears: Anthony Burgess and the Dissolution of the West." HC, 6 (April 1969), 1-11.

WILLIAM BURROUGHS (1914-), AMERICAN

NOVELS

JUNKIE (as William Lee). New York: Ace, 1953.

NAKED LUNCH. Paris: Olympia Press, 1959; New York: Grove Press, 1962.

THE SOFT MACHINE. Paris: Olympia Press, 1961; New York: Grove Press, 1966.

THE TICKET THAT EXPLODED. Paris: Olympia Press, 1962; New York: Grove Press, 1967.

DEAD FINGERS TALK. London: John Calder, 1963.

NOVA EXPRESS. New York: Grove Press, 1964.

CRITICAL ARTICLES

Adam, Ian W. "Society as Novelist." JAAC, 25 (Summer 1967), 375-86.

Cimatti, Pietro. "Burroughs e Updike." Fle, 17 (April 1962), 3.

Hassan, Ihab. "The Literature of Silence: From Henry Miller to Beckett and Burroughs." ENCOUNTER, 28 (January 1967), 74-82.

_____. "The Subtracting Machine: The Work of William Burroughs." Crit, 6 (1963), 4-23.

Knickerbocker, Conrad. "William Burroughs." ParisR, 35 (Fall 1965), 13-49.

William Burroughs

Kostelanetz, Richard. "From Nightmare to Seredipity [sic]: A Retrospective Look at William Burroughs." TCL, 11 (1965), 123-30.

Lodge, David. "Objections to William Burroughs." CritQ, 8 (1966), 203-12.

McCarthy, Mary. "Burroughs' NAKED LUNCH." ENCOUNTER, 20 (April 1963), 92-98.

McConnell, Frank D. "William Burroughs and the Literature of Addiction." MR, 8 (1967), 665-80.

McLuhan, Marshall. "Notes on Burroughs." NATION, 28 December 1964, pp. 517-18.

Manganotti, Donatella. "William Burroughs." SA, 8 (1962), 245-91.

Michelson, Peter. "Beardsley, Burroughs, Decadence, and the Poetics of Obscenity." TriQ, 12 (Spring 1968), 148-55.

Peterson, R.G. "A Picture is a Fact: Wittgenstein and THE NAKED LUNCH." TCL, 12 (1966), 78-86.

Phillips, William. "The New Immoralists." Com, 39 (April 1965), 66-69.

Solotaroff, Theodore. "The Algebra of Need." NRep, 157 (5 August 1967), 29-30.

Tanner, Tony. "The New Demonology." PR, 33 (1966), 547-72.

Weston, Ronald. "William Burroughs, High Priest of Hipsterism." FACT, 2 (November-December 1965), 11-17.

104

HORTENSE CALISHER (1911-), AMERICAN

NOVELS

FALSE ENTRY. Boston: Little, Brown, 1961.

TEXTURES OF LIFE. Boston: Little, Brown, 1963.

JOURNAL FROM ELLIPSIA. Boston: Little, Brown, 1965.

THE RAILWAY POLICE AND THE LAST TROLLEY RIDE (two novellas). Boston: Little, Brown, 1966.

THE NEW YORKERS. Boston: Little, Brown, 1969.

SHORT STORIES

IN THE ABSENCE OF ANGELS: STORIES. Boston: Little, Brown, 1951.

TALE FOR THE MIRROR: A NOVELLA AND OTHER STORIES. Boston: Little, Brown, 1962.

EXTREME MAGIC: A NOVELLA AND OTHER STORIES. Boston: Little, Brown, 1964.

CRITICAL ARTICLES

Hahn, Emily. "In Appreciation of Hortense Calisher." WSCL, 6 (Summer 1965), 243–49.

TRUMAN CAPOTE (1924-), AMERICAN

NOVELS

OTHER VOICES, OTHER ROOMS. New York: Random House, 1948.

THE GRASS HARP. New York: Random House, 1951.

BREAKFAST AT TIFFANY'S: A SHORT NOVEL AND THREE STORIES. New York: Random House, 1958.

SHORT STORIES

A TREE OF NIGHT AND OTHER STORIES. New York: Random House, 1949.

A CHRISTMAS MEMORY. New York: Random House, 1966.

BIBLIOGRAPHY

Wall, Richard J., and Curl L. Craycraft. "A Checklist of Works About Truman Capote." BYNPL, 71 (1967), 165-72.

CRITICAL ARTICLES

Aldridge, John W. "The Metaphorical World of Truman Capote." WR, 15 (Summer 1951), 247-60.

Antonini, Giacomo. "I filtri magici di Capote." FLe, 8 (22 November 1953), 1-2.

Baldanza, Frank. "Plato in Dixie." GaR, 12 (1958), 151-67.

Berger, Yves. "Truman Capote." CRITIQUE, 15 (1959), 491–507.

Bisel, Gaetano. "Truman Capote." LETTURE, 21 (1966), 403–22.

Bucco, Martin. "Truman Capote and the Country Below the Surface." FOUR QUARTERS, 7 (November 1957), 22–25.

_____. "Voice from a Cloud." Harper's, 235 (November 1967), 99–104.

Chapsal, Madeleine. "Truman Capote: s'engager dans l'aventure." QUIN-ZAINE LITTERAIRE, no. 11 (Spring 1960), 4–5.

Cimatti, Pietro. "Romanzieri americani." FLe, 15 (15 May 1960), 5.

Collins, Carvel. "Other Voices." ASch, 25 (1955), 108–16.

Goad, Craig. "Daylight and Darkness, Dream and Delusion: The Works of Truman Capote." ESRS, 16 (1967), 5–57.

Hassan, Ihab. "Birth of a Heroine." PrS, 34 (1960), 78–83.

_____. "The Daydream and Nightmare of Narcissus." WSCL, 1 (Spring–Summer 1960), 5–21.

Hill, Pati. "The Art of Fiction." ParisR, 16 (1957), 35–51.

Keith, Don Lee. "An Interview with Truman Capote." CONTEMPORA, 1, iv (1970), 36–40.

Le Clec'h, Guy. "Truman Capote poursuit a Paris un reportage sur l'Amerique." FL, 17 (1962), 3.

Lemaire, Marcel. "Fiction in U.S.A. from the South." RLV, 27 (1961), 244–53.

Levine, Paul. "Truman Capote: The Revelation of the Broken Image." VQR, 34 (1958), 600–617.

Mengeling, Marvin E. "OTHER VOICES, OTHER ROOMS: Oedipus Between the Covers." AI, 19 (1962), 361–74.

Moravia, Alberto. "Two American Writers (1949)." SR, 68 (1960), 473–81.

Norden, Eric. "PLAYBOY Interview: Truman Capote." PLAYBOY, 15 (March 1968), 51–53, 56, 58–62, 160–62, 164–70.

Pini, Richard. "Fiction et realite chez Truman Capote." LanM, 63 (1969), 176–85.

Saporta, Marc. "Truman Capote." INFORMATIONS ET DOCUMENTS, no. 162 (1962), 29–33.

Toebosch, Wim. "Recente Amerikaanse literatuur: Truman Capote en Oscar Lewis." VIG, 50 (1966), 402–8.

Trimmier, Diane B. "The Critical Reception of Capote's OTHER VOICES, OTHER ROOMS." WVUPP, 17 (1970), 94–101.

JOHN CHEEVER (1912-), AMERICAN

NOVELS

THE WAPSHOT CHRONICLE. New York: Harper, 1957.

THE WAPSHOT SCANDAL. New York: Harper, 1964.

BULLET PARK. New York: Knopf, 1969.

SHORT STORIES

THE WAY SOME PEOPLE LIVE: A BOOK OF STORIES. New York: Random House, 1943.

THE ENORMOUS RADIO AND OTHER STORIES. New York: Funk and Wagnalls, 1953.

THE HOUSEBREAKER OF SHADY HILL AND OTHER STORIES. New York: Harper, 1958.

SOME PEOPLE, PLACES, AND THINGS THAT WILL NOT APPEAR IN MY NEXT NOVEL. New York: Harper, 1961.

THE BRIGADIER AND THE GOLF WIDOW. New York: Harper, 1964.

CRITICAL ARTICLES

Auser, C.P. "John Cheever's Myth of Man and Time: 'The Swimmer.'" CEA, 29 (March 1967), 18-19.

Bartolini, Antonio. "Una vera America." FLe, 13 (26 October 1959), 5-6.

Bracher, Frederick. "John Cheever: A Vision of the World." ClareQ, 11 (Winter 1964), 47-57.

_____. "John Cheever and Comedy." Crit, 6 (1963), 66-77.

Garrett, George. "John Cheever and the Charm of Innocence: The Craft of THE WAPSHOT SCANDAL." HC, 1, ii (April 1964), 1-4, 6-12.

LEONARD COHEN (1934-), CANADIAN

NOVELS

THE FAVORITE GAME. London: Secker and Warburg, 1963.

BEAUTIFUL LOSERS. Toronto: McClelland and Stewart, 1966.

CRITICAL ARTICLES

Djwa, Sandra. "Leonard Cohen: Black Romantic." CanL, no. 34 (1967), 32-42.

Gose, E.B. "Of Beauty and Unmeaning." CanL, no. 29 (1966), 61-63.

Pacoy, Desmond. "The Phenomenon of Leonard Cohen." CanL, no. 34 (1967), 9-15.

EVAN S[HELBY]. CONNELL, JR. (1924-   ), AMERICAN

NOVELS

MRS. BRIDGE. New York: Viking Press, 1959.

THE PATRIOT. New York: Viking Press, 1960.

NOTES FROM A BOTTLE FOUND ON THE BEACH AT CARMEL. New York: Viking Press, 1963.

THE DIARY OF A RAPIST. New York: Simon and Schuster, 1966.

MR. BRIDGE. New York: Knopf, 1969.

SHORT STORIES

THE ANATOMY LESSON AND OTHER STORIES. New York: Viking Press, 1957.

AT THE CROSSROADS: STORIES. New York: Simon and Schuster, 1965.

CRITICAL ARTICLES

Blaisdell, Gus. "After Ground Zero: The Writings of Evan S. Connell, Jr." NMQ, 36 (1966), 200-206.

Van Bark, Bella S. "The Alienated Person in Literature." AJP, 21 (1961), 189-91.

WILLIAM COOPER [HARRY S. HOFF] (1910-), ENGLISH

NOVELS

TRINA (as H.S. Hoff). London: Heinemann, 1934. As IT HAPPENED IN PRK. New York: Coward McCann, 1934.

RHEA (as H.S. Hoff). London: Heinemann, 1935.

LISA (as H.S. Hoff). London: Heinemann, 1937.

THREE MARRIAGES (as H.S. Hoff). London: Heinemann, 1946.

SCENES FROM PROVINCIAL LIFE. London: Cape, 1950.

SCENES FROM METROPOLITAN LIFE. 1951. Suppressed.

THE STRUGGLES OF ALBERT WOODS. London: Cape, 1952.

THE EVER-INTERESTING TOPIC. London: Cape, 1953.

DISQUIET AND PEACE. London: Macmillan, 1956.

YOUNG PEOPLE. London: Macmillan, 1958.

SCENES FROM MARRIED LIFE. London: Macmillan, 1961.
   Contains SCENES FROM PROVINCIAL LIFE and SCENES FROM MARRIED LIFE.

SCENES FROM LIFE. New York: Scribner, 1961.

MEMOIRS OF A NEW MAN. London: Macmillan, 1966.

CRITICAL ARTICLES

Deakin, Nicholas. "An Appraisal of William Cooper: In Search of Banality." T&T, 42 (1961), 140-41.

Johnson, Pamela Hansford. "Smart Chap Grows Up." REPORTER, 14 (16 March 1961), 55-56.

ROBERT COOVER (1932-), AMERICAN

NOVELS

THE ORIGIN OF THE BRUNISTS. New York: Putnam, 1966.

THE UNIVERSAL BASEBALL ASSOCIATION, INC., J. HENRY WAUGH, PROP. New York: Random House, 1968.

SHORT STORIES

PRICKSONGS & DESCANTS. New York: Dutton, 1969.

CRITICAL ARTICLES

Hertzel, Leo J. "An Interview with Robert Coover." Crit, 11 (1969), 25–29.

_____. "What's Wrong with the Christians." Crit, 11 (1969), 11–24.

NIGEL DENNIS (1912-), ENGLISH

NOVELS

BOYS AND GIRLS COME OUT TO PLAY. London: Eyre and Spottiswoode, 1949. As SEA CHANGE. Boston: Houghton Mifflin, 1949.

CARDS OF IDENTITY. London: Weidenfeld and Nicolson, 1955.

A HOUSE IN ORDER. London: Weidenfeld and Nicolson, 1966.

CRITICAL ARTICLES

Ewart, Gavin. "Nigel Dennis--Identity Man." LonM, n.s. 3 (November 1963), 35-38.

Peake, Charles. "CARDS OF IDENTITY: An Intellectual Satire." IHY, 1 (July 1960), 49-57.

PETER DEVRIES (1910-   ), AMERICAN

NOVELS

BUT WHO WAKES THE BUGLER? Boston: Houghton Mifflin, 1940.

THE HANDSOME HEART. New York: Coward-McCann, 1943.

ANGELS CAN'T DO BETTER. New York: Coward-McCann, 1944.

THE TUNNEL OF LOVE (with Joseph Fields). Boston: Little, Brown, 1954.

COMFORT ME WITH APPLES. Boston: Little, Brown, 1956.

THE MACKEREL PLAZA. Boston: Little, Brown, 1958.

THE TENTS OF WICKEDNESS. Boston: Little, Brown, 1959.

THROUGH THE FIELDS OF CLOVER. Boston: Little, Brown, 1961.

THE BLOOD OF THE LAMB. Boston: Little, Brown, 1962.

REUBEN, REUBEN. Boston: Little, Brown, 1964.

LET ME COUNT THE WAYS. Boston: Little, Brown, 1965.

THE VALE OF LAUGHTER. Boston: Little, Brown, 1967.

THE CAT'S PAJAMAS AND WITCH'S MILK. Boston: Little, Brown, 1968.

MRS. WALLOP. Boston: Little, Brown, 1970.

SHORT STORIES

NO, BUT I SAW THE MOVIE. Boston: Little, Brown, 1952.

BIBLIOGRAPHY

Bowden, Edwin T. "Peter De Vries--The First Thirty Years: A Bibliography, 1934-1964." TSLL, 6 (1965), 543-70.

CRITICAL BOOKS

Jellema, Roderick. PETER DE VRIES: A CRITICAL ESSAY. Grand Rapids, Mich.: Eerdmans, 1966.

CRITICAL ARTICLES

Davis, Douglas M. "An Interview with Peter De Vries." CE, 28 (1967), 524-28.

Sale, Richard B. "A STUDIES IN THE NOVEL Interview: An Interview in New York with Peter De Vries." SNNTS, 1 (1969), 364-69.

J[AMES]. P[ATRICK]. DONLEAVY (1926-   ), AMERICAN

NOVELS

THE GINGER MAN. Paris: Olympia Press, 1955; New York: McDowell, Obolensky, 1958; complete, unexpurgated edition, New York: Seymour Lawrence-Delacorte Press, 1965.

A SINGULAR MAN. Boston: Little, Brown, 1963.

THE SADDEST SUMMER OF SAMUEL S. New York: Seymour Lawrence-Delacorte Press, 1966.

THE BEASTLY BEATITUDES OF BALTHAZAR B. New York: Seymour Lawrence-Delacorte Press, 1968.

SHORT STORIES

MEET MY MAKER THE MAD MOLECULE. Boston: Little, Brown, 1964.

CRITICAL ARTICLES

Corrigan, Robert A. "The Artist as Censor: J.P. Donleavy and THE GINGER MAN." MASJ, 8 (1967), 60-72.

Moore, John R. "Hard Times and the Noble Savage: J.P. Donleavy's A SINGULAR MAN." HC, 1 (February 1964), 1-4, 6-11.

Sherman, William D. "J.P. Donleavy: Anarchic Man as Dying Dionysian." TCE, 13 (1968), 216-28.

Vintner, Maurice. "The Novelist as a Clown: The Fiction of J.P. Donleavy." Meanjin, 29 (1970), 108-14.

LAWRENCE DURRELL (1912-   ), ENGLISH

NOVELS

PIED PIPER OF LOVERS. London: Cassell, 1935.

PANIC SPRING (as Charles Norden). London: Faber, 1937.

THE BLACK BOOK: AN AGON. Paris: Obelisk Press, 1938.

CEFALU. London: Editions Poetry, 1947. As THE DARK LABYRINTH. London: Ace, 1958.

WHITE EAGLES OVER SERBIA. London: Faber, 1957.

THE ALEXANDRIA QUARTET:
   JUSTINE. London: Faber, 1957.
   BALTHAZAR. London: Faber, 1958.
   MOUNTOLIVE. London: Faber, 1958.
   CLEA. London: Faber, 1960.

AUT TUNC AUT NUNGUAM:
   TUNC. London: Faber, 1968.
   NUNQUAM. London: Faber, 1970.

SHORT STORIES

ESPRIT DE CORPS: SKETCHES FROM DIPLOMATIC LIFE. London: Faber, 1957.

STIFF UPPER LIP: LIFE AMONG THE DIPLOMATS. London: Faber, 1958.

SAUVE QUI PEUT. London: Faber, 1966.

BIBLIOGRAPHY

Beebe, Maurice. "Criticism of Lawrence Durrell: A Selected Checklist." MFS, 13 (1967), 417-21.

Knerr, Anthony. "Regarding a Checklist of Lawrence Durrell." PBSA, 55 (1961), 142-52.

Potter, Robert A., and Brooke Whiting, comps. LAWRENCE DURRELL: A CHECKLIST. Los Angeles: U.C.L.A. Library, 1961.

Thomas, Alan G. "Bibliography." In LAWRENCE DURRELL: A STUDY, by G.S. Fraser, pp. 177-233. London: Faber, 1968.

CRITICAL BOOKS

Fraser, G.S. LAWRENCE DURRELL: A STUDY. London: Faber, 1968.

Friedman, Alan W. LAWRENCE DURRELL AND THE ALEXANDRIA QUARTET: ART FOR LOVE'S SAKE. Norman: University of Oklahoma Press, 1970.

Moore, Harry T., ed. THE WORLD OF LAWRENCE DURRELL. Carbondale: Southern Illinois University Press, 1962.

Perles, Alfred. MY FRIEND LAWRENCE DURRELL. Northwood, Middlesex: Scorpion, 1961.

Unterecker, John. LAWRENCE DURRELL. New York: Columbia University Press, 1964.

Weigel, John A. LAWRENCE DURRELL. New York: Twayne, 1966.

SPECIAL ISSUES

MODERN FICTION STUDIES, 13 (1967), "Lawrence Durrell Special Number."

CRITICAL ARTICLES

Arban, Dominique. "Lawrence Durrell." PREUVES, 109 (1960), 86-94.

Arthos, John. "Lawrence Durell's Gnosticism." Person, 43 (1962), 360-73.

Baldanza, Frank. "Lawrence Durrell's 'Word Continuum.'" Crit, 4 (1961), 3-17.

Becher, Father Hubert, S.J. "Lawrence Durrells Tetralogie und die literarische Kritik." SZ, 168 (1961), 360-69.

Bode, Carl. "Durrell's Way to Alexandria." CE, 22 (1961), 531-38.

Bork, Alfred M. "Durrell and Relativity." CRAS, 7 (1963), 191-203.

Bosquet, Alain. "Lawrence Durrell ou l'azur ironique." NRF, 14 (June 1966), 1116-23.

Cate, Curtis. "Lawrence Durrell." ATLANTIC MONTHLY, 208 (December 1961), 63-69.

Coleman, John. "Mr. Durrell's Dimensions." SPECTATOR, 19 February 1960, pp. 256-57.

Corke, Hilary. "Lawrence Durrell." LHY, 2 (January 1961), 43-49.

_____. "Mr. Durrell and Brother Criticus." ENCOUNTER, 14 (May 1960), 65-70.

Cortland, Peter. "Durrell's Sentimentalism." EngR, 14 (April 1964), 15-19.

Crowder, Richard. "Durrell, Libido, and Eros." BSTCF, 3, ii (1962), 34-39.

Dare, H. "The Quest for Durrell's Scobie." MFS, 10 (1965), 379-83.

Decancq, Roland. "What Lies Beyond? An Analysis of Darley's 'Quest' in Lawrence Durrell's ALEXANDRIA QUARTET." RLV, 34 (1968), 134-50.

DeMott, Benjamin. "Grading the Emanglons." HudR, 13 (1960), 457-64.

Dobree, Bonamy. "Durrell's Alexandrian Series." SR, 69 (1961), 61-79.

Enright, D.J. "Alexandrian Nights' Entertainments: Lawrence Durrell's QUARTET." ILA, 3 (1961), 30-39.

Eskin, Stanley G.   "Durrell's Themes in THE ALEXANDRIA QUARTET."   TQ, 5, iv (1962), 43–60.

Flint, R.W.   "A Major Novelist."   Com, 27 (April 1959), 353–56.

Friedman, Alan W.   "A 'Key' to Lawrence Durrell."   WSCL, 8 (Winter 1967), 31–42.

Glicksberg, Charles I.   "The Fictional World of Lawrence Durrell."   BuR, 11, ii (1963), 118–33.

Goldberg, Gerald J.   "The Search for the Artist in Some Recent British Fiction."   SAQ, 62 (1963), 387–92.

Gossman, Ann.   "Some Characters in Search of a Mirror."   Crit, 8 (1966), 79–84.

Goulianos, Joan.   "Lawrence Durrell and Alexandria."   VQR, 45 (1969), 664–73.

Green, Martin.   "Lawrence Durrell, II: A Minority Report."   YR, 49 (1960), 496–508.

Hagergard, Sture.   "Om medvetandets struktur."   HORISONT, 13, ii (1966), 21–23.

Hagopian, John V.   "The Resolution of the ALEXANDRIA QUARTET."   Crit, 7 (1964), 97–106.

Hamard, J.P.   "L'espace et le temps dans les romans de Lawrence Durrell."   CRITIQUE, 7 (1960), 387–413.

_____.   "Lawrence Durrell: A European Writer."   DUJ, 29 (1968), 171–81.

_____.   "Lawrence Durrell, renovateur assagi."   CRITIQUE, 163 (1960), 1025–33.

Hauge, Ingvar.   "Lawrence Durrell fram til ALEXANDRIAKVARTETTEN."   SAMTIDEN, 71 (1962), 220–26.

Highet, Gilbert.   "The Alexandrians of Lawrence Durrell."   HORIZON, 2 (1960), 113–18.

Howarth, Herbert.   "Lawrence Durrell and Some Early Masters."   BA, 37

(1963), 5-11.

_____. "A Segment of Durrell's QUARTET." UTQ, 32 (1963), 282-93.

Hutchens, Eleanor H. "The Heraldic Universe in THE ALEXANDRIA QUAR-
TET." CE, 24 (1962), 56-61.

Katope, Christopher G. "Cavafy and Durrell's 'The Alexandria Quartet.'"
CL, 21 (1969), 125-38.

Kelly, John C. "Lawrence Durrell: THE ALEXANDRIA QUARTET." STUDIES,
52 (1963), 52-68.

_____. "Lawrence Durrell's Style." STUDIES, 52 (1963), 199-204.

Kermode, Frank. "Fourth Dimension." REL, 1 (April 1960), 73-77.

Kihlman, Christer. "Lawrence Durrell och den moderna romanen." NyA, 55
(1962), 139-41, 155-59.

Lebas, Gerard. "Lawrence Durrell's ALEXANDRIA QUARTET and the Critics:
A Survey of Published Criticism." CALIBAN, 6 (1969), 91-114.

_____. "The Mechanisms of Space-Time in THE ALEXANDRIA QUARTET."
CALIBAN, 7 (1970), 80-97.

Lemon, Lee T. "THE ALEXANDRIA QUARTET: Form and Fiction." WSCL,
4 (Autumn 1963), 327-38.

Leslie, Ann. "This Infuriating Man--Lawrence Durrell." IRISH DIGEST, 82
(February 1965), 67-70.

Littlejohn, David. "Lawrence Durrell: The Novelist as Entertainer."
MOTIVE, 23 (November 1962), 14-16.

_____. "The Permanence of Lawrence Durrell." ColQ, 14 (Summer 1965),
63-71.

Lombardo, Agostino. "IL QUARTETTO DI ALESSANDRIA." TP, 1 (1961),
186-92.

Lund, Mary Graham. "The Alexandrian Projection." AR, 21 (1961), 193-
204.

_____. "The Big Rock Crystal Mountain." FQ, 11 (May 1962), 15-18.

_____. "Durrell: Soft Focus on Crime." PrS, 35 (1961), 339-44.

_____. "Eight Aspects of Melissa." ForumH, 3, ix (1962), 18-22.

_____. "Submerge for Reality: The New Novel Form of Lawrence Durrell." SWR, 64 (1959), 229-35.

Mackworth, Cecily. "Lawrence Durrell and the New Romanticism." TC, 167 (1960), 203-13.

Manzalaoui, Mahmoud. "Curate's Egg: An Alexandrian Opinion of Durrell's QUARTET." EA, 15 (1962), 248-60.

Michot, Paulette. "Lawrence Durrell's ALEXANDRIA QUARTET." RLV, 5 (1960), 361-67.

Neifer, Leo J. "Durrell's Method and Purpose of Art." WisSL, 3 (1966), 99-103.

O'Brien, R.A. "Time, Space and Language in Lawrence Durrell." WATER-LOO REVIEW, 6 (Winter 1961), 16-24.

Ozana, Anna. "Auf dem Wege zum modernen Roman: Gedanken bei der Lekture der Romane Lawrence Durrells." WuW, 14 (1959), 237-42.

Proser, Matthew N. "Darley's Dilemma: The Problem of Structure in Durrell's ALEXANDRIA QUARTET." Crit, 4 (1961), 18-28.

Rexroth, Kenneth. "The Artifice of Convincing Immodesty." THE GRIFFIN, 9 (September 1960), 3-9.

Robinson, W.R. "Intellect and Imagination in THE ALEXANDRIA QUARTET." SHENANDOAH, 18 (Summer 1967), 55-68.

Russo, John Paul. "Love in Lawrence Durrell." PrS, 43 (1970), 396-407.

Scholes, Robert. "Return to Alexandria: Lawrence Durrell and the Western Narrative Tradition." VQR, 40 (1964), 411-20.

Serpieri, Alessandro. "IL QUARTETTO DI ALESSANDRO di Lawrence Durrell." Ponte, 18 (1962), 48-57.

Sertoli, Giuseppe. "Lawrence Durrell e il QUARTETTO DI ALESSANDRIA."
EM, 18 (1967), 207-56.

Servotte, Herman. "THE ALEXANDRIA QUARTET van Lawrence Durrell."
DWB, 108 (1963), 646-58.

Steiner, George. "Lawrence Durrell, I: The Baroque Novel." YR, 49
(1960), 488-95.

Sullivan, Nancy. "Lawrence Durrell's Epitaph for the Novel." Person, 44
(1963), 79-88.

Weatherhead, A.K. "Romantic Anachronism in THE ALEXANDRIA QUARTET."
MFS, 10 (1964), 128-36.

Weigel, John A. "Lawrence Durrell's First Novel." TCL, 14 (1968), 75-83.

Young, Kenneth. "A Dialogue with Durrell." ENCOUNTER, 13, vi (1959),
61-62, 64-68.

WILLIAM EASTLAKE (1917-), AMERICAN

NOVELS

GO IN BEAUTY. New York: Harper, 1956.

THE BRONC PEOPLE. New York: Harcourt, Brace, 1958.

PORTRAIT OF AN ARTIST WITH TWENTY-SIX HORSES. New York: Simon and Schuster, 1963.

CASTLE KEEP. New York: Simon and Schuster, 1965.

THE BAMBOO BED. New York: Simon and Schuster, 1969.

CRITICAL ARTICLES

Gold, Herbert. "Wit and Truth." NATION, 187 (20 September 1958), 158-59.

Phelps, Donald. "The Land of Grace and Isolation." NATION, 199 (12 October 1964), 225-27.

Woolf, Douglas. "One of the Truly Good Men." EVERGREEN REVIEW, 2, no. 8 (Spring 1959), 194-96.

Wylder, Delbert E. "The Novels of William Eastlake." NMQ, 34 (1964), 190-97.

STANLEY L[AWRENCE]. ELKIN (1930-), AMERICAN

NOVELS

BOSWELL. New York: Random House, 1964.

A BAD MAN. New York: Random House, 1967.

SHORT STORIES

CRIERS AND KIBITZERS, KIBITZERS AND CRIERS. New York: Random House, 1966.

CRITICAL ARTICLES

Guttmann, Allen. "Stanley Elkin's Orphans." MR, 7 (1966), 598–600.

GEORGE PAUL ELLIOTT (1918-), AMERICAN

NOVELS

PARKTILDEN VILLAGE. Boston: Beacon Press, 1958.

DAVID KNUDSEN. New York: Random House, 1962.

IN THE WORLD. New York: Viking Press, 1965.

SHORT STORIES

AMONG THE DANGS. New York: Holt Rinehart, 1961.

AN HOUR OF LAST THINGS AND OTHER STORIES. New York: Harper, 1968.

CRITICAL ARTICLES

Gelfant, Blanche H. "Beyond Nihilism: The Fiction of George P. Elliott." HC, 5 (December 1968), 1-12.

Slatoff, Walter. "George P. Elliott." EPOCH, 12 (Spring 1962), 60-62.

Trachtenberg, Alan. "George P. Elliott: David Knudsen." Crit, 5 (1962), 83-89.

RALPH ELLISON (1914-), AMERICAN

NOVELS

INVISIBLE MAN. New York: Random House, 1952.

CRITICAL BOOKS

Reilly, John M., ed. TWENTIETH CENTURY INTERPRETATIONS OF "IN-VISIBLE MAN": A COLLECTION OF CRITICAL ESSAYS. Englewood Cliffs, N.J.: Prentice-Hall, 1969.

SPECIAL ISSUES

COLLEGE LANGUAGE ASSOCIATION JOURNAL, 13 (1970), "Ralph Ellison Special Number."

BLACK WORLD, 20, ii (1970), "Ralph Ellison Issue."

CRITICAL ARTICLES

Alter, Robert. "The Apocalyptic Temper." Com, 41 (1966), 61-66.

Baumbach, Jonathan. "Nightmare of A Native Son: Ralph Ellison's INVISI-BLE MAN." Crit, 6 (1963), 48-65.

Bennett, John Z. "The Race and the Runner: Ellison's INVISIBLE MAN." XUS, 5 (1966), 12-26.

Bloch, Alice. "Sight Imagery in INVISIBLE MAN." EJ, 55 (1966), 1019-21, 1024.

Bluestein, Gene. "The Blues as a Literary Theme." MR, 8 (1967), 600-617.

Ralph Ellison

Bone, Robert A. "Ralph Ellison and the Uses of Imagination." TriQ, 6 (1966), 39-54.

Ducornet, Guy. "Ralph Ellison: Homme invisible, pour qui chantes-tu? Grasset, 1969, traduction de Robert Merle." LanM, 63 (1969), 394-401.

Ellison, Ralph. "Letters: No Apologies." Harper's, 235 (March 1967), 4-20.

_____. "Light on INVISIBLE MAN." CRISIS, 60 (March 1953), 157-58.

_____. "On Becoming a Writer." Com, 38 (October 1964), 57-60.

Fraiberg, Selma. "Two Modern Incest Heroes." PR, 28 (1961), 646-61.

Geller, Allen. "An Interview with Ralph Ellison." TamR, 32 (Summer 1964), 3-24.

Gerard, Albert. "Ralph Ellison et le dilemme noir (Le roman afro-americain)." RGB, 97 (1961), 89-104.

Girson, Rochelle. "Sidelights on Invisibility." SatR, 36 (14 March 1953), 20, 49.

Glicksberg, Charles I. "The Symbolism of Vision." SWR, 39 (1954), 259-65.

Greene, Maxine. "Against Invisibility." CE, 30 (1969), 430-36.

Griffin, Edward M. "Notes from a Clean, Well-Lighted Place: Ralph Ellison's INVISIBLE MAN." TCL, 15 (1959), 129-44.

Hays, Peter L. "The Incest Theme in INVISIBLE MAN." WHR, 23 (1969), 335-39.

Horowitz, Floyd Ross. "The Enigma of Ellison's Intellectual Man." CLAJ, 7 (1963), 126-32.

_____. "Ralph Ellison's Modern Version of Brer Bear and Brer Rabbit in IN-VISIBLE MAN." MASJ, 4 (1963), 21-27.

Howe, Irving. "Black Boys and Native Sons." DISSENT, 10 (August 1963), 353-68.

Hyman, Stanley Edgar, and Ralph Ellison. "The Negro Writer in America:

An Exchange." PR, 25 (1958), 197-222.

Isaacs, Harold R. "Five Writers and Their African Ancestors." PHYLON, 21 (1960), 243-65, 317-36.

Jackson, Esther M. "The American Negro and the Image of the Absurd." PHYLON, 23 (1962), 368-71.

Kostelanetz, Richard. "The Politics of Ellison's Booker: INVISIBLE MAN As Symbolic History." ChiR, 19, ii (1967), 5-26.

_____. "Ralph Ellison: Novelist as Brown Skinned Aristocrat." SHENAN-DOAH, 20, iv (1969), 56-77.

Lee, A. Robert. "Sight and Mask: Ralph Ellison's INVISIBLE MAN." NALF, 4 (1970), 22-33.

Lehan, Richard. "Existentialism in Recent American Fiction: The Demonic Quest." TSLL, 1 (1959), 181-202.

_____. "The Strange Silence of Ralph Ellison." CEJ, 1, ii (1965), 63-68.

Levant, Howard. "Aspiraling We Should Go." MASJ, 4 (1963), 3-20.

Ludington, Charles T., Jr. "Protest and Anti-Protest: Ralph Ellison." SHR, 4 (1970), 31-39.

Mengeling, Marvin E. "Whitman and Ellison: Older Symbols in a Modern Mainstream." WWR, 12 (1966), 67-70.

Nichols, William W. "Ralph Ellison's Black American Scholar." PHYLON, 31 (1970), 70-75.

O'Daniel, Therman B. "The Image of Man as Portrayed by Ralph Ellison." CLAJ, 10 (1967), 277-84.

Olderman, Raymond M. "Ralph Ellison's Blues and INVISIBLE MAN." WSCL, 7 (Summer 1966), 142-59.

Plessner, Monika. "Bildnis des Kunstlers als Volksaufwiegler." MERKUR, 24 (1970), 629-43.

"Ralph Ellison: Fiction Winner." CRISIS, 60 (March 1953), 154-56.

Ralph Ellison

Randall, John H. III. "Ralph Ellison: INVISIBLE MAN." RLV, 31 (1965), 24-45.

Rodnon, Stewart. "Ralph Ellison's INVISIBLE MAN: Six Tentative Approaches." CLAJ, 12 (1969), 244-56.

Rogge, Heinz. "Die amerikanische Negerfrage im Licht der Literatur von Richard Wright und Ralph Ellison." NS, 2 (1958), 59-69, 103-17.

Rovit, Earl. "Ralph Ellison and the American Comic Tradition." WSCL, 1 (February 1960), 34-42.

Schafer, William J. "Irony from Underground--Satiric Elements in INVISIBLE MAN." SNL, 7 (1969), 22-29.

_____. "Ralph Ellison and the Birth of the Anti-Hero." Crit, 10 (1968), 81-93.

Singleton, M.K. "Leadership Mirages as Antagonists in INVISIBLE MAN." ArQ, 22 (1966), 157-71.

Thompson, James; Lennox Raphael; and Steve Cannon. "'A Very Stern Discipline': An Interview with Ralph Ellison." Harper's, 234 (March 1967), 76-95.

Waghmare, J.M. "Invisibility of the American Negro: Ralph Ellison's INVISIBLE MAN." QUEST, 59 (1969), 23-30.

Whittemore, Reed. "Beating that Boy Again." NRep, 151 (14 November 1964), 25-26.

HOWARD [MELVIN] FAST (1914-   ), AMERICAN

NOVELS

TWO VALLEYS. New York: Dial Press, 1933.

STRANGE YESTERDAY. New York: Dodd, Mead, 1934.

PLACE IN THE CITY. New York: Harcourt, Brace, 1937.

CONCEIVED IN LIBERTY: A NOVEL OF VALLEY FORGE. New York: Simon and Schuster, 1939.

THE LAST FRONTIER. New York: Duell, Sloan, 1941.

THE UNVANQUISHED. New York: Duell, Sloan, 1942.

THE TALL HUNTER. New York: Harper, 1942.

CITIZEN TOM PAINE. New York: Duell, Sloan, 1943.

FREEDOM ROAD. New York: Duell, Sloan, 1944.

THE AMERICAN: A MIDDLE WESTERN LEGEND. New York: Duell, Sloan, 1946.

THE CHILDREN. New York: Duell, Sloan, 1947.

CLARKTON. New York: Duell, Sloan, 1947.

MY GLORIOUS BROTHERS. Boston: Little, Brown, 1948.

THE PROUD AND THE FREE. Boston: Little, Brown, 1950.

SPARTACUS. New York: privately printed, 1951; New York: Citadel Press, 1952.

FALLEN ANGEL (as Walter Erickson). Boston: Little, Brown, 1952.

SILAS TIMBERMAN. New York: Blue Heron Press, 1954.

THE STORY OF LOLA GREGG. New York: Blue Heron Press, 1956.

MOSES, PRINCE OF EGYPT. New York: Crown, 1958.

THE WINSTON AFFAIR. New York: Crown, 1959.

THE GOLDEN RIVER, in THE HOWARD FAST READER. New York: Crown, 1960.

SYLVIA (as E.V. Cunningham). Garden City, N.Y.: Doubleday, 1960.

APRIL MORNING. New York: Crown, 1961.

POWER. Garden City, N.Y.: Doubleday, 1962.

PHYLLIS (as E.V. Cunningham). Garden City, N.Y.: Doubleday, 1962.

ALICE (as E.V. Cunningham). Garden City, N.Y.: Doubleday, 1963.

AGRIPPA'S DAUGHTER. Garden City, N.Y.: Doubleday, 1964.

SHIRLEY (as E.V. Cunningham). Garden City, N.Y.: Doubleday, 1964.

LYDIA (as E.V. Cunningham). Garden City, N.Y.: Doubleday, 1964.

PENELOPE (as E.V. Cunningham). Garden City, N.Y.: Doubleday, 1965.

TORQUEMADA. Garden City, N.Y.: Doubleday, 1966.

HELEN (as E.V. Cunningham). Garden City, N.Y.: Doubleday, 1966.

MARGIE (as E.V. Cunningham). New York: Morrow, 1966.

THE HUNTER AND THE TRAP. New York: Dial Press, 1967.

SALLY (as E.V. Cunningham). New York: Morrow, 1967.

SAMANTHA (as E.V. Cunningham). New York: Morrow, 1967.

CYNTHIA (as E.V. Cunningham). New York: Morrow, 1968.

THE ASSASSIN WHO GAVE UP HIS GUN (as E.V. Cunningham). New York: Morrow, 1969.

THE GENERAL ZAPPED AN ANGEL. New York: Morrow, 1970.

SHORT STORIES

PATRICK HENRY AND THE FRIGATE'S KEEL AND OTHER STORIES OF A YOUNG NATION. New York: Duell, 1945.

DEPARTURES AND OTHER STORIES. Boston: Little, Brown, 1949.

THE LAST SUPPER AND OTHER STORIES. New York: Blue Heron Press, 1955.

THE EDGE OF TOMORROW. New York: Bantam, 1961.

CRITICAL ARTICLES

Fast, Howard. "Reply to the Critics." MASSES AND MAINSTREAM, 3 (December 1950), 53–64.

Hicks, Granville. "Howard Fast's One-Man Reformation." CE, 7 (1945), 1–6.

Lifka, Marion. "Howard Fast: Wool Puller?" CathW, 177 (September 1953), 446–51.

Meisler, Stanley. "The Lost Dreams of Howard Fast." NATION, 188 (30 May 1959), 498–500.

GABRIEL FIELDING [ALAN GABRIEL BARNSLEY]
(1916-), ENGLISH

NOVELS

BROTHERLY LOVE. London: Hutchinson, 1954.

IN THE TIME OF GREENBLOOM. London: Hutchinson, 1956.

EIGHT DAYS. London: Hutchinson, 1958.

THROUGH STREETS BROAD AND NARROW. London: Hutchinson, 1960.

THE BIRTHDAY KING. London: Hutchinson, 1962.

GENTLEMEN IN THEIR SEASON. London: Hutchinson, 1966.

CRITICAL ARTICLES

Bowers, Frederick. "Gabriel Fielding's THE BIRTHDAY KING." QQ, 74 (1967), 149-58.

Grande, Brother Luke M., F.S.C. "Gabriel Fielding, New Master of the Catholic Classic?" CathW, 197 (June 1963), 172-79.

Kunkel, Francis L. "Clowns and Saviors: Two Contemporary Novels." Ren, 18 (1965), 40-44.

Stanford, Derek. "Gabriel Fielding and the Catholic Novel." MONTH, 212 (December 1961), 352-56.

SHELBY FOOTE (1916-), AMERICAN

NOVELS

TOURNAMENT. New York: Dial Press, 1949.

FOLLOW ME DOWN. New York: Dial Press, 1950.

LOVE IN A DRY SEASON. New York: Dial Press, 1951.

SHILOH. New York: Dial Press, 1952.

JORDAN COUNTY: A LANDSCAPE IN NARRATIVE. New York: Dial Press, 1954.

CRITICAL ARTICLES

Carr, John. "It's Worth a Grown Man's Time: An Interview with Shelby Foote." CONTEMPORA, I, ii (1970), 2-16.

JOHN FOWLES (1926-), ENGLISH

NOVELS

THE COLLECTOR. London: Cape; Boston: Little, Brown, 1963.

THE MAGUS. London: Cape; Boston: Little, Brown, 1966.

THE FRENCH LIEUTENANT'S WOMAN. London: Cape; Boston: Little, Brown, 1969.

CRITICAL ARTICLES

Allen, Walter. "The Achievement of John Fowles." ENCOUNTER, 35 (August 1970), 64–67.

Churchill, Thomas. "Waterhouse, Storey, and Fowles: Which Way Out of the Room?" Crit, 10 (1968), 72–87.

WILLIAM H[OWARD]. GASS (1924-   ), AMERICAN

NOVELS

OMENSETTER'S LUCK. New York: New American Library, 1966.

WILLIE MASTERS' LONESOME WIFE. Evanston, Ill.: Northwestern University Press, 1968.

SHORT STORIES

IN THE HEART OF THE HEART OF THE COUNTRY AND OTHER STORIES. New York: Harper, 1968.

RUMER GODDEN (1907-), ENGLISH

NOVELS

CHINESE PUZZLE. London: Davies, 1936.

THE LADY AND THE UNICORN. London: Davies, 1938.

BLACK NARCISSUS. London: Davies, 1939.

GYPSY, GYPSY. London: Davies, 1940.

BREAKFAST WITH THE NIKOLIDES. London: Davies, 1942.

RUNCLI-RUNGLIOT (THUS FAR AND NO FURTHER). London: Davies, 1944.

FUGUE IN TIME. London: Joseph, 1945.

THE RIVER. London: Joseph, 1946.

A CANDLE FOR ST. JUDE. London: Joseph, 1948.

A BREATH OF AIR. London: Joseph, 1950.

KINGFISHERS CATCH FIRE. London: Macmillan, 1953.

AN EPISODE OF SPARROWS. London: Macmillan, 1956.

THE GREENGAGE SUMMER. London: Macmillan, 1958.

CHINA COURT. London: Macmillan, 1961.

THE BATTLE OF THE VILLA FIORITA. London: Macmillan, 1963.

IN THIS HOUSE OF BREDE. London: Macmillan, 1969.

SHORT STORIES

MOOLTIKI. London: Macmillan, 1957.

SWANS AND TURTLES. London: Macmillan, 1968.

CRITICAL ARTICLES

Hartley, Lois. "The Indian Novels of Rumer Godden." MAHFIL, 3, ii-iii (1966), 65-75.

Tindall, William York. "Rumer Godden, Public Symbolist." CE, 13 (1952), 297-303.

HERBERT GOLD (1924-), AMERICAN

NOVELS

BIRTH OF A HERO. New York: Viking Press, 1951.

THE PROSPECT BEFORE US. Cleveland: World, 1954. As ROOM CLERK. New York: New American Library, 1955.

THE MAN WHO WAS NOT WITH IT. Boston: Little, Brown, 1956.

THE OPTIMIST. Boston: Little, Brown, 1959.

THEREFORE BE BOLD. New York: Dial Press, 1960.

SALT. New York. Dial Press, 1963.

FATHERS: A NOVEL IN THE FORM OF A MEMOIR. New York: Random House, 1967.

THE GREAT AMERICAN JACKPOT. New York: Random House, 1969.

SHORT STORIES

15 X 3, with R.V. Cassill and James B. Hall. New York: New Directions, 1957.

LOVE AND LIKE. New York: Dial Press, 1960.

CRITICAL ARTICLES

Dommergues, Pierre. "Entretien avec Herbert Gold." LanM, 58 (1964), 256–60.

Sainte Phalle, Therese. "Herbert Gold fait le proces d'un continent trop heureux." FL, 20 (1965), 11.

Seiden, Melvin. "Characters and Ideas: The Modern Novel." NATION, 188 (25 April 1959), 387-92.

WILLIAM GOLDING (1911-), ENGLISH

NOVELS

LORD OF THE FLIES. London: Faber, 1954.

THE INHERITORS. London: Faber, 1955.

PINCHER MARTIN. London: Faber, 1956. As THE TWO DEATHS OF CHRISTOPHER MARTIN. New York: Harcourt, Brace, 1957.

FREE FALL. London: Faber, 1960.

THE SPIRE. London: Faber, 1964.

THE PYRAMID. London: Faber, 1967.

CRITICAL BOOKS

Babb, Howard S. THE NOVELS OF WILLIAM GOLDING. Columbus: Ohio State University Press, 1970.

Baker, James R. WILLIAM GOLDING: A CRITICAL STUDY. New York: St. Martin's, 1965.

Dick, Bernard F. WILLIAM GOLDING. New York: Twayne, 1967.

Elmen, Paul. WILLIAM GOLDING: A CRITICAL STUDY. Grand Rapids, Mich.: Eerdmans, 1967.

Hodson, Leighton. GOLDING. Edinburgh: Oliver & Boyd, 1969.

Hynes, Samuel. WILLIAM GOLDING. New York and London: Columbia University Press, 1964.

Kinkead-Weekes, Mark, and Ian Gregor. WILLIAM GOLDING: A CRITICAL STUDY. New York: Harcourt, Brace, 1968.

Moody, Philippa. A CRITICAL COMMENTARY ON WILLIAM GOLDING'S "LORD OF THE FLIES." London: Macmillan, 1966.

Nelson, William. WILLIAM GOLDING'S "LORD OF THE FLIES": A SOURCE BOOK. New York: Odyssey Press, 1963.

Oldsey, Bernard S., and Stanley Weintraub. THE ART OF WILLIAM GOLD-ING. New York: Harcourt, Brace, 1965.

Pemberton, Clive. WILLIAM GOLDING. London: Longmans, Green, 1969.

SPECIAL ISSUES

STUDIES IN THE LITERARY IMAGINATION (Georgia State College), 2, ii (1969), "William Golding Issue."

CRITICAL ARTICLES

Adriaens, Mark. "Style in W. Golding's THE INHERITORS." ES, 51 (1970), 16-30.

Ali, Masood Amjad. "THE INHERITORS: An Experiment in Technique." VENTURE, 5 (1969), 123-31.

Antonini, Maria. "FREE FALL di William Golding." CONVIVIUM, 37 (1969), 486-93.

Babb, Howard S. "Four Passages from William Golding's Fiction." MinnR, 5 (1965), 50-58.

_____. "On the Ending of PINCHER MARTIN." EIC, 14 (1964), 106-8.

Baker, James R. "The Decline of LORD OF THE FLIES." SAQ, 69 (1970), 446-60.

_____. "Why It's No Go: A Study of William Golding's LORD OF THE FLIES." ArQ, 19 (1963), 293-305.

Biles, Jack I. "Piggy: Apologia Pro Vita Sua." SLitl, 1, ii (1968), 83-109.

Blake, Ian. "PINCHER MARTIN: William Golding and 'Taffrail.'" N&Q, 9 (1962), 309-10.

Boyle, Ted E. "The Denial of the Spirit: An Explication of William Golding's FREE FALL." WascanaR, 1 (1966), 3-10.

Braybrooke, Neville. "The Return of Pincher Martin." Cweal, 89 (25 October 1968), 115-18.

_____. "Two William Golding Novels: Two Aspects of His Work." QQ, 76 (1969), 92-100.

Brockway, James. "Niet God marr Golding." TIRADE, 8 (1964), 402-6.

Bufkin, E.C. "The Ironic Art of William Golding's THE INHERITORS." TSLL, 9 (1968), 567-78.

_____. "LORD OF THE FLIES: An Analysis." GaR, 19 (1965), 40-57.

Carmichael, D. "A God in Ruins." Quadrant, no. 33 (January 1965), 72-75.

Cixous-Berger, Helene. "L'allegorie du mal dans l'oeuvre de William Golding." CRITIQUE, 22 (1966), 309-20.

Cohn, Alan M. "The Berengaria Allusion in LORD OF THE FLIES." N&Q, 13 (1966), 419-20.

Coskren, Thomas M., O.P. "Is Golding Calvinistic?" AMERICA, 109 (6 July 1963), 18-20.

Cox, C.B. "LORD OF THE FLIES." CritQ, 2 (1960), 112-17.

Crompton, D.W. "THE SPIRE." CritQ, 9 (1967), 63-79.

Davies, Cecil W. "The Novels Foreshadowed: Some Recurring Themes in Early Poems by William Golding." ENGLISH, 17 (1969), 86-89.

Davies, Harold. "Moral Choice in the Novels of William Golding." ModSp, 11, v (1969), 1-2, 35-45.

Davis, W. Eugene. "Mr. Golding's Optical Delusion." ELN, 3 (1965), 125-26.

Delbaere-Garant, Jeanne. "The Evil Plant in William Golding's THE SPIRE." RLV, 35 (1969), 623-31.

Dick, Bernard F. "'The Novelist Is a Displaced Person': An Interview With William Golding." CE, 26 (1965), 480-82.

Dick, Bernard F., and Raymond J. Porter. "Jocelin and Oedipus." CITHARA, 6, i (1966), 43-48.

Dierickx, J. "Le theme de la chute dans les romans de W. Golding." EA, 16 (1963), 230-42.

Drew, Philip. "Second Reading." CamR, 78 (1956), 79-84.

Duncan, Kirby L. "William Golding and Vardis Fisher: A Study in Parallels and Extensions." CE, 27 (1965), 232-35.

Ely, Sister M. Amanda, O.P. "The Adult Image in Three Novels of Adolescent Life." EJ, 56 (1967), 1127-28.

Engelborghs, Maurits. "Engelse letteren: De romans van William Golding." DWB, 105 (1957), 515-27.

Fackler, Herbert V. "Paleontology and Paradise Lost: A Study of Golding's Modifications of Fact in THE INHERITORS." BSUF, 10, ii (1969), 64-66.

Filipi, Zivan. "Moralna deterioracija u romanima Williama Goldinga." IZRAZ, 23 (1968), 576-85.

Freedman, Ralph. "The New Realism: The Fancy of William Golding." Per, 10 (1958), 118-28.

Freehof, Solomon B. "Nostalgia for the Middle Ages: William Golding's THE SPIRE." CARNEGIE MAGAZINE, 39 (January 1965), 13-16.

Gallagher, Michael P. "The Human Image in William Golding." STUDIES, 54 (1965), 197-216.

Gaskin, J.C.A. "Beelzebub." HJ, 66 (1968), 58-61.

Gindin, James. "'Gimmick' and Metaphor in the Novels of William Golding."

MFS, 6 (1960), 145-152.

Goldberg, Gerald J. "The Search for the Artist in Some Recent British Fiction." SAQ, 62 (1963), 392-94.

Gordon, Robert C. "Classical Themes in LORD OF THE FLIES." MFS, 11 (1966), 424-27.

Green, Peter. "The World of William Golding." EDH, 32 (1963), 37-57.

_____. "The World of William Golding." REL, 1, ii (1960), 62-72.

Green, Martin. "Distaste for the Contemporary." NATION, 190 (21 May 1960), 451-54.

Gregor, Ian, and Mark Kinkead-Weekes. "The Strange Case of Mr. Golding and His Critics." TC, 167 (1960), 115-25.

Gulbin, Suzanne. "Parallels and Contrasts in LORD OF THE FLIES and ANIMAL FARM." EJ, 55 (1966), 86-90, 92.

Hampton, T. "An Error in LORD OF THE FLIES." N&Q, 12 (1965), 275.

Harris, Wendell V. "Golding's FREE FALL." Expl, 23 (1965), Item 76.

Henry, Avril. "William Golding: THE PYRAMID." SoRA, 3 (1968), 5-31.

Herndl, George C. "Golding and Salinger: A Clear Choice." WiseR, no. 502 (Winter 1964), 309-22.

Hollahan, Eugene. "Running in Circles: A Major Motif in LORD OF THE FLIES." SNNTS, 2, 1 (1970), 22-30.

Hurt, James R. "Grendel's Point of View: BEOWULF and William Golding." MFS, 13 (1967), 264-65.

Hynes, Samuel. "Novels of a Religious Man." Cweal, 71 (18 March 1960), 673-75.

Irwin, Joseph J. "The Serpent Coiled Within." MOTIVE, 23 (May 1963), 1-5.

Kearns, Francis E., and L.M. Grande. "An Exchange of Views." Cweal, 77 (22 February 1963), 569-71.

Kermode, Frank. "The Novels of William Golding." ILA, 3 (1961), 16-19.

Kort, Wesley. "The Groundless Glory of Golding's Spire." Ren, 20 (1968), 75-78.

LaChance, Paul R. "PINCHER MARTIN: The Essential Dilemma of Modern Man." CITHARA, 8, ii (1969), 55-60.

Lederer, Richard H. "Student Reactions to LORD OF THE FLIES." EJ, 53 (1964), 575-79.

Leed, Jacob. "Golding's LORD OF THE FLIES, Chapter 7." Expl, 24 (1965), Item 8.

MacLure, Millar. "Allegories of Innocence." DR, 40 (Summer 1960), 149-51.

_____. "William Golding's Survivor Stories." TamR, 5 (Summer 1957), 60-67.

MacShane, Frank. "The Novels of William Golding." DR, 42 (Summer 1962), 171-83.

Marcus, Steven. "The Novel Again." PR, 29 (1962), 180-84.

Marsden, Arthur. "The Novels of William Golding." Delta, no. 10 (Autumn 1956), 26-29.

Michel-Michot, Paulette. "The Myth of Innocence." RLV, 28 (1962), 510-20.

Mitchell, Charles. "THE LORD OF THE FLIES and the Escape from Freedom." ArQ, 22 (1966), 27-40.

Mitchell, Juliet. "Concepts and Technique in William Golding." NEW LEFT REVIEW, no. 15 (May-June 1962), 63-71.

Morgan, Edwin. "PINCHER MARTIN and THE CORAL ISLAND." N&Q, 7 (1960), 150.

Mueller, William R. "An Old Story Well Told." ChC, 80 (2 October 1963), 1203-6.

Niemeyer, Carl. "The Coral Island Revisited." CE, 22 (1961), 241-45.

Nossen, Evon. "The Beast-Man Theme in the Work of William Golding." BSUF, 9, ii (1968), 60-69.

O'Hara, J.D. "Mute Choirboys and Angelic Pigs: The Fable in LORD OF THE FLIES." TSLL, 7 (1966), 411-20.

Oldsey, Bernard S., and Stanley Weintraub. "LORD OF THE FLIES: Beelzebub Revisited." CE, 25 (1963), 90-99.

Pearson, Anthony. "H.G. Wells and PINCHER MARTIN." N&Q, 12 (1965), 275-76.

Pendry, E.D. "William Golding and 'Mankind's Essential Illness.'" MSpr, 55 (1961), 1-7.

Perez Minik, Domingo. "William Golding de LA PIRAMIDE a MARTIN EL NAUFRAGO." INSULA, 25 (June 1970), 5.

Peter, John. "The Fables of William Golding." KR, 19 (1957), 577-92.

Pira, Gisela. "Die Macht des Bosen in Goldings Roman LORD OF THE FLIES." NS, 18 (1969), 67-73.

Pritchett, V.S. "God's Folly." NStat, 67 (10 April 1964), 562-63.

Quinn, Michael. "An Unheroic Hero: William Golding's PINCHER MARTIN." CritQ, 4 (1962), 247-56.

Rexroth, Kenneth. "William Golding." ATLANTIC MONTHLY, 215 (May 1965), 96-90.

Rocco-Bergera, Niny. "William Golding." RLMC, 22 (1969), 204-29.

Roper, Derek. "Allegory and Novel in Golding's THE SPIRE." WSCL, 8 (Winter 1967), 19-30.

Rosenberg, Bruce A. "Lord of the Fire-Flies." CentR, 11 (1967), 128-39.

Rosenfield, Claire. "'Men of a Smaller Growth': A Psychological Analysis of William Golding's LORD OF THE FLIES." L&P, 11 (Autumn 1961), 93-101.

_____. "Reply by Miss Rosenfield." L&P, 12 (Winter 1962), 11-12.

Sasso, Laurence J., Jr. "A Note on the Dwarf in PINCHER MARTIN." MSE,

1 (1968), 66-68.

Servotte, Herman. "Sterfelijkheid en Licht." DWB, 109 (1964), 590-95.

_____. "William Golding, religieus romancier zonder dogma's." DWB, 108 (1963), 437-44.

Spitz, David. "Power and Authority: An Interpretation of Golding's LORD OF THE FLIES." AR, 30 (1970), 21-33.

Sternlicht, Sanford. "PINCHER MARTIN: A Freudian Crusoe." EngR, 15 (April 1965), 2-4.

_____. "Songs of Innocence and Songs of Experience in LORD OF THE FLIES and THE INHERITORS." MQ, 9 (1968), 383-90.

_____. "A Source for Golding's LORD OF THE FLIES: Peter Pan?" EngR, 14 (December 1963), 41-42.

Sullivan, Walter. "The Long Chronicle of Guilt: William Golding's THE SPIRE." HC, 1, iii (1964), 1-12.

_____. "William Golding: The Fables and the Art." SR, 71 (Autumn 1963), 660-64.

Talon, Henri. "Irony in LORD OF THE FLIES." EIC, 18 (1968), 296-309.

Taylor, Harry H. "The Case Against William Golding's Simon-Piggy." ContempR, September 1966, pp. 155-60.

Temple, E.R.A. "William Golding's THE SPIRE: A Critique." Ren, 20 (1968), 171-73.

Thomson, George H. "The Real World of William Golding." ALPHABET, no. 9 (November 1964), 26-33.

_____. "William Golding: Between God-Darkness and God-Light." CRESSET, 32, vii (1969), 8-12.

Townsend, R.C. "LORD OF THE FLIES: Fool's Gold?" JGE, 16 (1964), 153-60.

Veidemanis, Gladys. "LORD OF THE FLIES in the Classroom--No Passing Fad." EJ, 53 (1964), 569-74.

Vizioli, Paulo. "Paradiso perdido de William Golding." ESPSL, 6 January 1968, p. 1.

Wain, John. "Lord of the Agencies." ASPECT, no. 3 (April 1963), 56-67.

Walters, Margaret. "Two Fabulists: Golding and Camus." MCR, no. 4 (1961), 18-29.

Warner, Oliver. "Mr. Golding and Marryat's LITTLE SAVAGE." REL, 5, i (1964), 51-55.

Watson, Kenneth. "A Reading of LORD OF THE FLIES." ENGLISH, 15 (1964), 2-7.

White, Robert J. "Butterfly and Beast in LORD OF THE FLIES." MFS, 10 (1964), 163-70.

Whitehead, John. "A Conducted Tour to the Pyramid." LonM, n.s. 7 (June 1967), 100-104.

Wicht, Wolfgang. "'Oh, the continent of a man!' Das Menschenbild in William Goldings Romanen FREE FALL, THE SPIRE und THE PYRAMID." ZAA, 18 (1970), 59-70.

SHIRLEY ANN GRAU (1929-), AMERICAN

NOVELS

THE HARD BLUE SKY. New York: Knopf, 1958.

THE HOUSE ON COLISEUM STREET. New York: Knopf, 1961.

THE KEEPERS OF THE HOUSE. New York: Knopf, 1964.

SHORT STORIES

THE BLACK PRINCE AND OTHER STORIES. New York: Knopf, 1955.

CRITICAL ARTICLES

Berland, Alwyn. "The Fiction of Shirley Ann Grau." Crit, 6 (1963), 78-84.

Going, William T. "Alabama Geography in Shirley Ann Grau's THE KEEPERS OF THE HOUSE." AlaR, 20 (January 1967), 62-68.

ROBERT GRAVES (1895-), ENGLISH

NOVELS

THE REAL DAVID COPPERFIELD. London: Barker, 1933. I, CLAUDIUS: FROM THE AUTOBIOGRAPHY OF TIBERIUS CLAUDIUS, EMPEROR OF THE ROMANS, BORN B.C. 10, MURDERED AND DEIFIED A.D. 54. London: Barker, 1934.

CLAUDIUS THE GOD AND HIS WIFE MESSALINA. THE TROUBLESOME REIGN OF TIBERIUS CLAUDIUS CAESAR, EMPEROR OF THE ROMANS (BORN B.C. 10, DIED A.D. 54), AS DESCRIBED BY HIMSELF; ALSO HIS MURDER AT THE HANDS OF THE NOTORIOUS AGRIPPINA (MOTHER OF THE EMPEROR NERO) AND HIS SUBSEQUENT DEIFICATION, AS DESCRIBED BY OTHERS. London: Barker, 1934.

"ANTIGUA, PENNY, PUCE." London: Constable, 1936. As THE ANTIGUA STAMP. New York: Random House, 1937.

COUNT BELISARIUS. London: Cassell, 1938.

SERGEANT LAMB OF THE NINTH. London: Methuen, 1940. As SERGEANT LAMB'S AMERICA. New York: Random House, 1940.

PROCEED, SERGEANT LAMB. London: Methuen, 1941.

THE STORY OF MARIE POWELL: WIFE TO MR. MILTON. London: Cassell, 1943. As WIFE TO MR. MILTON: THE STORY OF MARIE POWELL. New York: Creative Age Press, 1944.

THE GOLDEN FLEECE. London: Cassell, 1944. As HERCULES, MY SHIPMATE. New York: Creative Age Press, 1945.

KING JESUS. London: Cassell, 1946.

173

WATCH THE NORTH WIND RISE. New York: Creative Age Press, 1949.
As SEVEN DAYS IN CRETE. London: Cassell, 1949.

THE ISLANDS OF UNWISDOM. Garden City, N.Y.: Doubleday, 1949.
As THE ISLES OF UNWISDOM. London: Cassell, 1950.

HOMER'S DAUGHTER. London: Cassell, 1955.

SHORT STORIES

THE SHOUT. London: Elkin Mathews and Marrot, 1929.

CATACROK! MOSTLY STORIES, MOSTLY FUNNY. London: Cassell, 1956.

COLLECTED SHORT STORIES. London: Cassell, 1965.

BIBLIOGRAPHY

Higginson, Fred H. A BIBLIOGRAPHY OF THE WORKS OF ROBERT GRAVES.
London: Nicholas Vane, 1966.

CRITICAL BOOKS

Cohen, J.M. ROBERT GRAVES. Edinburgh: Oliver & Boyd, 1960.

Stade, George. ROBERT GRAVES. New York: Columbia University Press,
1967.

CRITICAL ARTICLES

Auden, W.H., et al. "A Symposium on Robert Graves." SHENANDOAH,
13 (1962), 5-62.

Fauchereau, Serge. "L'oeuvre de Robert Graves." CRITIQUE, 21 (1965),
526-34.

"Graves, 1965." TLS, 7 October 1965, p. 898.

Haller, John. "Conversations with Robert Graves." SWR, 42 (1957), 237-41.

_____. "Robert Graves in Lecture and Talk." ArQ, 15 (1959), 150-56.

Leiber, Fritz. "Utopia for Poets and Witches." RQ, 4 (1970), 194–205.

Peeters, E. "Apologie voor een fantast." TVUB, 5 (1963), 222–30.

Peschmann, Hermann. "Salute to Robert Graves." ENGLISH, 14 (1962), 2–8.

Steiner, George. "The Genius of Robert Graves." KR, 22 (1957), 340–65.

GRAHAM GREENE (1904-), ENGLISH

NOVELS

THE MAN WITHIN. London: Heinemann, 1929.

THE NAME OF ACTION. London: Heinemann, 1930.

RUMOUR AT NIGHTFALL. London: Heinemann, 1931.

STAMBOUL TRAIN: AN ENTERTAINMENT. London: Heinemann, 1932. As ORIENT EXPRESS: AN ENTERTAINMENT. Garden City, N.Y.: Doubleday, 1932.

IT'S A BATTLEFIELD. London: Heinemann, 1934.

ENGLAND MADE ME. London: Heinemann, 1935. As THE SHIPWRECKED. New York: Viking Press, 1935.

GUN FOR SALE: AN ENTERTAINMENT. London: Heinemann, 1936. As THIS GUN FOR HIRE: AN ENTERTAINMENT. Garden City, N.Y.: Double-day, 1936.

BRIGHTON ROCK. London: Heinemann, 1938.

THE CONFIDENTIAL AGENT. London: Heinemann, 1939.

THE POWER AND THE GLORY. London: Heinemann, 1940. As THE LABY-RINTHINE WAYS. New York: Viking Press, 1940.

THE MINISTRY OF FEAR: AN ENTERTAINMENT. London: Heinemann, 1943.

THE HEART OF THE MATTER. London: Heinemann, 1948.

THE THIRD MAN: AN ENTERTAINMENT. New York: Viking Press, 1950.

THE THIRD MAN AND THE FALLEN IDOL. London: Heinemann, 1950.

THE END OF THE AFFAIR. London: Heinemann, 1951.

LOSER TAKES ALL: AN ENTERTAINMENT. London: Heinemann, 1955.

THE QUIET AMERICAN. London: Heinemann, 1955.

OUR MAN IN HAVANA: AN ENTERTAINMENT. London: Heinemann, 1958.

A BURNT-OUT CASE. London: Heinemann, 1961.

THE COMEDIANS. London: Bodley Head, 1966.

TRAVELS WITH MY AUNT. London: Bodley Head, 1969.

SHORT STORIES

THE BASEMENT ROOM AND OTHER STORIES. London: Cresset Press, 1935.

THE BEAR FELL FREE. London: Grayson, 1935.

TWENTY-FOUR STORIES, with James Laver and Sylvia Townsend Warner. London: Cresset Press, 1939.

NINETEEN STORIES. London: Heinemann, 1947. Augmented edition, as TWENTY-ONE STORIES. London: Heinemann, 1954.

A VISIT TO MORIN. [n.p.]: privately printed, 1959.

A SENSE OF REALITY. London: Bodley Head, 1963.

MAY WE BORROW YOUR HUSBAND? AND OTHER COMEDIES OF THE SEXUAL LIFE. London: Bodley Head, 1967.

BIBLIOGRAPHY

Beebe, Maurice. "Criticism of Graham Greene: A Selected Checklist with an Index to Studies of Separate Works." MFS, 3 (1957), 281-88.

Birmingham, William. "Graham Greene Criticism: A Bibliographical Study." THOUGHT, 27 (Spring 1952), 72-100.

Hargreaves, Phylis. "Graham Greene: A Selected Bibliography." MFS, 3 (1957), 269-80.

Vann, J. Donn. GRAHAM GREENE. Kent, Ohio: Kent State University Press, 1970.

CRITICAL BOOKS

Allott, Kenneth, and Miriam Farris. THE ART OF GRAHAM GREENE. London: Hamish Hamilton, 1951.

Atkins, John. GRAHAM GREENE. London: Calder, 1957.

Cargas, Harry J., ed. GRAHAM GREENE. St. Louis, Mo.: Herder, 1969.

DeVitis, A.A. GRAHAM GREENE. New York: Twayne, 1964.

Evans, Robert O., ed. GRAHAM GREENE: SOME CRITICAL CONSIDERATIONS. Lexington: University of Kentucky Press, 1963.

Kohn, Lynette. GRAHAM GREENE: THE MAJOR NOVELS. Stanford, Calif.: Stanford University Press, 1961.

Kunkel, Francis L. THE LABYRINTHINE WAYS OF GRAHAM GREENE. New York: Sheed & Ward, 1960.

Lodge, David. GRAHAM GREENE. New York: Columbia University Press, 1966.

Madaule, Jacques. GRAHAM GREENE. Paris: Editions du Temps Present, 1949.

Mathews, Ronald. MON AMI, GRAHAM GREENE. Paris: Desclee de Brouwer, 1957.

Mesnet, Marie-Beatrice. GRAHAM GREENE AND THE HEART OF THE MATTER. London: Cresset, 1954.

Pryce-Jones, David. GRAHAM GREENE. Edinburgh: Oliver & Boyd, 1963.

Rischik, Josef. GRAHAM GREENE UND SEIN WERK. Bern: Francke, 1951.

Rostenne, Paul. GRAHAM GREENE TEMOIN DES TEMPS TRAGIQUES. Paris: Juliard, 1949.

Stratford, Philip. FAITH AND FICTION: CREATIVE PROCESS IN GREENE AND MAURIAC. Notre Dame, Ind.: University of Notre Dame Press, 1964.

Turnell, Martin. GRAHAM GREENE: A CRITICAL ESSAY. Grand Rapids, Mich.: Eerdmans, 1967.

Wyndham, Francis. GRAHAM GREENE. London: Longmans, Greene, 1955.

SPECIAL ISSUES

MODERN FICTION STUDIES, 3 (1957), "Graham Greene Number."

RENASCENCE, 23, i (1970), "Special: Graham Greene."

CRITICAL ARTICLES

Allen, W. Gore. "Evelyn Waugh and Graham Greene." IrM, 97 (January 1949), 16-22.

_____. "The World of Graham Greene." IrEccRec, 71 (January 1949), 42-49.

Allen, Walter. "Awareness of Evil: Graham Greene." NATION, 182 (21 April 1956), 344-46.

Alloway, Lawrence. "Symbolism in THE THIRD MAN." WoR, (March 1950), 57-60.

Arnold, G.L. "Adam's Tree." TC, 154 (1951), 337-42.

Auden, W.H. "The Heresy of Our Time." Ren, 1 (1949), 23-24.

Barnes, Robert J. "Two Modes of Fiction: Hemingway and Greene." Ren, 14 (1962), 193-98.

Barratt, Harold. "Adultery as Betrayal in Graham Greene." DR, 45 (1965), 324-32.

Battock, Marjorie. "The Novels of Graham Greene." NORSEMAN, 13 (January-February 1955), 45-52.

Beary, Thomas J. "Religion and the Modern Novel." CathW, 166 (December 1947), 204-5.

Bedford, Sybille. "Tragic Comedians." NYRB, 6 (3 March 1966), 25-27.

Boardman, Gwenn R. "Greene's 'Under the Garden': Aesthetic Explorations." Ren, 17 (1965), 180-90, 194.

Boyle, Alexander. "Graham Greene." IrM, 77 (November 1949), 519-25.

_____. "Symbolism of Graham Greene." IrM, 80 (March 1952), 98-102.

Braybrooke, Neville. "Graham Greene." ENVOY, 3 (September 1950), 10-23.

_____. "Graham Greene: A Pioneer Novelist." CE, 12 (1950), 1-9.

_____. "Graham Greene--The Double Man: An Approach to His Novel, THE END OF THE AFFAIR." DubR, no. 455 (1952), 61-73.

Bryden, Ronald. "Graham Greene, Alas." SPECTATOR (28 September 1962), 441-42.

Burgess, Anthony. "The Politics of Graham Greene." NYTBR, 10 September 1967, pp. 2, 32, 34.

Calder-Marshall, Arthur. "The Works of Graham Greene." HORIZON, 1 (1940), 367-75.

Celeste, Sister Marie, S.C. "Bernanos and Graham Greene on the Role of the Priest." CULTURE, 30 (1969), 287-98.

Clancy, L.J. "Graham Greene's Battlefield." CritR, 10 (1967), 99-108.

Connolly, Francis X. "Inside Modern Man: The Spiritual Adventures of Graham Greene." Ren, 1 (1949), 16-24.

Consolo, Dominick P. "Music as Motif: The Unity of BRIGHTON ROCK." Ren, 15 (1962), 12-20.

Cosman, Max. "Disquieted Graham Greene." ColQ, 6 (Winter 1958), 319-25.

_____. "An Early Chapter in Graham Greene." ArQ, 11 (1955), 143-47.

Costello, Donald P. "Graham Greene and the Catholic Press." Ren, 12 (1959), 3-28.

_____. "The Latest in Greene Criticism." Ren, 12 (1959), 38-40.

Cummingham, Lawrence. "The Alter Ego of Greene's 'Whiskey Priest.'" ELN, 8 (1970), 50-52.

Davidson, Arnold C. "Graham Greene's Spiritual Lepers." IEY, 15 (1970), 50-55.

De Hegedus, Adam. "Graham Greene: The Man and His Work." WoR, August 1948, pp. 57-61.

_____. "Graham Greene and the Modern Novel." TOMORROW, 8 (October 1948), 54-56.

Desmond, John F. "Graham Greene and the Eternal Dimension." ABR, 20 (1969), 418-27.

DeVitis, A.A. "The Church and Major Scobie." Ren, 10 (1958), 115-20.

_____. "The Entertaining Mr. Greene." Ren, 14 (1961), 8-24.

_____. "Greene's THE COMEDIANS: Hollower Men." Ren, 18 (1966), 129-36, 146.

Dinkins, Paul. "Graham Greene: The Incomplete Version." CathW, 176 (November 1952), 96-102.

Dooley, D.J. "A BURNT-OUT CASE Reconsidered." WiseR, 237 (Summer 1963), 168-78.

_____. "The Suspension of Disbelief: Greene's BURNT-OUT CASE." DR, 43 (Autumn 1963), 343-52.

Duffy, Joseph M., Jr. "The Lost World of Graham Greene." THOUGHT, 33 (Summer 1958), 229-47.

Elistratova, Anna. "Graham Greene and His New Novel." SovL, 8 (1956), 149-55.

Ellis, William D., Jr. "The Grand Theme of Graham Greene." SWR, 41 (1956), 239-50.

Fielding, Gabriel. "Graham Greene: The Religious Englishman." LISTENER, 72 (24 September 1964), 465-66.

Fowler, Alastair. "Novelist of Damnation." THEOLOGY, 56 (July 1953), 259-64.

Freedman, Ralph. "Novel of Contention: THE QUIET AMERICAN." WR, 21 (Autumn 1956), 76-81.

Fytton, Francis. "Graham Greene: Catholicism and Controversy." CathW, 180 (December 1954), 172-75.

Gardiner, Harold C. "Graham Greene, Catholic Shocker." Ren, 1 (1949), 12-15.

Glicksberg, Charles I. "Graham Greene: Catholicism in Fiction." CRITI-CISM, 1 (1959), 339-53.

Gordon, Caroline. "Some Readings and Misreadings." SR, 61 (July-September 1953), 393-96.

Gregor, Ian. "The Green Baize Door." BLACKFRIARS, 36 (September 1955), 327-33.

Grob, Alan. "THE POWER AND THE GLORY: Graham Greene's Argument from Design." CRITICISM, 11 (1969), 1-30.

Grubbs, Henry A. "Albert Camus and Graham Greene." MLQ, 10 (1949), 33-42.

Harmer, Ruth M. "Greene World of Mexico: The Birth of a Novelist." Ren, 15 (1963), 171-82, 194.

Herling, Gustav. "Two Sanctities: Greene and Camus." ADAM: INTER-NATIONAL REVIEW, no. 201 (December 1949), 10-18.

Hess, M.W. "Graham Greene's Travesty on THE RING AND THE BOOK." CathW, 194 (October 1961), 37-42.

Hinchliffe, Arnold P. "The Good American." TC, 168 (1960), 534-37.

Hoggart, Richard. "The Force of Caricature: Aspects of the Art of Graham Greene with Particular Reference to THE POWER AND THE GLORY." EIC, 3 (1953), 447-62.

Hortmann, Wilhelm. "Graham Greene: The Burnt-Out Catholic." TCL, 10 (1964), 64-76.

Howes, Jane. "Out of the Pit." CathW, 171 (April 1950), 36-40.

Hughes, Catharine. "Innocence Revisited." Ren, 12 (1959), 29-34.

Hughes, R.E. "THE QUIET AMERICAN: The Case Reopened." Ren, 12 (1959), 41-42, 49.

Jacobsen, Josephine. "A Catholic Quartet." ChS, 47 (1964), 143-46.

Jefferson, Mary E. "THE HEART OF THE MATTER: The Responsible Man." CarQ, 9 (Summer 1957), 23-31.

Jerrold, Douglas. "Graham Greene, Pleasure-Hater." Harper's, 205 (August 1952), 50-52.

Jones, Grahame C. "Graham Greene and the Legend of Peguy." CL, 21 (1969), 139-45.

Jones, James L. "Graham Greene and the Structure of the Moral Imagination." PHOENIX, no. 2 (1966), 34-56.

Kenny, Herbert A. "Graham Greene." CathW, 185 (August 1957), 326-29.

Kermode, Frank. "Mr. Greene's Eggs and Crosses." ENCOUNTER, 16 (April 1961), 69-75.

King, Bruce. "Graham Greene's Inferno." EA, 21 (1968), 35-51.

King, James. "In the Lost Boyhood of Judas: Graham Greene's Early Novels of Hell." DR, 49 (Summer 1969), 229-36.

Knipp, Thomas R. "Gide and Greene: Africa and the Literary Imagination." Serif, 6, ii (1969), 3-14.

Kort, Wesley. "The Obsession of Graham Greene." THOUGHT, 45 (Spring 1970), 20-44.

Lanina, T. "Paradoxes of Graham Greene." INOSTRANNAJA LITERATURA, no. 3 (March 1959), 188-96.

Lees, F.N. "Graham Greene: A Comment." SCRUTINY, 19 (October 1952), 31-42.

Lerner, Laurence. "Graham Greene." CritQ, 5 (1963), 217-31.

Lewis, R.W.B. "The Fiction of Graham Greene: Between the Horror and the Glory." KR, 19 (Winter 1957), 56-75.

Lodge, David. "The Use of Key-Words in the Novels of Graham Greene-- Love, Hate, and THE END OF THE AFFAIR." BLACKFRIARS, 42 (November 1961), 468-74.

Lohf, Kenneth A. "Graham Greene and the Problem of Evil." CathW, 173 (June 1951), 196-99.

McCall, Dan. "BRIGHTON ROCK: The Price of Order." ELN, 3 (1966), 290-94.

McCormick, John O. "The Rough and Lurid Vision: Henry James, Graham Greene and the International Novel." JA, 2 (1957), 158-67.

McGowan, F.A. "Symbolism in BRIGHTON ROCK." Ren, 8 (1955), 25-35.

McMahon, J. "Graham Greene and THE QUIET AMERICAN." JAMMU AND KASHMIR UNIVERSITY REVIEW, 1 (November 1958), 64-73.

MacSween, R.J. "Exiled from the Garden: Graham Greene." AntigR, 1,ii (1970), 41-48.

Marian, Sister, I.H.M. "Graham Greene's People: Becoming and Becoming." Ren, 18 (1965), 17-18.

Markovic, Vida E. "Graham Greene in Search of God." TSLL, 5 (1963), 271-82.

Marshall, Bruce. "Graham Greene and Evelyn Waugh." Cweal, 51 (3 March 1950), 551-53.

Maxwell, J.C. "'The Dry Salvages': A Possible Echo of Graham Greene." N&Q, 11 (1964), 387.

Michener, Richard L. "Apocalyptic Mexico: THE PLUMED SERPENT and THE POWER AND THE GLORY." UR, 34 (1968), 313-16.

Miller, J.D.B. "Graham Greene." Meanjin, 5 (1946), 193-97.

Monroe, N. Elizabeth. "The New Man in Fiction." Ren, 6 (1953), 9-12.

More, Marcel. "The Two Holocausts of Scobie." CC, 1 (Winter 1951), 44-63.

Neis, Edgar. "Zum Sprachstil Graham Greenes." NS, 6 (1957), 166-73.

Noxon, James. "Kierkegaard's Stages and A BURNT-OUT CASE." REL, 3 (January 1962), 90-101.

O'Donnell, Donat. "Graham Greene." CHIMERA, 5 (Summer 1947), 18-30.

O'Faolain, Sean. "The Novels of Graham Greene: THE HEART OF THE MATTER." BRITAIN TODAY, no. 148 (August 1948), 32-36.

Osterman, Robert. "Interview with Graham Greene." CathW, 170 (February 1950), 356-61.

Peters, W. "The Concern of Graham Greene." MONTH, 10 (November 1953), 281-90.

Poole, Roger C. "Graham Greene's Indirection." BLACKFRIARS, 45 (June 1964), 257-68.

_____. "'Those Sad Arguments': Two Novels of Graham Greene." RMS, 13 (1969), 148-60.

Puentevella, Renato. "Ambiguity in Greene." Ren, 12 (1959), 35-37.

Rahv, Philip. "Wicked American Innocence." Com, 21 (May 1956), 488-90.

Rolo, Charles J. "Graham Greene: The Man and the Message." ATLANTIC MONTHLY, 207 (May 1961), 60-65.

Ruotolo, Lucio P. "BRIGHTON ROCK'S Absurd Heroine." MLQ, 25 (1964), 425-33.

Sackville-West, Edward. "The Electric Hare: Some Aspects of Graham Greene." MONTH, 6 (September 1951), 141-47.

Sandra, Sister Mary, S.S.A. "The Priest-Hero in Modern Fiction." Person, 46 (1965), 538-42.

Scott, Nathan A., Jr. "Graham Greene: Christian Tragedian." VOLUSIA REVIEW, 1, i (1954), 29-42.

Seward, Barbara. "Graham Greene: A Hint of an Explanation." WR, 22 (Winter 1958), 83-95.

Sewell, Elizabeth. "Graham Greene." DubR, 228 (1954), 12-21.

_____. "The Imagination of Graham Greene." THOUGHT, 29 (March 1954), 51-60.

Shuttleworth, Martin, and Simon Raven. "The Art of Fiction III: Graham Greene." ParisR, 1 (Autumn 1953), 24-41.

Simon, John K. "Off the VOIE ROYALE: The Failure of Greene's A BURNT-OUT CASE." Sym, 18 (1964), 163-69.

Smith, A.J.M. "Graham Greene's Theological Thrillers." QQ, 68 (1961), 15-33.

Sternlicht, Sanford. "The Sad Comedies: Graham Greene's Later Novels." FQ, 1, iv (1968), 65-77.

_____. "Two Views of the Builder in Graham Greene's A BURNT-OUT CASE and William Golding's THE SPIRE." CalR, 1 (1970), 401-4.

Stratford, Philip. "Chalk and Cheese: A Comparative Study of A KISS FOR THE LEPER and A BURNT-OUT CASE." UTQ, 33 (1964), 200-218.

_____. "Graham Greene: Master of Melodrama." TamR, no. 19 (Spring 1961), 67-86.

Taylor, Marion A., and John Clark. "Further Sources for 'The Second Death' by Graham Greene." PELL, 1 (1965), 378-80.

Thomas, D.P. "Mr. Tench and Secondary Allegory in THE POWER AND THE GLORY." ELN, 7 (1969), 129-33.

Torres, Manuel. "El socio y OUR MAN IN HAVANA, novelas paralelas." MAPOCHO, 17 (1968), 61-67.

Tracy, Honor. "The Life and Soul of the Party." NRep, 140 (20 April 1959), 15-16.

Traversi, Derek. "Graham Greene." TC, 149 (1951), 231-40, 319-28.

Trilling, Diana, and Philip Rahv. "America and THE QUIET AMERICAN." Com, 12 (July 1956), 166-71.

Turnell, Martin. "Graham Greene: The Man Within." RAMPARTS, 4 (June 1965), 54-64.

_____. "The Religious Novel." Cweal, 55 (26 October 1951), 55-57.

Voorhees, Richard J. "Recent Greene." SAQ, 62 (1963), 244-55.

_____. "The World of Graham Greene." SAQ, 50 (1951), 389-98.

Wansbrough, John. "Graham Greene: The Detective in the Wasteland." HarvardA, 136 (December 1962), 11-13.

Wassmer, Thomas A. "Graham Greene: A Look at His Sinners." CRITIC, 18 (December 1959-January 1960), 16-17, 72-74.

_____. "The Problem and the Mystery of Sin in the Works of Graham Greene." ChS, 43 (1960), 309-15.

_____. "The Sinners of Graham Greene." DR, 39 (Autumn 1959), 326-32.

Waugh, Evelyn. "Felix Culpa?" Cweal, 48 (16 July 1948), 322-25.

Wichert, Robert A. "The Quality of Graham Greene's Mercy." CE, 25 (1963), 99-103.

Wilshere, A.D. "Conflict and Conciliation in Graham Greene." E&S, 19 (1966), 122-37.

Woodcock, George. "Mexico and the English Novelist." WR, 21 (Autumn 1956), 29-32.

Zabel, Morton D. "Graham Greene." NATION, 157 (3 July 1943), 18-20.

L[ESLIE]. P[OLES]. HARTLEY (1895-   ), ENGLISH

NOVELS

SIMONETTA PERKINS. London: Putnam, 1925.

THE SHRIMP AND THE ANEMONE. London: Putnam, 1944. As THE WEST WINDOW. Garden City, N.Y.: Doubleday, 1945.

THE SIXTH HEAVEN. London: Putnam, 1946.

EUSTACE AND HILDA. London: Putnam, 1947.

THE BOAT. London: Putnam, 1950.

MY FELLOW DEVILS. London: Barrie, 1951.

THE GO-BETWEEN. London: Hamish Hamilton, 1953.

A PERFECT WOMAN. London: Hamish Hamilton, 1955.

THE HIRELING. London: Hamish Hamilton, 1957.

EUSTACE AND HILDA (a trilogy). London: Putnam, 1958.

FACIAL JUSTICE. London: Hamish Hamilton, 1960.

THE BRICKFIELD. London: Hamish Hamilton, 1964.

THE BETRAYAL. London: Hamish Hamilton, 1966.

POOR CLARE. London: Hamish Hamilton, 1968.

THE LOVE-ADEPT: A VARIATION ON A THEME. London: Hamish Hamilton, 1969.

MY SISTER'S KEEPER. London: Hamish Hamilton, 1970.

SHORT STORIES

NIGHT FEARS AND OTHER STORIES. London: Putnam, 1924.

THE KILLING BOTTLE. London: Putnam, 1932.

THE TRAVELLING GRAVE AND OTHER STORIES. London: Barrie, 1951.

THE WHITE WAND AND OTHER STORIES. London: Hamish Hamilton, 1954.

TWO FOR THE RIVER. London: Hamish Hamilton, 1961.

THE COLLECTED SHORT STORIES OF L.P. HARTLEY. London: Hamish Hamilton, 1968.

CRITICAL BOOKS

Bergonzi, Bernard, and Paul Bloomfield. ANTHONY POWELL AND L.P. HARTLEY. London: Longmans, Green, 1962.

CRITICAL ARTICLES

Athos, John. "L.P. Hartley and the Gothic Infatuation " TCL, 7 (1962), 172-79.

Davison, Richard A. "Graham Greene and L.P. Hartley: 'The Basement Room' and THE GO-BETWEEN." N&Q, 13 (1966), 101-2.

Kitchin, Laurence. "Imperial Weekend." LISTENER, 74 (28 October 1965), 662-63, 667.

Kreutz, Irving. "L.P. Hartley, Who Are U? or, Luncheon in the Lounge." KR, 25 (1963), 150-54.

Melchiori, Giorgio. "The English Novelist and the American Tradition." SR, 68 (1960), 502-15.

Webster, Harvey C. "The Novels of L.P. Hartley." Crit, 4 (1961), 39-51.

JOHN HAWKES (1925-   ), AMERICAN

NOVELS

THE CANNIBAL. New York: New Directions, 1949.

THE BEETLE LEG. New York: New Directions, 1951.

THE LIME TWIG. New York: New Directions, 1961.

SECOND SKIN. New York: New Directions, 1964.

SHORT STORIES

THE GOOSE ON THE GRAVE AND THE OWL: TWO SHORT NOVELS. New York: New Directions, 1954.

LUNAR LANDSCAPES: STORIES AND SHORT NOVELS 1949-1963. New York: New Directions, 1969.

BIBLIOGRAPHY

Bryer, Jackson R. "John Hawkes." Crit, 6 (1963), 89-94.

SPECIAL ISSUES

CRITIQUE: STUDIES IN MODERN FICTION, 6 (Fall 1963), "John Hawkes and John Barth Issue."

CRITICAL ARTICLES

Edenbaum, Robert I. "John Hawkes: THE LIME TWIG and Tenuous Horrors." MR, 7 (1966), 462-75.

Enck, John. "John Hawkes: An Interview." WSCL, 6 (Summer 1965), 141-55.

Fiedler, Leslie A. "A Lonely American Eccentric: The Pleasures of John Hawkes." NewL, 43 (12 December 1960), 12-14.

Frohock, W.M. "John Hawkes's Vision of Violence." SWR, 50 (1965), 69-79.

Graham, John. "John Hawkes on His Novels; An Interview." MR, 7 (1966), 449-53.

Greiner, Donald J. "The Thematic Use of Color in John Hawkes' SECOND SKIN." ConL, 11 (1970), 389-400.

Guerard, Albert J. "The Prose Style of John Hawkes." Crit, 5 (1963), 19-29.

Matthews, Charles. "The Destructive Vision of John Hawkes." Crit, 6 (1963), 38-52.

Ratner, Marc L. "The Constructed Vision: The Fiction of John Hawkes." SA, 11 (1965), 345-57.

Reutlinger, D.P. "THE CANNIBAL: 'The Reality of Victim.'" Crit, 6 (1963), 30-37.

Rovit, Earl. "The Fiction of John Hawkes: An Introductory View." MFS, 11 (1964), 150-62.

Trachtenberg, Alan. "Barth and Hawkes: Two Fabulists." Crit, 6 (1963), 4-18.

JOSEPH HELLER (1923-), AMERICAN

NOVELS

CATCH-22. New York: Simon and Schuster, 1961.

CRITICAL ARTICLES

Alter, Robert. "The Apocalyptic Temper." Com, 41 (June 1966), 61-66.

Brewer, J.E. "The Anti-Hero in Contemporary Literature." IEY, 12 (1967), 55-60.

Castelli, Jim. "CATCH-22 and the New Hero." CathW, 211 (August 1970), 199-202.

Denniston, Constance. "The American Romance Parody: A Study of Purdy's MALCOLM and Heller's CATCH-22." ESRS, 14 (1965), 42-59, 63-64.

Doskow, Minna. "The Night Journey In CATCH-22." TCL, 12 (1967), 106-93.

Gaukroger, Doug. "Time Structure in CATCH-22." Crit, 12 (1970), 70-85.

Gordon, Caroline, and Jeanne Richardson. "Flies in Their Eyes? A Note on Joseph Heller's CATCH-22." SoR, 3 (1967), 96-105.

Henry, G.B. McK. "Significant Corn: CATCH-22." CritR, 9 (1966), 133-44.

Lehan, Richard, and Jerry Patch. "CATCH-22: The Making of a Novel." MinnR, 7 (1967), 238-44.

McDonald, James M. "I See Everything Twice: The Structure of Joseph Heller's CATCH–22." UR, 34 (1968), 175–80.

Milne, Victor J. "Heller's 'Bologniad': A Theological Perspective on CATCH–22." Crit, 12 (1970), 50–69.

Muste, John M. "Better to Die Laughing: The War Novels of Joseph Heller and John Ashmead." Crit, 5 (1962), 16–27.

Pinsker, Sanford. "Heller's CATCH–22: The Protest of a PUER ETERNIS." Crit, 7 (1965), 150–62.

Solomon, Eric. "From Christ in Flanders to CATCH–22: An Approach to War Fiction." TSLL, 11 (1969), 851–66.

Solomon, Jan. "The Structure of Joseph Heller's CATCH–22." Crit, 9 (1967), 46–57.

Stern, J.P. "War and the Comic Muse." CL, 20 (Summer 1968), 193–216.

Wain, John. "A New Novel About Old Troubles." CritQ, 5 (1963), 168–73.

Waldmeir, Joseph J. "Two Novelists of the Absurd: Heller and Kesey." WSCL, 5 (Autumn 1964), 192–204.

Way, Brian. "Formal Experiment and Social Discontent: Joseph Heller's CATCH–22." JAMS, 2 (1968), 253–70.

JOHN HERSEY (1914-), AMERICAN

NOVELS

A BELL FOR ADANO. New York: Knopf, 1944.

THE WALL. New York: Knopf, 1950.

THE MARMOT DRIVE. New York: Knopf, 1953.

A SINGLE PEBBLE. New York: Knopf, 1956.

THE WAR LOVER. New York: Knopf, 1959.

THE CHILD BUYER. A NOVEL IN THE FORM OF HEARINGS BEFORE THE STANDING COMMITTEE ON EDUCATION, WELFARE AND PUBLIC MORALITY OF A CERTAIN STATE SENATE INVESTIGATING THE CONSPIRACY OF MR. WISSEY JONES, WITH OTHERS, TO PURCHASE A MALE CHILD. New York: Knopf, 1960.

WHITE LOTUS. New York: Knopf, 1965.

TOO FAR TO WALK. New York: Knopf, 1966.

UNDER THE EYE OF THE STORM. New York: Knopf, 1967.

CRITICAL BOOKS

Sanders, David. JOHN HERSEY. New York: Twayne, 1967.

CRITICAL ARTICLES

Burton, Arthur. "Existential Conceptions in John Hersey's Novel, THE CHILD BUYER." JOURNAL OF EXISTENTIAL PSYCHOLOGY, 2 (Fall 1961), 243-58.

Green, L.C. "The Wall." AMERICAN HEBREW, 159 (31 March 1950), 7-8, 60.

Guilfoil, Kelsey. "John Hersey: Fact and Fiction." EJ, 34 (1950), 355-60.

Hudspeth, Robert N. "A Definition of Modern Nihilism: Hersey's THE WAR LOVER." UR, 35 (1969), 243-49.

Lampell, Millard. "Bringing 'The Wall' to the Stage." MIDSTREAM, 6 (August 1960), 14-19.

McDonnell, T.P. "Hersey's Allegorical Novels." CathW, 95 (July 1962), 240-45.

Ross, G.M. "'The Wall' on Broadway." Com, 31 (January 1961), 66-69.

Werner, Alfred. "With a Pen of Iron." AMERICAN HEBREW, 160 (11 August 1950), 4-5.

RICHARD HUGHES [ARTHUR WARREN]
(1900-   ), ENGLISH

NOVELS

A HIGH WIND IN JAMAICA. London: Chatto and Windus, 1929. As THE INNOCENT VOYAGE. New York: Harper, 1929.

IN HAZARD: A SEA STORY. London: Chatto and Windus, 1938.

THE FOX IN THE ATTIC. Volume I of a projected long novel, THE HUMAN PREDICAMENT. London: Chatto and Windus, 1961.

SHORT STORIES

A MOMENT OF TIME. London: Chatto and Windus, 1926.

CRITICAL ARTICLES

Bosano, J. "Richard Hughes." EA, 16 (1963), 262-69.

Brown, Daniel R. "A HIGH WIND IN JAMAICA." BSUF, 9, i (1968), 6-12.

Henighan, T.J. "Nature and Convention in A HIGH WIND IN JAMAICA." Crit, 9 (1967), 5-18.

Schone, Annemarie. "Richard Hughes--Ein Meister der tragischen Ironie." GRM, 9 (1959), 75-86.

Woodward, Daniel H. "The Delphic Voice: Richard Hughes's A HIGH WIND IN JAMAICA." PLL, 3 (1967), 57-74.

CHRISTOPHER ISHERWOOD (1904-), ENGLISH

NOVELS

ALL THE CONSPIRATORS. London: Cape, 1928.

THE MEMORIAL: PORTRAIT OF A FAMILY. London: Hogarth Press, 1932.

MR. NORRIS CHANGES TRAINS. London: Hogarth Press, 1935. As THE LAST OF MR. NORRIS. New York: Morrow, 1935.

SALLY BOWLES. London: Hogarth Press, 1937.

LIONS AND SHADOWS. London: Hogarth Press, 1938.

GOODBYE TO BERLIN. London: Hogarth Press, 1939.

PRATER VIOLET. London: Methuen, 1946.

THE BERLIN STORIES. (THE LAST OF MR. NORRIS and GOODBYE TO BER-LIN). New York· New Directions, 1946.

THE WORLD IN THE EVENING. London: Methuen, 1954.

DOWN THERE ON A VISIT. London: Methuen, 1962.

A SINGLE MAN. London: Methuen, 1964.

A MEETING BY THE RIVER. London: Methuen, 1967.

BIBLIOGRAPHY

Westby, Selmer, and Clayton M. Brown. CHRISTOPHER ISHERWOOD: A BIBLIOGRAPHY 1923-1967. Los Angeles: California State College, 1968.

CRITICAL BOOKS

Heilbrun, Carolyn G. CHRISTOPHER ISHERWOOD. New York: Columbia University Press, 1970.

CRITICAL ARTICLES

Isherwood, Christopher. "A Conversation on Tape." LonM, n.s. 1 (June 1961), 41-58.

Mayne, Richard. "The Novel and Mr. Norris." CAMBRIDGE JOURNAL, 6 (June 1953), 561-70.

Perez Minik, Domingo. "Christopher Isherwood, un novelista famoso, pero frustrado." INSULA, 23 (February 1968), 5.

Pryce-Jones, David. "Isherwood Reassessed." T&T, 41 (1960), 1162-63.

Solway, Clifford. "An Interview with Christopher Isherwood." TamR, 39 (Spring 1966), 22-35.

Whitehead, John. "Christophananda: Isherwood at Sixty." LonM, n.s. 5 (July 1965), 90-100.

Wickes, Gerald. "An Interview with Christopher Isherwood." SHENAN-DOAH, 16 (Spring 1965), 23-52.

Wilde, Alan. "Irony and Style: The Example of Christopher Isherwood." MFS, 16 (1970), 475-89.

PAMELA HANSFORD JOHNSON (1912-), ENGLISH

NOVELS

THIS BED THY CENTRE. London: Chapman and Hall, 1935.

BLESSED ABOVE WOMEN. London: Chapman and Hall, 1936.

HERE TODAY. London: Chapman and Hall, 1937.

WORLD'S END. London: Chapman and Hall, 1937.

THE MONUMENT. London: Chapman and Hall, 1938.

GIRDLE OF VENUS. London: Chapman and Hall, 1939.

TOO DEAR FOR MY POSSESSING. London: Collins, 1940.

TIDY DEATH, with Neil Stewart (as Nap Lombard). London: Cassell, 1940.

THE FAMILY PATTERN. London: Collins, 1942.

WINTER QUARTERS. London: Collins, 1943.

MURDER'S A SWINE, with Neil Stewart (as Nap Lombard). London: Hutchinson, 1943. As THE GRINNING PIG. New York: Simon and Schuster,
1943.

THE TROJAN BROTHERS. London: Joseph, 1944.

AN AVENUE OF STONE. London: Joseph, 1947.

A SUMMER TO DECIDE. London: Joseph, 1948.

THE PHILISTINES. London: Joseph, 1949.

CATHERINE CARTER. London: Macmillan, 1952.

AN IMPOSSIBLE MARRIAGE. London: Macmillan, 1954.

THE LAST RESORT. London: Macmillan, 1956. As THE SEA AND THE WEDDING. New York: Harcourt, Brace, 1957.

THE HUMBLER CREATION. London: Macmillan, 1959.

THE UNSPEAKABLE SKIPTON. London: Macmillan, 1959.

AN ERROR OF JUDGEMENT. London: Macmillan, 1962.

NIGHT AND SILENCE, WHO IS HERE? AN AMERICAN COMEDY. London: Macmillan, 1963.

CORK STREET, NEXT TO THE HATTER'S: A NOVEL IN BAD TASTE. London: Macmillan, 1965.

THE SURVIVAL OF THE FITTEST. London: Macmillan, 1968.

THE HONOURS BOARD. London: Macmillan, 1970.

CRITICAL BOOKS

Quigly, Isabel. PAMELA HANSFORD JOHNSON. London: Longman, 1968.

JAMES JONES (1921-), AMERICAN

NOVELS

FROM HERE TO ETERNITY. New York: Scribner, 1951.

SOME CAME RUNNING. New York: Scribner, 1957.

THE PISTOL. New York: Scribner, 1958.

THE THIN RED LINE. New York: Scribner, 1962.

GO TO THE WIDOW-MAKER. New York: Delacorte Press, 1967.

SHORT STORIES

THE ICE-CREAM HEADACHE AND OTHER STORIES. New York: Delacorte Press, 1968.

CRITICAL ARTICLES

Adams, Richard P. "A Second Look at FROM HERE TO ETERNITY." CE, 17 (1956), 205-10.

Brierre, Annie. "Pourquoi preferez-vous Paris?" NL, no. 1642 (1959), 1-4.

Bromberg, Jan. "En Amerikan i Paris." HORISONT, 11 (1964), 19-22.

Burress, L.A. "James Jones on Folklore and Ballad." CE, 21 (1959), 161-65.

DeVoto, Bernard. "Dull Novels Make Dull Reading." Harper's, 202 (June 1951), 67-70.

Fiedler, Leslie A. "James Jones' Dead-End Young Werther." Com, 12 (September 1951), 252-55.

Glicksberg, Charles I. "Racial Attitudes in FROM HERE TO ETERNITY." PHYLON, 14 (1953), 384-89.

Griffith, Benjamin W. "Rear Rank Robin Hood: James Jones's Folk Hero." GaR, 10 (1956), 41-46.

Jaesrich, Helmut. "Null-acht Funfzehn auf Hawaii. Uber 'Verdammt in alle Ewigkeit.'" Monat, 6 (April 1954), 55-60.

Jones, James, and William Styron. "Two Writers Talk it Over." ESQUIRE, 60 (July 1963), 57-59.

Michel-Michot, Paulette. "Jones's THE THIN RED LINE: The End of Innocence." RLV, 30 (1964), 15-26.

Ray, David. "Mrs. Handy's Writing Mill." LonM, 5 (July 1958), 35-41.

Rizzardi, Alfredo. "L'eredita della guerra nel romanzo di James Jones." GALLERIA, 13 (1963), 89-95.

Sheed, Wilfrid. "The Jones Boy Forever." ATLANTIC MONTHLY, 219 (June 1967), 68-72.

JACK KEROUAC (1922-69), AMERICAN

NOVELS

THE TOWN AND THE CITY. New York: Harcourt, 1950.

ON THE ROAD. New York: Viking Press, 1957.

THE DHARMA BUMS. New York: Viking Press, 1958.

THE SUBTERRANEANS. New York: Grove Press, 1958.

DOCTOR SAX. New York: Grove Press, 1959.

MAGGIE CASSIDY. New York: Avon, 1959.

TRISTESSA. New York: Avon, 1960.

EXCERPTS FROM VISIONS OF CODY. Norfolk, Conn.: New Directions, 1960.

BOOK OF DREAMS. San Francisco: City Lights, 1961.

BIG SUR. New York: Farrar, Straus, 1962.

VISIONS OF GERARD. New York: Farrar, Straus, 1963.

DESOLATION ANGELS. New York: Coward-McCann, 1965.

VANITY OF DULUOZ. New York: Coward-McCann, 1968.

BIBLIOGRAPHY

Charters, Ann. A BIBLIOGRAPHY OF WORKS BY JACK KEROUAC. New York: Phoenix Book Shop, 1967.

CRITICAL ARTICLES

Ashida, Margaret E. "Frogs and Frozen Zen." PrS, 34 (1960), 199-206.

Askew, Melvin W. "Quests, Cars, and Kerouac." UKCR, 29 (March 1962), 231-40.

Bellman, Samuel I. "On the Mountain." ChiR, 13 (1959), 68-72.

Berrigan, Ted. "The Art of Fiction, XLI: Jack Kerouac." ParisR, 11 (1968), 60-105.

Champney, Freeman. "Beat-up or Beatific." AR, 19 (1959), 114-21.

Cimatti, Pietro. "Jack Kerouac: scrittore o divo?" FLe, 16 (1961), 4.

Dommergues, Pierre. "Le dernier roman de Jack Kerouac." LanM, 58 (1964), 149-52.

Gleason, Ralph. "Kerouac's 'Beat Generation.'" SatR, 41 (11 January 1958), 75.

Gold, Herbert. "Hip, Cool, Beat--and Frantic." NATION, 185 (16 November 1957), 349-55.

Gresset, Michel. "Les clochards celestes." MdF, no. 1201 (1963), 620-21.

Kerouac, Jack. "Beatific: On the Origins of a Generation." ENCOUNTER, 13 (August 1959), 57-61.

Krim, Seymour. "King of the Beats." CWEAL, 69 (2 January 1959), 359-60.

Leer, Norman. "Three American Novels and Contemporary Society." WSCL, 3 (Fall 1962), 67-86.

Podhoretz, Norman. "The Know-Nothing Bohemians." PR, 25 (1958), 305-18.

Rubin, Louis D. "Two Gentlemen of San Francisco: Notes on Kerouac and Responsibility." WR, 23 (Spring 1959), 278-83.

Russell, William. "Kerouac's THE SUBTERRANEANS." MAINSTREAM, 15, vi (June 1962), 61-64.

Tallman, Warren. "Kerouac's Sound." TamR, 11 (1959), 58-74.

Van den Haag, Ernest. "Jack Kerouac et la 'Beat Generation.'" TM, (1959), 568-76.

KEN KESEY (1935-), AMERICAN

NOVELS

ONE FLEW OVER THE CUCKOO'S NEST. New York: Viking Press, 1962.

SOMETIMES A GREAT NOTION. New York: Viking Press, 1964.

CRITICAL ARTICLES

Barsness, John A. "Ken Kesey: The Hero in Modern Dress." BRMMLA, 23 (1969), 27–33.

Malin, Irving. "Ken Kesey: ONE FLEW OVER THE CUCKOO'S NEST." Crit, 5 (1962), 81–84.

Waldmeir, Joseph J. "Two Novelists of the Abusrd: Heller and Kesoy." WSCL, 5 (Autumn 1964), 196–204.

Witke, Charles. "Pastoral Convention in Virgil and Kesey." PCP, I (1966), 20–24.

JOHN KNOWLES (1926-), AMERICAN

NOVELS

A SEPARATE PEACE. New York: Macmillan, 1960.

MORNING IN ANTIBES. New York: Macmillan, 1962.

INDIAN SUMMER. New York: Random House, 1966.

SHORT STORIES

PHINEAS: 6 STORIES. New York: Random House, 1968.

CRITICAL ARTICLES

Crabbe, John K. "On the Playing Fields of Devon." EJ, 52 (1963), 109-11.

Ellis, James. "A SEPARATE PEACE: The Fall from Innocence." EJ, 53 (1964), 313-10.

Ely, Sister M. Amanda, O.P. "The Adult Image in Three Novels of Adolescent Life." EJ, 56 (1967), 1128-30.

Foster, Milton P. "Levels of Meaning in A SEPARATE PEACE." EngR, 18 (Winter 1968), 34-40.

Greiling, F.L. "The Theme of Freedom in A SEPARATE PEACE." EJ, 56 (1967), 1269-72.

Halio, Jay L. "John Knowles's Short Novels." SSF, 1 (1964), 107-12.

McDonald, J.L. "The Novels of John Knowles." ArQ, 23 (1967), 335-42.

Mellard, K.M. "Counterpoint and 'Double Vision' in A SEPARATE PEACE." SSF, 4 (1967), 127-34.

Nora, Sister M., S.S.N.D. "A Comparison of Actual and Symbolic Landscape in A SEPARATE PEACE." DISCOURSE, 11 (1968), 356-62.

Weber, Ronald. "Narrative Method in A SEPARATE PEACE." SSF, 3 (1965), 63-72.

Witherington, Paul. "A SEPARATE PEACE: A Study in Structural Ambiguity." EJ, 54 (1965), 795-800.

JERZY [NIKODEM] KOSINSKI (1933-), AMERICAN

NOVELS

THE PAINTED BIRD. Boston: Houghton Mifflin, 1965; rev. ed., New York: Modern Library, 1970.

STEPS. New York: Random House, 1968.

DORIS LESSING (1919-), ENGLISH

NOVELS

THE GRASS IS SINGING. London: Joseph, 1950.

CHILDREN OF VIOLENCE:
    MARTHA QUEST. London: Joseph, 1952.
    A PROPER MARRIAGE. London: Joseph, 1954.
    A RIPPLE FROM THE STORM. London: Joseph, 1958.
    LANDLOCKED. London: MacGibbon and Kee, 1965.
    THE FOUR-GATED CITY. London: MacGibbon and Kee, 1969.

RETREAT TO INNOCENCE. London: Joseph, 1956.

THE GOLDEN NOTEBOOK. London: Joseph, 1962.

SHORT STORIES

THIS WAS THE OLD CHIEF'S COUNTRY: STORIES. London: Joseph, 1951.

THE HABIT OF LOVING. London: MacGibbon and Kee, 1957.

A MAN AND TWO WOMEN: STORIES. London: Joseph, 1964.

AFRICAN STORIES. London: Joseph, 1964.

NINE AFRICAN STORIES. London: Longman, 1968.

BIBLIOGRAPHY

Burkom, Selma R. "A Doris Lessing Checklist." Crit, 11 (1969), 69–81.

Ipp, C. DORIS LESSING. Johannesburg: University of Witwatersrand Department of Bibliography, Librarianship, and Typography, 1967.

CRITICAL BOOKS

Brewster, Dorothy. DORIS LESSING. New York: Twayne, 1965.

CRITICAL ARTICLES

Brewer, J.E. "The Anti-Hero in Contemporary Literature." IEY, 12 (1967), 55–60.

Burkom, Selma R. "'Only Connect': Form and Content in the Works of Doris Lessing." Crit, 11 (1969), 51–68.

Graustein, Gottfried. "Entwicklungstandenzen in Schaffen Doris Lessings." WZUR, 12 (1963), 529–33.

Hartwig, Dorothea. "Die Widerspiegelung afrikanischer Probleme im Werk Doris Lessings." WZUR, 12 (1963), 87–104.

McDowell, Frederick P.W. "The Devious Involutions of Human Character and Emotions: Reflections on Some Recent British Novels." WSCL, 4 (Autumn 1963), 346–50.

_____. "The Fiction of Doris Lessing: An Interim View." ArQ, 21 (1965), 314–45.

RICHARD LLEWELLYN (1907-), ENGLISH

NOVELS

HOW GREEN WAS MY VALLEY. London: Joseph, 1939.

NONE BUT THE LONELY HEART. London: Joseph, 1943.

A FEW FLOWERS FOR SHINER. London: Joseph, 1950.

A FLAME FOR DOUBTING THOMAS. London: Joseph, 1954.

SWEET WITCH. London: Joseph, 1955.

MR. HAMISH GLEAVE. London: Joseph, 1956.

THE FLAME OF HERCULES. London: Joseph, 1957.

WARDEN OF THE SMOKE AND BELLS. London: Joseph, 1958.

CHEZ PAVAN. London: Joseph, 1959.

UP, INTO THE SINGING MOUNTAIN. London: Joseph, 1963.

A MAN IN A MIRROR. London: Joseph, 1964.

SWEET MORN OF JUDAS' DAY. London: Joseph, 1965.

DOWN WHERE THE MOON IS SMALL. London: Joseph, 1966.

THE END OF THE RUG. London: Joseph, 1966.

BUT WE DIDN'T GET THE FOX. London: Joseph, 1970.

MARY McCARTHY (1912-), AMERICAN

NOVELS

THE COMPANY SHE KEEPS. New York: Simon and Schuster, 1942.

THE OASIS. New York: Random House, 1949.

THE GROVES OF ACADEME. New York: Harcourt, Brace, 1952.

A CHARMED LIFE. New York: Harcourt, Brace, 1955.

THE GROUP. New York: Harcourt, Brace, 1963.

SHORT STORIES

CAST A COLD EYE. New York: Harcourt, Brace, 1950.

BIBLIOGRAPHY

Goldman, Sherli. MARY McCARTHY: A BIBLIOGRAPHY. New York: Harcourt, Brace, 1968.

CRITICAL BOOKS

Grumbach, Doris. THE COMPANY SHE KEPT. New York: Coward-McCann, 1967.

McKenzie, Barbara. MARY McCARTHY. New York: Twayne, 1967.

Stock, Irvin. MARY McCARTHY. Minneapolis: University of Minnesota Press, 1968.

CRITICAL ARTICLES

Brower, Brock. "Mary McCarthyism." ESQUIRE, 58 (July 1962), 62-67, 113.

Cook, Bruce. "Mary McCarthy: One of Ours?" CathW, 199 (April 1964), 34-42.

Fitch, Robert E. "The Cold Eye of Mary McCarthy." NRep, 138 (5 May 1958), 17-19.

Heissenbuttel, Helmut. "Mary McCarthy: Versuch eines Portrats." Monat, no. 189 (1964), 54-66.

Kauffmann, Stanley. "Miss McCarthy's Era." NRep, 144 (31 August 1963), 25-30.

McCarthy, Mary. "Characters in Fiction." PR, 28 (1961), 171-91.

_____. "Letters to a Translator: About THE GROUP." ENCOUNTER, 23 (November 1964), 69-71, 74-76.

Mathewson, Ruth. "The Vassar Joke." CUF, 6 (1963), 10-16.

Neibuhr, Elisabeth. "The Art of Fiction, XXVII: Mary McCarthy." ParisR, no. 27 (Winter-Spring 1962), 58-94.

Poli, Sara. "La narrativa di Mary McCarthy." SA, 7 (1961), 215-59.

Ross, Theodore J. "Passion--Moral and Otherwise." NRep, 139 (18 August 1958), 23-26.

CARSON McCULLERS (1917-67), AMERICAN

NOVELS

THE HEART IS A LONELY HUNTER. Boston: Houghton Mifflin, 1940.

REFLECTIONS IN A GOLDEN EYE. Boston: Houghton Mifflin, 1941.

THE MEMBER OF THE WEDDING. Boston: Houghton Mifflin, 1946.

THE BALLAD OF THE SAD CAFE. Boston: Houghton Mifflin, 1951.

CLOCK WITHOUT HANDS. Boston: Houghton Mifflin, 1961.

BIBLIOGRAPHY

Phillips, Robert S. "Carson McCullers: 1956-1964: A Selective Checklist." BB, 24 (1964), 113-16.

Stewart, Stanley. "Carson McCullers, 1940-1956: A Selected Checklist." BB, 22 (1959), 182-85.

CRITICAL BOOKS

Edmonds, Dale. CARSON McCULLERS. Austin, Tex.: Steck-Vaughn, 1969.

Evans, Oliver. CARSON McCULLERS: HER LIFE AND WORK. London: Peter Owen, 1965.

Graver, Lawrence. CARSON McCULLERS. Minneapolis: University of Minnesota Press, 1969.

CRITICAL ARTICLES

Baldanza, Frank. "Plato in Dixie." GaR, 12 (1958), 151-67.

Dodd, Wayne D. "The Development of Theme Through Symbol in the Novels of Carson McCullers." GaR, 17 (1963), 206-13.

Durham, Frank. "God and No God in THE HEART IS A LONELY HUNTER." SAQ, 56 (1956), 494-99.

Emerson, Donald. "The Ambiguities of CLOCK WITHOUT HANDS." WSCL, 3 (Fall 1962), 15-28.

Evans, Oliver. "The Achievement of Carson McCullers." EJ, 51 (1962), 301-308.

_____. "The Case of Carson McCullers." GaR, 18 (1964), 40-45.

_____. "The Case of the Silent Singer: A Revaluation of THE HEART IS A LONELY HUNTER." GaR, 19 (1965), 188-203.

Folk, Barbara N. "The Sweet Sad Music of Carson McCullers." GaR, 16 (1962), 202-9.

Gozzi, Francesco. "La narrativa di Carson McCullers." SA, 14 (1968), 339-76.

Hamilton, Alice. "Loneliness and Alienation: The Life and Work of Carson McCullers." DR, 50 (1969), 215-29.

Hart, Jane. "Carson McCullers, Pilgrim of Loneliness." GaR, 11 (1957), 53-58.

Hassan, Ihab. "Carson McCullers: The Alchemy of Love and Aesthetics of Pain." MFS, 5 (1959), 311-26.

Hendrick, George. "'Almost Everyone Wants to Be the Lover': The Fiction of Carson McCullers." BA, 42 (1968), 389-91.

Hughes, Catherine. "A World of Outcasts." Cweal, 75 (13 October 1961), 73-75.

Jaworski, Philippe. "La double quete de l'identite et de la realite chez Carson McCullers." NRF (17 July 1969), 93-101.

Kohler, Dayton. "Carson McCullers: Variations on a Theme." EJ, 40 (1951), 415-22; CE, 13 (1951), 1-8.

Lubbers, Klaus. "The Necessary Order: A Study of Theme and Structure in Carson McCuller's Fiction." JA, 8 (1963), 187-204.

McPherson, Hugo. "Carson McCullers: Lonely Huntress." TamR, no. 11 (1959), 28-40.

Madden, David. "The Paradox of the Need for Privacy and the Need for Understanding in Carson McCullers' THE HEART IS A LONELY HUNTER." L&P, 17, ii-iii (1967), 128-40.

Micha, Rene. "Carson McCullers ou la cabane de l'enfance." CRITIQUE, nos. 183-84 (1963), 696-707.

Moore, Jack B. "Carson McCullers: The Heart is a Timeless Hunter." TCL, 11 (1965), 76-81.

Phillips, Robert S. "Dinesen's 'Monkey' and McCullers' 'Ballad': A Study in Literary Affinity." SSF, 1 (1964), 184-90.

_____. "The Gothic Architecture of THE MEMBER OF THE WEDDING." Ren, 16 (1964), 59-72.

_____. "Painful Love: Carson McCullers' Parable." SWR, 51 (1966), 80-86.

Rechnitz, Robert M. "The Failure of Love: The Grotesque in Two Novels of Carson McCullers." GaR, 22 (1968), 454-58.

Rios Ruiz, Manuel. "Carson McCullers, la novelistia del fatalismo." CHA, 76 (1968), 763-71.

Robinson, W.R. "The Life of Carson McCullers' Imagination." SHR, 2 (1968), 291-302.

Sherill, Rowland A. "McCullers' THE HEART IS A LONELY HUNTER: The Missing Ego and the Problem of the Norm." KyR, 2 (1968), 5-17.

Tinkham, Charles B. "The Member of the Sideshow." PHYLON, 18 (1958), 383-90.

Vickery, John B. "Carson McCullers: A Map of Love." WSCL, 1 (Winter 1960), 13-24.

COLIN MacINNES (1914-), ENGLISH

NOVELS

TO THE VICTORS THE SPOILS. London: MacGibbon and Kee, 1950.

JUNE IN HER SPRING. London: MacGibbon and Kee, 1952.

CITY OF SPADES. London: MacGibbon and Kee, 1957.

ABSOLUTE BEGINNERS. London: MacGibbon and Kee, 1959.

MR. LOVE AND JUSTICE. London: MacGibbon and Kee, 1960.

ALL DAY SATURDAY. London: MacGibbon and Kee, 1966.

WESTWARD TO LAUGHTER. London: MacGibbon and Kee, 1969.

THREE YEARS TO PLAY. London: MacGibbon and Kee, 1970.

NORMAN MAILER (1923-), AMERICAN

NOVELS

THE NAKED AND THE DEAD. New York: Rinehart, 1948.

BARBARY SHORE. New York: Rinehart, 1951.

THE DEER PARK. New York: Putnam, 1955.

AN AMERICAN DREAM. New York: Dial Press, 1965.

WHY ARE WE IN VIETNAM? New York: Putnam, 1967.

SHORT STORIES

NEW SHORT NOVELS 2 ("The Man Who Studied Yoga"), with others. New York: Ballantine, 1956.

ADVERTISEMENTS FOR MYSELF. New York: Putnam, 1959.

BIBLIOGRAPHY

Sokoloff, B.A. A COMPREHENSIVE BIBLIOGRAPHY OF NORMAN MAILER. Folcroft, Pa.: Folcroft Press, 1970.

CRITICAL BOOKS

Foster, Richard. NORMAN MAILER. Minneapolis: University of Minnesota Press, 1968.

Kaufmann, Donald L. NORMAN MAILER: THE COUNTDOWN. Carbondale: Southern Illinois University Press, 1969.

Leeds, Barry H. THE STRUCTURED VISION OF NORMAN MAILER. New York: New York University Press, 1969.

CRITICAL ARTICLES

Arnavon, Cyrille. "Les cauchemars de Norman Mailer," EUROPE, 477 (1969), 93-116.

Baldwin, James. "The Black Boy Looks at the White Boy: Norman Mailer." ESQUIRE, 55 (May 1961), 102-6.

Bersani, Leo. "The Interpretation of Dreams." PR, 32 (1965), 603-8.

Cimatti, Pietro. "L'inferno di Mailer." FLe, 14 (12 April 1959), 4.

Cook, Bruce. "Norman Mailer: The Temptation to Power." Ren, 14 (1966), 206-15, 222.

Corona, Mario. "Norman Mailer." SA, 11 (1965), 359-407.

Corrington, J.W. "An American Dreamer." ChiR, 18, i (Spring 1965), 58-66.

DeMott, Benjamin. "Docket No. 15883." AScH, 30 (1961), 232-37.

Dupee, F.W. "The American Norman Mailer." Com, 29 (February 1960), 128-32.

Fiedler, Leslie A. "Antic Mailer--Portrait of a Middle-Aged Artist." NewL, 43 (25 January 1960), 23-24.

Finn, James. "Virtues, Failures, and Triumphs of an American Writer." Cweal, 71 (12 February 1960), 551-52.

Foster, Richard. "Mailer and the Fitzgerald Tradition." NOVEL, 1 (1968), 219-30.

Glicksberg, Charles I. "Norman Mailer: The Angry Young Novelist in America." WSCL, 1 (Winter 1960), 25-34.

_____. "Sex in Contemporary Literature." ColQ, 9 (Winter 1961), 277-87.

Goldstone, Herbert. "The Novels of Norman Mailer." EJ, 45 (1956), 113-21.

Gordon, Andrew. "THE NAKED AND THE DEAD: The Triumph of Impotence." L&P, 19 (1969), 3-13.

Hampshire, Stuart. "Mailer United." NStat, 62 (13 October 1961), 515-16.

Hoffman, Frederick J. "Norman Mailer and the Revolt of the Ego: Some Observations on Recent American Literature." WSCL, 1 (Fall 1960), 5-12.

Howe, Irving. "A Quest for Peril." PR, 27 (1960), 143-48.

Hux, Samuel. "Mailer's Dream of Violence." MinnR, 8 (1968), 152-57.

Iwamoto, Iwao. "Gendai wo Ikiru Messiah." EigoS, 115 (1969), 554-55.

Krim, Seymour. "A Hungry Mental Lion." EVERGREEN REVIEW, no. 4 (1960), 178-85.

_____. "An Open Letter to Norman Mailer." EVERGREEN REVIEW, no. 45 (February 1967), 89-96.

Lakin, R.D. "D.W.'s: The Displaced Writer in America." MQ, 4 (1963), 295-303.

Langbaum, Robert. "Mailer's New Style." NOVEL, 2 (1968), 69-78.

Leffalaar, H.L. "Norman Mailer in Chicago." LITTERAIR PASPOORT, 15 (April 1960), 79-81.

MacDonald, Dwight. "Massachusetts vs. Mailer." NY, 36 (8 October 1960), 154-66.

Mailer, Norman. "Advertisements for Myself on the Way Out." PR, 25 (1958), 519-40.

_____. "Norman Mailer versus Nine Writers." ESQUIRE, 60 (July 1963), 63-69, 105.

_____. "PLAYBOY Interview." PLAYBOY, 15 (January 1968), 69-84.

_____. "Up the Family Tree." PR, 35 (1968), 234-52.

Materassi, Mario. "La rauca voce di Norman Mailer." Ponte, 23 (1967), 630-35.

_____. "Undici domande a Norman Mailer." Ponte, 18 (1962, 1010-13.

Miller, Jonathan. "Black-Mailer." PR, 21 (1964), 103-7.

Mudrick, Marvin. "Mailer and Styron: Guests of the Establishment." HudR, 17 (1964), 346-66.

Newman, Paul B. "Mailer: The Jew as Existentialist." NORTH AMERICAN REVIEW, 2, iii (1965), 48-55.

Podhoretz, Norman. "Norman Mailer: The Embattled Vision." PR, 26 (1959), 371-91.

Pritchard, William H. "Norman Mailer's Extravagances." MR, 8 (1967), 562-68.

Richler, Mordecai. "Norman Mailer." ENCOUNTER, 25 (July 1965), 61-64.

Rijpens, John. "Mailer weer op oorlogspad." VIG, 52, iii (1968), 27-29.

Schein, Harry. "Norman Mailer." BLM, 26 (1957), 232-40.

Schrader, George Alfred. "Norman Mailer and the Despair of Defiance." YR, 52 (1962), 267-80.

Schroth, Raymond A., S.J. "Mailer and His Gods." Cweal, 90 (1969), 226-29.

Schulz, Max F. "Mailer's Divine Comedy." ConL, 9 (Winter 1968), 36-57.

Shaw, Peter. "The Tough Guy Intellectual." CritQ, 8 (1966), 13-28.

Solotaroff, Robert. "Down Mailer's Way." ChiR, 19, iii (June 1967), 11-25.

Steiner, George. "Naked But Not Dead." ENCOUNTER, 17 (December 1961), 67-70.

Stern, Richard G. "Hip, Hell, and The Navigator: An Interview with Norman Mailer." WR, 23 (Winter 1959), 101-9.

Tanner, Tony. "On Norman Mailer." PR, 34 (1967), 465-71.

_____. "On the Parapet: A Study of the Novels of Norman Mailer." CritQ, 12 (1970), 153-76.

Toback, James. "Norman Mailer Today." Com, 64 (October 1967), 68-76.

Trilling, Diana. "Norman Mailer." ENCOUNTER, 19 (November 1962), 45-56.

Wagenheim, Allan J. "Square's Progress: AN AMERICAN DREAM." Crit, 10 (1968), 45-68.

Weatherby, W.J. "Talking of Violence: An Interview with Norman Mailer." TC, 173 (1964-65), 109-14.

Weber, Brom. "A Fear of Dying: Norman Mailer's AN AMERICAN DREAM." HC, 2, iii (1965), 1-6, 8-11.

Witt, Grace. "The Bad Man as Hipster: Norman Mailer's Use of Frontier Metaphor." WAL, 4 (1969), 203-17.

Wood, Margery. "Norman Mailer and Nathalie Sarraute: A Comparison of Existential Novels." MinnR, 6 (1966), 67-72.

Wustenhagen, Heinz. "Instinkt kontra Vernunft: Norman Mailers ideologische und ästhetische Konfusion." ZAA, 16 (1968), 362-89.

Yamamoto, Hiroshi. "The Realistic Consciousness of Norman Mailer." AMERICAN LITERARY REVIEW, 34 (April 1961), 10-11.

BERNARD MALAMUD (1914-), AMERICAN

NOVELS

THE NATURAL. New York: Harcourt, Brace, 1952.

THE ASSISTANT. New York: Farrar, Straus, 1957.

A NEW LIFE. New York: Farrar, Straus, 1961.

THE FIXER. New York: Farrar, Straus, 1966.

PICTURES OF FIDELMAN: AN EXHIBITION. New York: Farrar, Straus, 1969.

SHORT STORIES

THE MAGIC BARREL. New York: Farrar, Straus, 1958.

IDIOTS FIRST. New York: Farrar, Straus, 1963.

BIBLIOGRAPHY

Kosofsky, R.N. BERNARD MALAMUD. Kent, Ohio: Kent State University Press, 1969.

CRITICAL BOOKS

Field, Leslie, and Joyce Field, eds. BERNARD MALAMUD AND THE CRITICS. New York: New York University Press, 1970.

Meeter, Glenn. BERNARD MALAMUD AND PHILIP ROTH: A CRITICAL ES-
SAY. Grand Rapids, Mich.: Eerdmans, 1968.

Richman, Sidney. BERNARD MALAMUD. New York: Twayne, 1966.

CRITICAL ARTICLES

Alley, Alvin D., and Hugh Agee. "Existential Heroes: Frank Alpine and
Rabbit Angstrom." BSUF, 9 (Winter 1968), 3-5.

Alter, Robert. "Malamud as Jewish Writer." Com, 42 (September 1966),
71-76.

Bailey, Anthony. "Insidious Patience." Cweal, 66 (21 June 1957), 307-8.

Barsness, John A. "A NEW LIFE: The Frontier Myth in Perspective." WAL,
3 (1969), 297-302.

Baumbach, Jonathan. "The Economy of Love: The Novels of Bernard Malamud." KR, 25 (1963), 438-57.

_____. "Malamud's Heroes." Cweal 85 (28 October 1966), 97-99.

Bellman, Samuel I. "Women, Children and Idiots First: The Transformation
Psychology of Bernard Malamud." Crit, 7 (1965), 123-38.

Bluefarb, Sam. "Bernard Malamud: The Scope of Caricature." EJ, 53
(1964), 319-26, 335.

Dupee, F.W. "The Power of Positive Sex." PR, 31 (1964), 425-30.

Eigner, Edwin M. "Malamud's Use of the Quest Romance." GENRE, 1
(January 1968), 55-74.

Elman, Richard M. "Malamud on Campus." Cweal, 75 (27 October 1961),
114-15.

Featherstone, Joseph. "Bernard Malamud." ATLANTIC MONTHLY, 219
(March 1967), 95-98.

Francis, H.E. "Bernard Malamud's Everyman." MIDSTREAM, 7 (Winter 1961),
93-97.

Frankel, Haskel. "Interview with Bernard Malamud." SatR, 49 (10 September 1966), 39-40.

Freese, Peter. "Parzival als Baseballstar: Bernard Malamuds THE NATURAL." JA, 13 (1968), 143-57.

Friedberg, Maurice. "History and Imagination: Two Views of The Beiliss Case." MIDSTREAM, 12 (November 1966), 72-76.

Friedman, Alan W. "Bernard Malamud: The Hero as Schnook." SoR, 4 (1968), 927-44.

Goldman, Mark. "Bernard Malamud's Comic Vision and the Theme of Identity." Crit, 7 (1965), 92-109.

Goodman, Oscar B. "There are Jews Everywhere." JUDAISM, 19 (1970), 283-94.

Graber, Ralph S. "Baseball in American Fiction." EJ, 56 (1967), 1107-14.

Greenfield, Josh. "Innocence and Punishment." BOOK WEEK, 11 September 1966, pp. 1, 10.

Greiff, Louis K. "Quest and Defeat in THE NATURAL." THOTH, 8 (Winter 1967), 23-24.

Hays, Peter L. "The Complex Pattern of Redemption in THE ASSISTANT." CentR, 13 (Spring 1969), 200-214.

Hicks, Granville. "One Man to Stand for Six Million." SatR, 49 (10 September 1966), 37-39.

Hill, John S. "Malamud's 'The Lady of the Lake': A Lesson in Rejection." UR, 36 (1969), 149-50.

Hoad, Gerald. "Malamud's Trial: THE FIXER and the Critics." WHR, 24 (1970), 1-12.

Hollander, John. "To Find the Westward Path." PR, 29 (1962), 137-39.

Kattan, Naim. "Deux ecrivains americains." ECRITS DU CANADA FRANCAIS, 17 (1964), 87-135.

Kazin, Alfred. "Fantasist of the Ordinary." Com, 24 (July 1957), 89-92.

Kermode, Frank. "Bernard Malamud." NStat, 63 (30 March 1962), 452-53.

Leer, Norman. "Three American Novels and Contemporary Society: A Search for Commitment." WSCL, 3 (Fall 1962), 67-86.

Lefcowitz, Barbara F. "The Hybris of Neurosis: Malamud's PICTURES OF FIDELMAN." L&P, 20 (1970), 115-20.

Mandel, Ruth B. "Bernard Malamud's THE ASSISTANT and A NEW LIFE: Ironic Affirmation." Crit, 7 (1965), 110-21.

Marcus, Steven. "The Novel Again." PR, 29 (1962), 171-95.

May, Charles E. "The Bread of Tears: Malamud's 'The Loan.'" SSF, 7 (1970), 652-54.

Mellard, James M. "Malamud's Novels: Four Versions of Pastoral." Crit, 9 (1969), 5-19.

_____. "Malamud's THE ASSISTANT: The City Novel as Pastoral." SSF, 5 (1969), 1-11.

Miller, Letizia Ciotti. "L'arte di Bernard Malamud." SA, 7 (1961), 261-97.

Mudrick, Marvin. "Who Killed Herzog? Or, Three American Novelists." UDQ, 1 (1966), 61-97.

Perrine, Laurence. "Malamud's 'Take Pity.'" SSF, 2 (1964), 84-86.

Pinsker, Sanford. "The Achievement of Bernard Malamud." MQ, 10 (1969), 379-89.

_____. "A Note on Bernard Malamud's 'Take Pity.'" SSF, 6 (1969), 212-13.

Ratner, Marc L. "The Humanism of Malamud's THE FIXER." Crit, 9 (1967), 81-84.

_____. "Style and Humanity in Malamud's Fiction." MR, 5 (1964), 663-83.

Rovit, Earl. "Bernard Malamud and the Jewish Literary Tradition." Crit, 3 (1960), 3-10.

Schulz, Max F. "Malamud's A NEW LIFE: The New Wasteland of the

Fifties." WR, 6, i (1969), 37-44.

Shear, Walter. "Culture Conflict in THE ASSISTANT." MQ, 7 (1966), 367-80.

Siegel, Ben. "Victims in Motion: Bernard Malamud's Sad and Bitter Clowns." NWR, 5 (1962), 69-80.

Solotaroff, Theodore. "Bernard Malamud's Fiction: The Old Life and the New." Com, 33 (March 1962), 197-204.

Stamerra, Silvana. "Il protagonists nelle narrativa di Bernard Malamud." ZAGAGLIA, 10 (1968), 333-43.

Swados, Harvey. "The Emergence of an Artist." WR, 32 (Winter 1958), 149-51.

Tanner, Tony. "Bernard Malamud and the New Life." CritQ, 10 (1968), 151-68.

Turner, Frederick W. III. "Myth Inside and Out: Malamud's THE NATURAL." NOVEL, 1 (1968), 133-39.

Wasserman, Earl R. "THE NATURAL: Malamud's World Ceres." CRAS, 9 (1965), 438-60.

Weiss, Samuel A. "Passion and Purgation in Bernard Malamud." UWR, 2 (1966), 93-99.

OLIVIA MANNING (?-   ), ENGLISH

NOVELS

THE WIND CHANGES. London: Cape, 1937.

ARTIST AMONG THE MISSING. London: Heinemann, 1949.

SCHOOL FOR LOVE. London: Heinemann, 1951.

A DIFFERENT FACE. London: Heinemann, 1953.

THE DOVES OF VENUS. London: Heinemann, 1955.

THE BALKAN TRILOGY:
 THE GREAT FORTUNE. London: Heinemann, 1960.
 THE SPOILT CITY. London: Heinemann, 1962.
 FRIENDS AND HEROES. London: Heinemann, 1965.

THE PLAY ROOM. London: Heinemann, 1969. As THE CAMPERLEA GIRLS.
New York: Coward-McCann, 1969.

SHORT STORIES

GROWING UP. London: Heinemann, 1948.

A ROMANTIC HERO AND OTHER STORIES. London: Heinemann, 1967.

NICHOLAS MONSARRAT [JOHN TURNEY]
(1910-), ENGLISH

NOVELS

THINK OF TOMORROW. London: Hurst and Blackett, 1934.

AT FIRST SIGHT. London: Hurst and Blackett, 1935.

THE WHIPPING BOY. London: Jarrolds, 1937.

THIS IS THE SCHOOLROOM. London: Cassell, 1939.

H.M. CORVETTE. London: Cassell, 1943.

EAST COAST CORVETTE. London: Cassell, 1943.

CORVETTE COMMAND. London: Cassell, 1944.

LEAVE CANCELLED. New York: Knopf, 1945.

H.M. FRIGATE. London: Cassell, 1946.

DEPENDS WHAT YOU MEAN BY LOVE: HEAVY RESCUE, LEAVE CAN-CELLED, H.M.S. MARLBOROUGH WILL ENTER HARBOUR. London: Cassell, 1947.

MY BROTHER DENYS. London: Cassell, 1948.

THE CRUEL SEA. London: Cassell, 1951.

THE STORY OF ESTHER COSTELLO. London: Cassell, 1953.

CASTLE GARAC. New York: Knopf, 1955.

THE TRIBE THAT LOST ITS HEAD. London: Cassell, 1956.

THE NYLON PIRATES. London: Cassell, 1960.

THE WHITE RAJAH. London: Cassell, 1961.

THE TIME BEFORE THIS. London: Cassell, 1962.

SMITH AND JONES. London: Cassell, 1963.

A FAIR DAY'S WORK. London: Cassell, 1964.

THE PILLOW FIGHT. London: Cassell, 1965.

SOMETHING TO HIDE. London: Cassell, 1966.

RICHER THAN ALL HIS TRIBE. London: Cassell, 1968.

SHORT STORIES

THE SHIP THAT DIED OF SHAME AND OTHER STORIES. London: Cassell, 1959.

BRIAN MOORE (1921-), CANADIAN

NOVELS

JUDITH HEARNE. Toronto: Collins, 1955. As THE LONELY PASSION OF JUDITH HEARNE. Boston: Little, Brown, 1956.

THE FEAST OF LUPERCAL. Boston: Little, Brown, 1957.

THE LUCK OF GINGER COFFEY. Boston: Little, Brown, 1960.

AN ANSWER FROM LIMBO. Boston: Little, Brown, 1962.

THE EMPEROR OF ICE-CREAM. London: Deutsch, 1966.

I AM MARY DUNNE. Toronto: McClelland and Stewart, 1968.

FERGUS. Toronto: McClelland and Stewart, 1970.

CRITICAL BOOKS

Dahlie, Hallvard. BRIAN MOORE. Toronto: Copp, Clark, 1969.

CRITICAL ARTICLES

Brady, Charles A. "I AM MARY DUNNE, by Brian Moore." Eire, 3 (1968), 136-40.

Cronin, John. "Ulster's Alarming Novels." Erie, 4 (1969), 27-34.

Dahlie, Hallvard. "Brian Moore: An Interview." TamR, no. 46 (Winter 1968), 7-29.

_____. "Brian Moore's Broader Vision: THE EMPEROR OF ICE-CREAM." Crit, 9 (1967), 43-55.

Foster, John W. "Crisis and Ritual in Brian Moore's Belfast Novels." Eire, 3 (1968), 66-74.

French, Philip. "The Novels of Brian Moore." LonM, n.s. 5 (February 1966), 86-91.

Kersnowski, Frank L. "Exit the Anti-Hero." Crit, 10 (1968), 60-71.

Ludwig, Jack. "Brian Moore: Ireland's Loss, Canada's Novelist." Crit, 5 (1963), 5-13.

_____. "A Mirror of Moore." TamR, no. 17 (Winter 1961), 19-23.

Sale, Richard B. "An Interview in London with Brian Moore." SNNTS, 1 (1969), 67-80.

WRIGHT MORRIS (1910-), AMERICAN

NOVELS

MY UNCLE DUDLEY. New York: Harcourt, Brace, 1942.

THE MAN WHO WAS THERE. New York: Scribner, 1945.

THE HOME PLACE. New York: Scribner, 1948.

THE WORLD IN THE ATTIC. New York: Scribner, 1949.

MAN AND BOY. New York: Knopf, 1951.

THE WORKS OF LOVE. New York: Knopf, 1952.

THE DEEP SLEEP. New York: Scribner, 1953.

THE HUGE SEASON. New York: Viking Press, 1954.

THE FIELD OF VISION. New York: Harcourt, Brace, 1956.

LOVE AMONG THE CANNIBALS. New York: Harcourt, Brace, 1957.

CEREMONY IN LONE TREE. New York: Atheneum, 1960.

WHAT A WAY TO GO. New York: Atheneum, 1962.

CAUSE FOR WONDER. New York: Atheneum, 1963.

ONE DAY. New York: Atheneum, 1965.

IN ORBIT. New York: New American Library, 1967.

SHORT STORIES

GREEN GRASS, BLUE SKY, WHITE HOUSE. Los Angeles: Black Sparrow Press, 1970.

BIBLIOGRAPHY

Linden, Stanton J., and David Madden. "A Wright Morris Bibliography." Crit, 4 (1962), 77-87.

CRITICAL BOOKS

Madden, David. WRIGHT MORRIS. New York: Twayne, 1964.

SPECIAL ISSUES

CRITIQUE: STUDIES IN MODERN FICTION, 4 (Winter 1961-62), "Wright Morris Issue."

CRITICAL ARTICLES

Baumbach, Jonathan. "Wake Before Bomb: CEREMONY IN LONE TREE." Crit, 4 (1962), 56-71.

Bluefarb, Sam. "Point of View: An Interview with Wright Morris." AC-CENT, 19 (Winter 1959), 34-46.

Booth, Wayne C. "The Two Worlds in the Fiction of Wright Morris." SR, 65 (Summer 1957), 375-99.

Carpenter, Frederic I. "Wright Morris and the Territory Ahead." CE, 21 (1959), 147-56.

Garrett, George. "Morris the Magician: A Look at IN ORBIT." HC, 4, ii (June 1967), 1-12.

Guettinger, Roger J. "The Problem with Jigsaw Puzzles: Form in the Fiction of Wright Morris." TQ, 11 (1968), 209-20.

Hunt, John W., Jr. "The Journey Back: The Early Novels of Wright Morris." Crit 5, (1962) 41-60.

Leer, Norman. "Three American Novels and Contemporary Society." WSCL, 3 (Fall 1962), 67-86.

Madden, David. "The Great Plains in the Novels of Wright Morris." Crit, 4 (1962), 5-23.

_____. "The Hero and the Witness in Wright Morris's FIELD OF VISION." PrS, 34 (1960), 263-78.

_____. "Wright Morris' IN ORBIT: An Unbroken Series of Poetic Gestures." Crit, 10 (1968), 102-19.

Miller, James E., Jr. "The Nebraska Encounter: Willa Cather and Wright Morris." PrS, 41 (1967), 165-67.

Morris, Wright. "Letter to a Young Critic." MR, 6 (1964-65), 93-100.

_____. "'The Lunatic, the Lover, and the Poet.'" KR, 27 (1965), 727-37.

_____. "National Book Award Address." Crit, 4 (1962), 72-75.

_____. "The Origin of the Species, 1952-1957." MR, 7 (1966), 121-35.

Trachtenberg, Alan. "The Craft of Vision." Crit, 4 (1962), 41-55.

Tucker, Martin. "The Landscape of Wright Morris." LHR, no. 7 (1965), 43-51.

Waterman, Arthur E. "The Novels of Wright Morris: An Escape from Nostalgia." Crit, 4 (1962), 24-40.

_____. "Wright Morris's ONE DAY: The Novel of Revelation." FurmS, 15 (May 1968), 29-36.

PENELOPE MORTIMER (1918-), ENGLISH

NOVELS

JOHANNA (as Penelope Dimont). London: Secker and Warburg, 1947.

A VILLA IN SUMMER. London: Joseph, 1954.

THE BRIGHT PRISON. London: Joseph, 1956.

DADDY'S GONE A-HUNTING. London: Joseph, 1958. As CAVE OF ICE.
New York: Harcourt, Brace, 1959.

SATURDAY LUNCH WITH THE BROWNINGS. London: Hutchinson, 1960.

THE PUMPKIN EATER. London: Hutchinson, 1962.

MY FRIEND SAYS IT'S BULLET-PROOF. London: Hutchinson, 1967.

IRIS MURDOCH (1919-), ENGLISH

NOVELS

UNDER THE NET. London: Chatto and Windus, 1954.

THE FLIGHT FROM THE ENCHANTER. London: Chatto and Windus, 1956.

THE SANDCASTLE. London: Chatto and Windus, 1957.

THE BELL. London: Chatto and Windus, 1958.

A SEVERED HEAD. London: Chatto and Windus, 1961.

AN UNOFFICIAL ROSE. London: Chatto and Windus, 1962.

THE UNICORN. London: Chatto and Windus, 1963.

THE ITALIAN GIRL. London: Chatto and Windus, 1964.

THE RED AND THE GREEN. London: Chatto and Windus, 1965.

THE TIME OF THE ANGELS. London: Chatto and Windus, 1966.

THE NICE AND THE GOOD. London: Chatto and Windus, 1968.

BRUNO'S DREAM. London: Chatto and Windus, 1969.

A FAIRLY HONOURABLE DEFEAT. London: Chatto and Windus, 1970.

BIBLIOGRAPHY

Civin, Laraine. IRIS MURDOCH: A BIBLIOGRAPHY. Johannesburg: University of Witwatersrand, Department of Bibliography, Librarianship, and Typography, 1968.

Cully, Ann, and John Feaster. "Criticism of Iris Murdoch: A Selected Checklist." MFS, 15 (1969), 449–57.

Widmann, R.L. "An Iris Murdoch Checklist." Crit, 10 (1968), 17–29.

CRITICAL BOOKS

Byatt, A.S. DEGREES OF FREEDOM: THE NOVELS OF IRIS MURDOCH. London: Chatto and Windus, 1965.

Rabinovitz, Rubin. IRIS MURDOCH. New York: Columbia University Press, 1968.

Wolfe, Peter. THE DISCIPLINED HEART: IRIS MURDOCH AND HER NOVELS. Columbia: University of Missouri Press, 1966.

SPECIAL ISSUES

MODERN FICTION STUDIES, 15 (1969), "Iris Murdoch Special Number."

CRITICAL ARTICLES

Baldanza, Frank. "Iris Murdoch and the Theory of Personality." CRITICISM, 7 (Spring 1965), 176–89.

_____. "The Murdoch Manuscripts at the University of Iowa: An Addendum." MFS, 16 (1970), 201–2.

Batchelor, Billie. "Revision in Iris Murdoch's UNDER THE NET." BI, 8 (1968), 30–36.

Berthoff, Warner. "The Enemy of Freedom is Fantasy." MR, 8 (1967), 580–84.

_____. "Fortunes of the Novel: Muriel Spark and Iris Murdoch." MR, 8 (1967), 314–32.

Bradbury, Malcolm. "Iris Murdoch's UNDER THE NET." CritQ, 4 (1962), 47-54.

DeMott, Benjamin. "Dirty Words?" HudR, 18 (1965), 37-40.

Dick, Bernard F. "The Novels of Iris Murdoch: A Formula for Enchantment." BuR, 14 (May 1966), 66-81.

Emerson, Donald. "Violence and Survival in the Novels of Iris Murdoch." TWA, 57 (1969), 21-28.

Felheim, Marvin. "Symbolic Characterization in the Novels of Iris Murdoch." TSLL, 2 (1960), 189-97.

Fraser, G.S. "Iris Murdoch and the Solidity of the Normal." ILA, 2 (1959), 37-54.

Gindin, James. "Images of Illusion in the Works of Iris Murdoch." TSLL, 2 (1960), 180-88.

Gregor, Ian. "Towards a Christian Literary Criticism." MONTH, 33 (October 1965), 239-49.

Hall, James. "Blurring the Will: The Growth of Iris Murdoch." ELH, 32 (1965), 256-73.

Hall, William. "The Third Way: The Novels of Iris Murdoch." DR, 46 (Autumn 1966), 306-18.

Hebblethwaite, Peter. "Out Hunting Unicorns." MONTH, 30 (October 1963), 224-28.

Heyd, Ruth. "An Interview with Iris Murdoch." UWR, 1 (Spring 1965), 138-43.

Hoffman, Frederick J. "Iris Murdoch: The Reality of Persons." Crit, 7 (1964), 48-57.

_____. "The Miracle of Contingency: The Novels of Iris Murdoch." SHENANDOAH, 17 (Autumn 1965), 49-56.

Hope, Francis. "The Novels of Iris Murdoch." LonM, n.s. 1 (August 1961), 84-87.

Jones, Dorothy. "Love and Morality in Iris Murdoch's THE BELL." Meanjin, 26 (1967), 85–90.

Kaehele, Sharon, and Howard German. "The Discovery of Reality in Iris Murdoch's THE BELL." PMLA, 82 (1967), 554–63.

Kaufmann, R.J. "The Progress of Iris Murdoch." NATION, 188 (21 March 1959), 255–56.

Kogan, Pauline. "Beyond Solipsism to Irrationalism: A Study of Iris Murdoch's Novels." L&I, 2 (1969), 47–69.

McCabe, Bernard. "The Guises of Love." Cweal, 83 (3 December 1965), 270–73.

McDowell, Frederick P.W. "'The Devious Involutions of Human Character and Emotions': Reflections on Some Recent British Novels." WSCL, 4 (Autumn 1963), 355–59.

McGinnis, Robert M. "Murdoch's THE BELL." Expl, 28 (1969), Item 1.

Maes-Jelinek, Hena. "A House for Free Characters: The Novels of Iris Murdoch." RLV, 29 (1963), 45–69.

Martin, Graham. "Iris Murdoch and the Symbolist Novel." BJA, 5 (1965), 296–300.

Meidner, Olga M. "The Progress of Iris Murdoch." ESA, 4 (1961), 17–38.

_____. "Reviewer's Bane: A Study of Iris Murdoch's THE FLIGHT FROM THE ENCHANTER." EIC, 11 (1961), 435–47.

Micha, Rene. "Les romans a machines d'Iris Murdoch." CRITIQUE, 16 (1960), 291–301.

Miner, Earl. "Iris Murdoch: The Uses of Love." NATION, 194 (2 June 1962), 498–99.

Morrell, Roy. "Iris Murdoch: The Early Novels." CritQ, 9 (1967), 272–82.

O'Connor, William Van. "Iris Murdoch: A SEVERED HEAD." Crit, 5 (1962), 74–77.

_____. "Iris Murdoch: The Formal and the Contingent." Crit, 3 (1960),

34-46.

O'Sullivan, Kevin. "Iris Murdoch and the Image of Liberal Man." YLM, 131 (1962), 27-32.

Palmer, Tony. "Artistic Privilege." LonM, 8 (May 1968), 47-52.

Pearson, Gabriel. "Iris Murdoch and the Romantic Novel." NEW LEFT RE-VIEW, nos. 13-14 (January-April 1962), 137-45.

Pondrom, Cyrena N. "Iris Murdoch: An Existentialist." CLS, 5 (1968), 403-19.

_____. "Iris Murdoch: THE UNICORN." Crit, 6 (1963-64), 177-80.

Ricks, Christopher. "A Sort of Mystery Novel." NStat, (22 October 1965), 604-5.

Rose, W.K. "An Interview with Iris Murdoch." SHENANDOAH, 19 (Winter 1968), 3-22.

Shestakov, Dmitri. "An Iris Murdoch Novel in Russian." SovL, 7 (1966), 169-75.

Souvage, Jacques. "The Novels of Iris Murdoch." SGG, 4 (1962), 225-52.

_____. "Symbol as Narrative Device: An Interpretation of Iris Murdoch's THE BELL." ES, 43 (1962), 81-96.

_____. "Theme and Structure in Iris Murdoch's THE FLIGHT FROM THE ENCHANTER." SPIEGHEL HISTORIAEL VAN DE BOND VAN GLNISTE GERMANISTEN, 3 (1960-61), 73-88.

_____. "The Unresolved Tension: An Interpretation of Iris Murdoch's UNDER THE NET." RLV, 26 (1960), 420-30.

Thomson, P.W. "Iris Murdoch's Honest Puppetry--The Characters of BRUNO'S DREAM." CritQ, 11 (1969), 277-83.

Tucker, Martin. "The Odd Fish in Iris Murdoch's Kettle." NRep, 154 (5 February 1966), 26-28.

Wall, Stephen. "The Bell in THE BELL." EIC, 13 (1963), 265-73.

Weatherhead, A.K. "Backgrounds with Figures in Iris Murdoch." TSLL, 10 (1969), 635-48.

Whiteside, George. "The Novels of Iris Murdoch." Crit, 7 (1964), 27-47.

Widmann, R.L. "Murdoch's UNDER THE NET: Theory and Practice of Fiction." Crit, 10 (1968), 5-16.

VLADIMIR NABOKOV (1899-), AMERICAN

NOVELS

MASHEN'KA. Berlin: Slovo, 1926. Translated by the author and Michael Glenny as MARY. New York: McGraw-Hill, 1970.

KOROL', DAMA, VALET. Berlin: Slovo, 1928. Translated by the author and Dmitri Nabokov as KING, QUEEN, KNAVE. New York: McGraw-Hill, 1968.

ZASHCHITA LUZHINA. Berlin: Slovo, 1930. Translated by the author and M. Scammell as THE DEFENSE. New York: Putnam, 1964.

KAMERA OBSKURA. Paris: Sovremenniya Zapiski, 1932. Translated by the author as LAUGHTER IN THE DARK. Indianapolis: Bobbs-Merrill, 1938.

OTCHAYANIE. Berlin: Petropolis, 1936. Translated by the author as DE-SPAIR, 1937, Rev. ed. New York: Putnam, 1966.

DAR. Paris, 1937. Translated by D. Nabokov, M. Scammell, and the author as THE GIFT. New York: Putnam, 1963.

PRIGLOSHENIE NA KAZN'. Paris: Dom Knigi, 1938. Translated by D. Nabokov and the author as INVITATION TO A BEHEADING. New York: Putnam, 1959.

THE REAL LIFE OF SEBASTIAN KNIGHT. New York: New Directions, 1941.

BEND SINISTER. New York: Holt, 1947.

LOLITA. 2 vols. Paris: Olympia Press, 1955. New York: Putnam, 1958.

PNIN. Garden City, N.Y.: Doubleday, 1957.

PALE FIRE. New York: Putnam, 1962.

ADA; OR, ARDOR: A FAMILY CHRONICLE. New York: McGraw-Hill, 1969.

SHORT STORIES

SOGLYADATAY. Paris: Russkiya Zapiski, 1938. Translated by D. Nabokov and the author as THE EYE. New York: Phaedra, 1965.

NINE STORIES. (DIRECTION TWO issue). New York: New Directions, 1947.

NABOKOV'S DOZEN: A COLLECTION OF 13 STORIES (includes SPRING IN FIALTA, published in Russian, 1956). New York: Doubleday, 1958.

NABOKOV'S QUARTET (three of the four translated by D. Nabokov). New York: Phaedra, 1966.

BIBLIOGRAPHY

Bryer, Jackson R., and Thomas J. Bergin, Jr. "Vladimir Nabokov's Critical Reputation in English: A Note and a Checklist." WSCL, 8 (Spring 1967), 312-64.

CRITICAL BOOKS

Dembo, L.S. NABOKOV: THE MAN AND HIS WORK. Madison: University of Wisconsin Press, 1967.

Field, Andrew. NABOKOV: HIS LIFE IN ART. Boston: Little, Brown, 1967.

Proffer, Carl R. KEYS TO LOLITA. Bloomington: Indiana University Press, 1968.

Stegner, S. Page. ESCAPE INTO AESTHETICS: THE ART OF VLADIMIR NABOKOV. New York: Dial Press, 1967.

SPECIAL ISSUES

TRI-QUARTERLY, 17 (Winter 1970), "Nabokov Issue."

WISCONSIN STUDIES IN CONTEMPORARY LITERATURE, 8 (Spring 1967), "Special Nabokov Issue."

CRITICAL ARTICLES

Aldridge, A. Owen. "LOLITA and LES LIAISONS DANGEREUSES." WSCL, 2 (Fall 1961), 20-26.

Anderson, Quentin. "Nabokov in Time." NRep, 154 (4 June 1966), 23-28.

Appel, Alfred, Jr. "Nabokov's Puppet Show." NRep, 156 (14 January 1967), 27-30.

Baker, George. "LOLITA: Literature or Pornography?" SatR, 40 (22 June 1957), 18.

Brenner, Conrad. "Nabokov: The Art of the Perverse." NRep, 138 (23 June 1958), 18-21.

Brick, Allan. "The Madman in His Cell: Joyce, Beckett, Nabokov and the Stereotypes." MR, 1 (1959), 40-55.

Campbell, Felicia F. "A Princedom by the Sea." LHR, 10 (1968), 39-46.

Clark, A.F.B. "Nabokov's Pushkin." UTQ, 36 (1967), 302-7.

Delpech, Jeanine. "Nabokov sans Lolita." NL, (29 October 1959), 1, 2.

Dillard, R.H. "Not Text, But Texture: The Novels of Vladimir Nabokov." HC, 3, iii (1966), 1-12.

Dommergues, Pierre. "Nabokov n'appartient a personne." MAG LITTERAIRE, no. 12 (November 1967), 38-40.

DuBois, Arthur E. "Poe and LOLITA." CEA, 26, vi (1964), 1, 7.

Dupee, F.W. "LOLITA in America." ENCOUNTER, 12 (February 1959), 30-35.

Field, Andrew. "PALE FIRE: The Labyrinth of a Great Novel." TriQ, 8 (Winter 1967), 13-36.

Fromberg, Susan. "The Unwritten Chapters in The Real Life of SEBASTIAN

KNIGHT." MFS, 13 (1967), 427–42.

Gardner, Thomas. "Vladimir Nabokov." SG, 21 (1968), 94–100.

Gerschenkron, Alexander. "A Manufactured Moment?" MP, 63 (1965), 336–47.

Gold, Herbert. "Vladimir Nabokov––an Interview." PR, 41 (1967), 92–111.

Gold, Joseph. "The Morality of LOLITA." BAASB, n.s. 1 (1960), 50–54.

Green, Martin. "The Morality of Lolita." KR, 28 (1966), 352–77.

Grosshans, Henry. "The Great Vladimir." RS, 35 (1967), 264–68.

_____. "Vladimir Nabokov and the Dream of Old Russia." TSLL, 7 (1966), 401–9.

Handley, Jack. "To Die in English." NWR, 6 (1963), 23–40.

Harris, Harold J. "LOLITA and the Sly Foreword." MRR, 1 (1965), 29–38.

Hayman, John G. "After 'Lolita'––A Conversation with Vladimir Nabokov––with Digressions." TC, 166 (1959), 444–50.

Heidenry, John. "Vladimir in Dreamland." Cweal, 90 (1969), 231–34.

Hiatt, L.R. "Nabokov's LOLITA: A 'Freudian' Cryptic Crossword." AI, 24 (1967), 360–70.

Hinchliffe, Arnold P. "Belinda in America." SA, 6 (1960), 339–47.

Hughes, Daniel J. "Nabokov: Spiral and Glass." NOVEL, 1 (1968), 178–85.

_____. "Reality and the Hero: LOLITA and HENDERSON THE RAIN KING." MFS, 6 (1960), 345–64.

Ivask, George. "Nabokov, poeta dello spazio." INVENTARIO, 17 (1962), 105–11.

_____. "The World of Vladimir Nabokov." RusR, 20 (April 1961), 134–42.

Janeway, Elizabeth. "Nabokov the Magician." ATLANTIC MONTHLY, 220 (July 1967), 66-71.

Johnson, W.R. "THE REAL LIFE OF SEBASTIAN KNIGHT." CM, 4 (Fall 1963), 111-14.

Jones, David L. "DOLORES DISPARUE." Sym, 20 (1966), 135-40.

Josipovici, G.D. "LOLITA: Parody and the Pursuit of Beauty." CritQ, 6 (1964), 35-48.

Kermode, Frank. "Aesthetic Bliss." ENCOUNTER, 14 (June 1960), 81-86.

Krueger, John R. "Nabokov's Zemblan: A Constructed Language of Fiction." LINGUISTICS, 31 (1967), 44-49.

Lawrenson, Helen. "The Man Who Scandalized the World." ESQUIRE, 54 (February 1962), 70-74.

Lee, L.L. "Duplexity in V. Nabokov's Short Stories." SSF, 2 (1965), 307-15.

_____. "Vladimir Nabokov's Great Spiral of Being." WHR, 18 (1964), 225-36.

Levine, J.A. "The Design of A TALE OF A TUB (with a Digression on a Mad Modern Critic)." ELH, 33 (1966), 198-227.

McCarthy, Mary. "A Bolt from the Blue." NRep, 166 (4 June 1962), 21-27.

MacDonald, Dwight. "Virtuosity Rewarded or Dr. Kinbote's Revenge." PR, 29 (1962), 437-42.

Malcolm, Donald. "A Retrospect." NY, 40 (25 April 1964), 198-205.

Mason, Bruce. "A Fissure in Time: The Art of Vladimir Nabokov." NZSJ (1969), 1-16.

Mitchell, Charles. "Mythic Seriousness in LOLITA." TSLL, 5 (1963), 329-43.

Mizener, Arthur. "The Seriousness of Vladimir Nabokov." SR, 76 (1968), 655-64.

Moynahan, Julian. "A Russian Preface for Nabokov's BEHEADING." NOVEL, 1 (1967), 12-18.

Nabokov, Vladimir. "LOLITA and Mr. Girodias." EVERGREEN REVIEW, no. 45 (1967), 37-41.

_____. "On a Book Entitled LOLITA." AnRev, no. 2 (1957), 105-12.

_____. "PLAYBOY Interview: Vladimir Nabokov." PLAYBOY, 11 (January 1964), 35-41, 44-45.

Nabokov, Vladimir, and Peter Duval Smith. "Vladimir Nabokov on His Life and Work." LISTENER, 68 (22 November 1962), 856-58.

Nilsson, Nils Ake. "Fangar i spegelvarlden: Kring Vladimir Nabokovs for- fattarskap." OB, 77 (1968), 28-32.

_____. "A Hall of Mirrors: Nabokov and Olesha." SSI, 15 (1969), 5-12.

Pack, Claus. "Humbert Humbert und seine Lolita." WuWahr, 15 (1960), 55-57.

Phillips, Elizabeth. "The Hocus-Pocus of LOLITA." L&P, 10 (Summer 1960), 97-101.

Pifer, Ellen I. "Nabokov's INVITATION TO A BEHEADING: The Parody of a Tradition." PCP, 5 (1970), 46-53.

Purdy, Struther B. "Solus Rex: Nabokov and the Chess Novel." MFS, 14 (1968-69), 379-95.

Reimer, Andrew. "Dim Glow, Faint Blaze--The Meaning of PALE FIRE." BALCONY, 6 (1967), 41-48.

Rovet, Jeanine. "Vladimir Nabokov: Le demon de l'analogie." TM, 21 (1966), 2279-82.

Rubin, Louis D. "The Self Recaptured." KR, 25 (1963), 393-415.

Rubinstein, E. "Approaching LOLITA." MinnR, 6 (1966), 361-67.

Scott, W.J. "The LOLITA Case." LANDFALL, 15 (June 1961), 134-38.

Seldon, E.S. "LOLITA and JUSTINE." EVERGREEN REVIEW, 2, vi (1958), 156-59.

Slonim, Marc. "DOCTOR ZHIVAGO and LOLITA." ILA, no. 2 (1959), 213-25.

Stegner, S. Page. "The Immortality of Art: Vladimir Nabokov's THE REAL LIFE OF SEBASTIAN KNIGHT." SoR, 2 (1966), 286-96.

Stern, Richard G. "PNIN and the Dust-Jacket." PrS, 31 (1957), 161-64.

Strainchamps, Ethel. "Nabokov's Handling of English Syntax." AS, 36 (1962), 234-35.

Stuart, Dabney. "THE REAL LIFE OF SEBASTIAN KNIGHT: Angles of Perception." MLQ, 29 (1968), 312-28.

Teirlinch, Herman. "Notes on Nabokov's LOLITA." LitR, 7 (Spring 1964), 439-42.

Thiebaut, Marcel. "Nabokov et LOLITA." RdP, (August 1959), 143-52.

Trilling, Lionel. "The Last Lover: Vladimir Nabokov's LOLITA." ENCOUNTER, 11 (October 1958), 9-19.

Updike, John. "Grandmaster Nabokov." NRep, 151 (26 September 1964), 15-18.

Uphaus, Robert W. "Nabokov's KUNSTLERROMAN: Portrait of the Artist as a Dying Man." TCL, 13 (1967), 104-10.

Vortriede, Werner. "Die Masken des Vladimir Nabokov." MERKUR, 20 (1966), 138-51.

Williams, Carol T. "'Web of Sense': PALE FIRE in the Nabokov Canon." Crit, 6 (1963), 29-45.

Zall, Paul M. "Lolita and Gulliver." SNL, 3 (1965), 33-37.

Zapadov, V. "Derzavin i Pnin." RUSSKAJA LITERATURA, 8 (1965), 114-19.

V[IDIADHAR]. S[URAJPRASAD]. NAIPAUL
(1932-   ), ENGLISH

NOVELS

THE MYSTIC MASSEUR. London: Deutsch, 1957.

THE SUFFRAGE OF ELVIRA. London: Deutsch, 1958.

MIGUEL STREET. London: Deutsch, 1959.

A HOUSE FOR MR. BISWAS. London: Deutsch, 1961.

MR. STONE AND THE KNIGHTS COMPANION. London: Doutsch, 1963.

THE MIMIC MEN. London: Doutsch, 1967.

SHORT STORIES

A FLAG ON THE ISLAND. London: Deutsch, 1967.

HOWARD NEMEROV (1920-), AMERICAN

NOVELS

THE MELODRAMATISTS. New York: Random House, 1949.

FEDERIGO: OR, THE POWER OF LOVE. Boston: Little, Brown, 1954.

THE HOMECOMING GAME. New York: Simon and Schuster, 1957.

SHORT STORIES

A COMMODITY OF DREAMS AND OTHER STORIES. New York: Simon and
Schuster, 1959.

CRITICAL BOOKS

Meinke, Peter. HOWARD NEMEROV. Minneapolis: University of Minnesota
Press, 1968.

CRITICAL ARTICLES

Gerstenberger, Donna. "An Interview with Howard Nemerov." TRACE, no.
35 (1960), 22-25.

White, Robert L. "The Trying-Out of THE HOMECOMING GAME." ColQ,
10 (Summer 1961), 84-96.

P[ERCY]. H[OWARD]. NEWBY (1918-   ), ENGLISH

NOVELS

A JOURNEY TO THE INTERIOR.   London: Cape, 1945.

AGENTS AND WITNESSES.   London: Cape, 1947.

MARINER DANCES.   London: Cape, 1948.

THE SNOW PASTURE.   London: Cape, 1949.

THE YOUNG MAY MOON.   London: Cape, 1950.

A SEASON IN ENGLAND.   London: Cape, 1951.

A STEP TO SILENCE.   London: Cape, 1952.

THE RETREAT.   London: Cape, 1953.

THE PICNIC AT SAKKARA.   London: Cape, 1955.

REVOLUTION AND ROSES.   London: Cape, 1957.

A GUEST AND HIS GOING.   London: Cape, 1959.

THE BARBARY LIGHT.   London: Faber, 1962.

ONE OF THE FOUNDERS.   London: Faber, 1965.

SOMETHING TO ANSWER FOR.   London: Faber, 1968.

P[ercy]. H[oward]. Newby

SHORT STORIES

TEN MILES FROM ANYWHERE AND OTHER STORIES. London: Cape, 1958.

CRITICAL BOOKS

Mathews, Francis X. THE FICTION OF P.H. NEWBY. Madison: University of Wisconsin Press, 1964.

CRITICAL ARTICLES

Balakian, Nona. "Three English Novels." KR, 15 (1953), 490-94.

Bufkin, E.C. "Quest in the Novels of P.H. Newby." Crit, 8 (1965), 51-62.

Dickerson, Lucia. "Portrait of the Artist as a Jung Man." KR, 21 (1959), 58-83.

Halpern, Ben. "The Wisdom of Blindness." MIDSTREAM, 3 (Winter 1957), 104-7.

Mathews, Francis X. "Newby on the Nile." TCL, 14 (1968), 10-12.

"Novelist on his Own." TLS, 6 April 1962, p. 232.

Watts, Harold H. "P.H. Newby: Experience as Farce." Per, 10 (Summer-Autumn 1958), 106-17.

JOYCE CAROL OATES (1938-), AMERICAN

NOVELS

WITH SHUDDERING FALL. New York: Vanguard Press, 1964.

A GARDEN OF EARTHLY DELIGHTS. New York: Vanguard Press, 1967.

EXPENSIVE PEOPLE. New York: Vanguard Press, 1968.

THEM. New York: Vanguard Press, 1969.

SHORT STORIES

BY THE NORTH GATE. New York: Vanguard Press, 1963.

UPON THE SWEEPING FLOOD AND OTHER STORIES. New York: Vanguard Press, 1966.

THE WHEEL OF LOVE. New York: Vanguard Press, 1970.

FLANNERY O'CONNOR (1925-64), AMERICAN

NOVELS

WISE BLOOD. New York: Harcourt, Brace, 1952.

THE VIOLENT BEAR IT AWAY. New York: Farrar, Straus, 1960.

SHORT STORIES

A GOOD MAN IS HARD TO FIND AND OTHER STORIES. New York: Harcourt, Brace, 1955.

EVERYTHING THAT RISES MUST CONVERGE. New York: Farrar, Straus, 1965.

BIBLIOGRAPHY

Brittain, Joan T. "Flannery O'Connor: A Bibliography." BB, 25 (1967), 98-100, 123-24.

_____. "Flannery O'Connor--Addenda." BB, 25 (1967), 142.

Wedge, George F. "Two Bibliographies: Flannery O'Connor, J.F. Powers." Crit, 2 (1958), 59-70.

CRITICAL BOOKS

Drake, Robert. FLANNERY O'CONNOR. Grand Rapids, Mich.: Eerdmans, 1966.

Friedman, Melvin J., and Lewis A. Lawson, eds. THE ADDED DIMENSION:

THE ART AND MIND OF FLANNERY O'CONNOR. New York: Fordham University Press, 1966.

Hendin, Josephine. THE WORLD OF FLANNERY O'CONNOR. Bloomington: Indiana University Press, 1970.

Hyman, Stanley Edgar. FLANNERY O'CONNOR. Minneapolis: University of Minnesota Press, 1966.

Martin, Carter W. THE TRUE COUNTRY: THEMES IN THE FICTION OF FLANNERY O'CONNOR. Nashville, Tenn.: Vanderbilt University Press, 1968.

Reiter, Robert E., ed. FLANNERY O'CONNOR. St. Louis, Mo.: Herder, 1968.

SPECIAL ISSUES

SEWANEE REVIEW, 76 (1968), "Diverse Readings of Flannery O'Connor."

CRITICAL ARTICLES

Abbott, Louise H. "Remembering Flannery O'Connor." SLJ, 2, ii (1970), 3-25.

Alice, Sister Rose, S.S.J. "Flannery O'Connor: Poet to the Outcast." Ren, 16 (1964), 126-32.

Asals, Frederick. "Flannery O'Connor's 'The Lame Shall Enter First.'" MissQ, 23 (1970), 103-20.

_____. "The Mythic Dimensions of Flannery O'Connor's 'Greenleaf.'" SSF, 5 (1968), 137-40.

_____. "The Road to WISE BLOOD." Ren, 21 (1969), 181-94.

Ballif, Algene. "A Southern Allegory--THE VIOLENT BEAR IT AWAY." Com, 30 (October 1960), 358-62.

Bassan, Maurice. "Flannery O'Connor's Way: Shock, with Moral Intent." Ren, 15 (1963), 195-99, 211.

Baumbach, Jonathan. "The Creed of God's Grace: The Fiction of Flannery O'Connor." GaR, 17 (1963), 334-46.

Bertrande, Sister. "Four Stories of Flannery O'Connor." THOUGHT, 37 (August 1962), 410-26.

Bleikasten, Andre. "Aveugles et voyants: Le theme du regard dans WISE BLOOD." BFLS, 47 (1969), 291-302.

_____. "Theologie et derision chez Flannery O'Connor." LanM, 64 (1970), 124-38.

Bowen, Robert O. "Hope vs. Despair in the New Gothic Novel." Ren, 13 (1961), 147-52.

Brittain, Joan T. "O'Connor's A GOOD MAN IS HARD TO FIND." Expl, 26 (1967), Item 1.

Brittain, Joan T., and Leon Driskell. "O'Connor and the Eternal Crossroads." Ren, 22 (1969), 49-55.

Browning, Preston, Jr. "'Parker's Back: Flannery O'Connor's Iconography of Salvation by Profanity.'" SSF, 6 (1969), 525-35.

Burke, John J., Jr., S.J. "Convergence of Flannery O'Connor and Chardin." Ren, 14 (1966), 41-47, 52.

Burns, Stuart L. "The Evolution of WISE BLOOD." MFS, 16 (1970), 147-62.

_____. "Flannery O'Connor's Literary Apprenticeship." Ren, 22 (1969), 3-16.

_____. "Structural Patterns in WISE BLOOD." XUS, 8 (1969), 32-43.

_____. "'Torn By the Lord's Eye': Flannery O'Connor's Use of Sun Imagery." TCL, 13 (1967), 154-66.

Carlson, Thomas M. "Flannery O'Connor: The Manichaean Dilemma." SR, 77 (1969), 254-76.

Cheney, Brainard. "Flannery O'Connor's Campaign for Her Country." SR, 72 (Autumn 1964), 555-58.

_____. "Miss O'Connor Creates Unusual Humor Out of Ordinary Sin." SR, 71 (Autumn 1963), 644-52.

Coleman, Richard. "Flannery O'Connor: A Scrutiny of Two Forms of Her

Many-Leveled Art." PHOENIX, 1 (1966), 30-66.

Davis, Jack, and June Davis. "Tarwater and Jonah: Two Reluctant Prophets." XUS, 9 (1970), 19-27.

Detweiler, Robert. "The Curse of Christ in Flannery O'Connor's Fiction." CLS, 2 (1966), 235-45.

Dowell, Bob. "The Moment of Grace in the Fiction of Flannery O'Connor." CE, 27 (1965), 235-39.

Drake, Robert. "'The Bleeding Stinking Mad Shadow of Jesus' in the Fiction of Flannery O'Connor." CLS, 3 (1966), 183-96.

_____. "The Paradigm of Flannery O'Connor's True Country." SSF, 6 (1969), 433-42.

Driskell, Leon. "'Parker's Back' vs. 'The Partridge Festival': Flannery O'Connor's Critical Choice." GaR, 21 (1967), 476-90.

Duhamel, P. Albert. "Flannery O'Connor's Violent View of Reality." CathW, 190 (February 1960), 280-85.

Eggenschwiler, David. "Flannery O'Connor's True and False Prophets." Ren, 21 (1969), 151-61, 167.

Esch, Robert M. "O'Connor's 'Everything That Rises Must Converge,'" Expl, 27 (1969), Item 58.

Fahey, William A. "Flannery O'Connor's 'Parker's Back.'" Ren, 20 (1968), 162-64, 166.

_____. "Out of the Eater: Flannery O'Connor's Appetite for Truth." Ren, 20 (1968), 22-29.

Farnham, J.F. "The Grotesque in Flannery O'Connor." AMERICA, 105 (13 May 1961), 277, 280-81.

Feeley, Sister M. Kathleen, S.S.N.D. "Thematic Imagery in the Fiction of Flannery O'Connor." SHR, 3 (1968), 14-32.

_____. "O'Connor and Teilhard de Chardin: The Problem of Evil." Ren, 22 (1969), 34-42.

Ferris, Summer J. "The Outside and the Inside: Flannery O'Connor's THE VIOLENT BEAR IT AWAY." Crit, 4 (1961), 11-19.

Fitzgerald, Robert. "The Countryside and the True Country." SR, 70 (Summer 1962), 380-94.

Friedman, Melvin J. "By and About Flannery O'Connor." JML, 1 (1970), 288-92.

_____. "Flannery O'Connor: Another Legend in Southern Fiction." EJ, 51 (1962), 233-43.

Gordon, Caroline. "Flannery O'Connor's WISE BLOOD." Crit, 2 (1958), 3-10.

Gresset, Michel. "Le petit mode de Flannery O'Connor." MdF, no. 1203 (January 1964), 141-43.

Griffith, Albert J. "Flannery O'Connor's Salvation Road." SSF, 3 (1966), 329-33.

Hamblen, Abigail A. "Flannery O'Connor's Study of Innocence and Evil." UR, 34 (1968), 295-97.

Hart, Jane. "Strange Earth: The Stories of Flannery O'Connor." GaR, 12 (1958), 215-22.

Hawkes, John. "Flannery O'Connor's Devil." SR, 70 (Summer 1962), 395-407.

Hays, Peter L. "Dante, Tobit, and 'The Artificial Nigger.'" SSF, 5 (1968), 263-68.

Hendin, Josephine. "In Search of Flannery O'Connor." ColF, 13, i (1970), 38-41.

Hicks, Granville. "A Writer at Home with Her Heritage." SatR, 45 (12 May 1962), 22-23.

Jacobsen, Josephine. "A Catholic Quartet." ChS, 47 (1964), 139-54.

Jeremy, Sister, C.S.J. "THE VIOLENT BEAR IT AWAY: A Linguistic Education." Ren, 17 (1964), 11-16.

Jones, Bartlett C. "Depth Psychology and Literary Study." MASJ, 5 (1964), 50-56.

Joselyn, Sister M. "Thematic Centers in 'The Displaced Person.'" SSF, 1 (1964), 85-92.

Kann, Jean Marie, O.S.F. "Everything That Rises Must Converge." CathW, 204 (December 1966), 154-59.

Kitagaki, Muneharu. "The Valley of the Shadow of Death: An Interpretation of Flannery O'Connor's 'A Good Man is Hard to Find.'" STUDIES IN HUMANITIES, 85 (February 1966), 51-66.

Lawson, Lewis A. "Flannery O'Connor and the Grotesque: WISE BLOOD." Ren, 18 (1965), 137-47, 156.

Le Clezio, J.M.G. "L'univers de Flannery O'Connor." NRF, 13 (1965), 488-93.

Lensing, George. "De Chardin's Ideas in Flannery O'Connor." Ren, 18 (1966), 171-75.

Lipper, Mark. "Blessed Are the Destitute in Flannery O'Connor." SHIPPENSBURG STATE COLLEGE REVIEW, October 1968, pp. 20-23.

Littlefield, Daniel F., Jr. "Flannery O'Connor's WISE BLOOD: 'Unparalleled Prosperity' and Spiritual Chaos." MissQ, 23 (1970), 121-33.

Lorch, Thomas M. "Flannery O'Connor: Christian Allegorist." Crit, 10 (1968), 69-80.

McCarthy, John F. "Human Intelligence versus Divine Truth: The Intellectual in Flannery O'Connor's Works." EJ, 55 (1966), 1143-48.

McCown, Robert. "The Education of a Prophet: A Study of Flannery O'Connor's THE VIOLENT BEAR IT AWAY." KM, (1962), 73-78.

_____. "Flannery O'Connor and the Reality of Sin." CathW, 188 (January 1959), 285-91.

Maida, Patricia D. "'Convergence' in Flannery O'Connor's 'Everything That Rises Must Converge.'" SSF, 7 (1970), 549-55.

Male, Roy R. "The Two Versions of 'The Displaced Person.'" SSF, 7 (1970), 450-57.

Marks, W.S. III. "Advertisements for Grace: Flannery O'Connor's 'A Good Man Is Hard to Find.'" SSF, 4 (1966), 19-27.

Martin, Sister M. "O'Connor's 'A Good Man Is Hard To Find.'" Expl, 24 (1965), Item 19.

May, John R., S.J. "The Pruning Word: Flannery O'Connor's Judgment of Intellectuals." SHR, 4 (1970), 325-38.

Meador, Margaret. "Flannery O'Connor: Literary Witch." ColQ, 10 (Spring 1962), 377-86.

Mohrt, Michel. "L'evangile selon O'Connor." FL, no. 1030 (1966), 6.

Montgomery, Marion. "Flannery O'Connor's 'Leaden Tract Against Complacency and Contraception.'" ArQ, 24 (1968), 133-46.

_____. "Flannery O'Connor's Territorial Center." Crit, 11 (1969), 5-10.

_____. "Miss O'Connor and the Christ-Haunted." SoR, 4 (1968), 665-72.

_____. "A Note on Flannery O'Connor's Terrible and Violent Prophecy of Mercy." ForumH, 7, iii (1969), 4-7.

Muller, Gilbert H. "The City of Woe: Flannery O'Connor's Dantean Vision." GaR, 23 (1969), 206-13.

_____. "THE VIOLENT BEAR IT AWAY: Moral and Dramatic Sense." Ken, 22 (1969), 17-25.

Nance, William L. "Flannery O'Connor: The Trouble with Being a Prophet." UR, 36 (1969), 101-8.

Nolde, Sister M. Simon. "THE VIOLENT BEAR IT AWAY: A Study in Imagery." XUS, 1 (1962), 180-94.

Orvell, Miles D. "Flannery O'Connor." SR, 78 (Spring 1969), 184-92.

Quinn, Sister M. Bernetta. "View from a Rock: The Fiction of Flannery O'Connor and J.F. Powers." Crit, 2 (1958), 19-27.

Rechnitz, Robert M. "Passionate Pilgrim: Flannery O'Connor's WISE BLOOD." GaR, 19 (1965), 310-16.

Rubin, Louis D. "Flannery O'Connor: A Note on Literary Fashions." Crit, 2 (1958), 11–18.

_____. "Two Ladies of the South." SR, 63 (August 1962), 671–81.

Rupp, Richard H. "Flannery O'Connor." Cweal, 79 (6 December 1963), 304–7.

Shear, Walter. "Flannery O'Connor: Character and Characterization." Ren, 20 (1968), 140–46.

Sherry, G.E. "An Interview with Flannery O'Connor." CRITIC, 21 (1963), 29–31.

Shinn, Thelma J. "Flannery O'Connor and the Violence of Grace." WSCL, 9 (Winter 1968), 58–73.

Smith, Francis J., S.J. "O'Connor's Religious Viewpoint in THE VIOLENT BEAR IT AWAY." Ren, 22 (1969), 108–12.

Smith, J. Oates. "Ritual and Violence in Flannery O'Connor." THOUGHT, 41 (Winter 1966), 545–60.

Snow, Ollye Tine. "The Functional Gothic of Flannery O'Connor." SWR, 50 (1965), 286–99.

Spivey, Ted R. "Flannery O'Connor's View of God and Man." SSF, 1 (1964), 200–206.

Stelzmann, Rainulf. "Shock and Orthodoxy: An Interpretation of Flannery O'Connor's Novels and Short Stories." XUS, 2 (1963), 4–21.

_____. "Der Stein des Anstosses: Die Romane und Erzahlungen Flannery O'Connors." SZ, 174 (1964), 286–96.

Stephens, Martha. "Flannery O'Connor and the Sanctified–Sinner Tradition." ArQ, 24 (1968), 223–39.

Sullivan, Walter. "The Achievement of Flannery O'Connor." SHR, 2 (1968), 303–9.

_____. "Flannery O'Connor, Sin, and Grace: EVERYTHING THAT RISES MUST CONVERGE." HC, 2, iv (1965), 1–8, 10.

Taylor, Henry. "The Halt Shall Be Gathered Together: Physical Deformity in the Fiction of Flannery O'Connor." WHR, 22 (1968), 325-38.

True, Michael D. "Flannery O'Connor: Backwoods Prophet in the Secular City." PLL, 5 (1969), 209-23.

Walsh, Thomas F. "The Devils of Hawthorne and Flannery O'Connor." XUS, 5 (1966), 117-22.

JOHN O'HARA (1905-70), AMERICAN

NOVELS

APPOINTMENT IN SAMARRA. New York: Harcourt, Brace, 1934.

BUTTERFIELD 8. New York: Harcourt, Brace, 1935.

HOPE OF HEAVEN. New York: Harcourt, Brace, 1938.

A RAGE TO LIVE. New York: Random House, 1949.

THE FARMERS HOTEL. New York: Random House, 1951.

TEN NORTH FREDERICK. New York: Random House, 1955.

A FAMILY PARTY. New York: Random House, 1956.

FROM THE TERRACE. New York: Random House, 1958.

SERMONS AND SODA-WATER (a Trilogy). New York: Random House, 1960.

OURSELVES TO KNOW. New York: Random House, 1960.

THE BIG LAUGH. New York: Random House, 1962.

ELIZABETH APPLETON. New York: Random House, 1963.

THE LOCKWOOD CONCERN. New York: Random House, 1965.

MY TURN. New York: New American Library, 1966.

THE INSTRUMENT. New York: Random House, 1967.

LOVEY CHILDS: A PHILADELPHIAN'S STORY. New York: Random House, 1969.

SHORT STORIES

THE DOCTOR'S SON AND OTHER STORIES. New York: Harcourt, Brace, 1935.

FILES ON PARADE. New York: Harcourt, Brace, 1939.

PAL JOEY. New York: Duell, Sloan, 1940.

PIPE NIGHT. New York: Duell, Sloan, and Pearce, 1945.

HELLBOX. New York: Random House, 1947.

ASSEMBLY. New York: Random House, 1961.

THE CAPE COD LIGHTER. New York: Random House, 1962.

THE HAT ON THE BED. New York: Random House, 1963.

THE HORSE KNOWS THE WAY. New York: Random House, 1964.

WAITING FOR WINTER. New York: Random House, 1966.

AND OTHER STORIES. New York: Random House, 1968.

CRITICAL BOOKS

Carson, Edward R. THE FICTION OF JOHN O'HARA. Pittsburgh, Pa.: University of Pittsburgh Press, 1961.

Grebstein, Sheldon Norman. JOHN O'HARA. New York: Twayne, 1966.

CRITICAL ARTICLES

Antonini, Giacomo. "John O'Hara, pittore della societa americana." FLe, 9 (25 April 1954), 1-2.

Barrick, M.E. "Proverbs and Sayings from Gibbsville, Pennsylvania." KFQ, 12 (1967), 55-80.

Bier, Jesse. "O'Hara's APPOINTMENT IN SAMARRA: His First and Only Real Novel." CE, 25 (1963), 135-41.

Hierth, H.E. "The Class Novel." CEA, 27 (December 1964), 1-4.

Kazin, Alfred. "The Great American Bore." REPORTER, 19 (11 December 1958), 30-33.

McCormick, Bernard. "A John O'Hara Geography." JML, 1 (1970), 151-68.

Podhoretz, Norman. "Gibbsville and New Leeds: The America of John O'Hara and Mary McCarthy." Com, 21 (March 1956), 269-73.

Waterman, Rollene. "Appt. with O'Hara." SatR, 41 (29 November 1958), 15.

Weaver, Robert. "Twilight Area of Fiction: The Novels of John O'Hara." QQ, 64 (1959), 320-25.

ALAN PATON (1903-), SOUTH AFRICAN

NOVELS

CRY, THE BELOVED COUNTRY. London: Cape, 1948.

TOO LATE THE PHALAROPE. London: Cape, 1953.

SHORT STORIES

DEBBIE GO HOME: STORIES. London: Cape, 1961. As TALES FROM A
TROUBLED LAND. New York: Scribner, 1961.

CRITICAL BOOKS

Callan, Edward. ALAN PATON. New York: Twayne, 1968.

CRITICAL ARTICLES

Baker, Sheridan. "Paton's Beloved Country and the Morality of Geography."
CE, 19 (1957), 56-61.

_____. "Paton's Late Phalarope." ESA, 3 (1960), 152-59.

Bruell, Edwin. "Keen Scalpel on Racial Ills." EJ, 53 (1964), 658-61.

Collins, Harold R. "CRY, THE BELOVED COUNTRY and the Broken Tribe."
CE, 14 (1953), 379-83.

Davies, Horton. "Alan Paton: Literary Artist and Anglican." HJ, 50 (April
1952), 262-68.

Gailey, Harry A. "Sheridan Baker's 'Paton's Beloved Country.'" CE, 20 (1958), 143-44.

Hester, Sister Mary. "Greek Tragedy and the Novels of Alan Paton." WisSL, 1 (1964), 54-61.

Marcus, Fred H. "CRY, THE BELOVED COUNTRY and STRANGE FRUIT: Exploring Man's Inhumanity to Man." EJ, 51 (1962), 658-61.

Rooney, F. Charles. "The 'Message' of Alan Paton." CathW, 194 (November 1961), 94-95.

WALKER PERCY (1916-), AMERICAN

NOVELS

THE MOVIEGOER. New York: Knopf, 1961.

THE LAST GENTLEMAN. New York: Farrar, Straus, 1966.

CRITICAL ARTICLES

Atkins, Anselm. "Walker Percy and Post-Christian Search." CentR, 12 (1968), 73-95.

Blovin, Michael T. "The Novels of Walker Percy: An Attempt at Synthesis." XUS, 6 (1967), 29-42.

Brown, Ashley. "An Interview with Walker Percy." SHENANDOAH, 18, iii (1967), 3-10.

Cheney, Brainard. "To Restore a Fragmented Image." SR, 64 (1961), 691-700.

Cremeens, Carlton. "Walker Percy, The Man and the Novelist: An Interview." SoR, 4 (1968), 271-90.

Crews, Frederick C. "The Hero as 'Case.'" Com, 42 (September 1966), 100-102.

Henisey, Sarah. "Intersubjectivity in Symbolization." Ren, 20 (1968), 208-14.

Hoggard, James. "Death of the Vicarious." SWR, 44 (1964), 366-74.

Lawson, Lewis A. "Walker Percy's Southern Stoic." SLJ, 3 (1970), 5-31.

_____. "Walker Percy's Indirect Communications." TSLL, 11 (1969), 867-900.

Lehan, Richard. "The Way Back: Redemption in the Novels of Walker Percy." SoR, 4 (1968), 306-19.

Maxwell, Robert. "Walker Percy's Fancy." MinnR, 7 (1967), 231-37.

Thale, Jerome. "Alienation on the American Plan." ForumH, 6, iii (1968), 36-40.

Thale, Mary. "The Moviegoer of the 1950's." TCL, 14 (1968), 84-89.

Van Cleave, Jim. "Versions of Percy." SoR, 6 (1970), 990-1010.

ANTHONY POWELL (1905-), ENGLISH

NOVELS

AFTERNOON MEN. London: Duckworth, 1931.

VENUSBURG. London: Duckworth, 1932.

FROM A VIEW TO A DEATH. London: Duckworth, 1933. As MR. ZOUCH: SUPERMAN: FROM A VIEW TO A DEATH. New York: Vanguard Press, 1934. As FROM A VIEW TO A DEATH. Boston: Little, Brown, 1964.

AGENTS AND PATIENTS. London: Duckworth, 1936.

WHAT'S BECOME OF WARING. London: Cassell, 1939.

A DANCE TO THE MUSIC OF TIME:
    A QUESTION OF UPBRINGING. London: Heinemann, 1951.
    A BUYER'S MARKET. London: Heinemann, 1952.
    THE ACCEPTANCE WORLD. London: Heinemann, 1955.
    AT LADY MOLLY'S. London: Heinemann, 1957.
    CASANOVA'S CHINESE RESTAURANT. London: Heinemann, 1960.
    THE KINDLY ONES. London: Heinemann, 1962.
    THE VALLEY OF BONES. London: Heinemann, 1962.
    THE SOLDIER'S ART. London: Heinemann, 1966.
    THE MILITARY PHILOSOPHERS. London: Heinemann, 1968.

CRITICAL BOOKS

Bergonzi, Bernard, and Paul Bloomfield. ANTHONY POWELL AND L.P. HARTLEY. London: Longmans, 1962.

Morris, Robert K. THE NOVELS OF ANTHONY POWELL. Pittsburgh, Pa.: University of Pittsburgh Press, 1968.

Russell, John. ANTHONY POWELL: A QUINTET, SEXTET AND WAR. Bloomington: Indiana University Press, 1970.

SPECIAL ISSUES

SUMMARY (Autumn 1970), "Anthony Powell Issue."

CRITICAL ARTICLES

Bergonzi, Bernard. "Anthony Powell: 9/12." CritQ, 11 (1969), 76–86.

Brooke, Jocelyn. "From Wauchop to Widmerpol." LonM, 7 (September 1960), 60–64.

Davis, Douglas M. "An Interview with Anthony Powell, Frome, England, June, 1962." CE, 24 (1963), 533–36.

Glazebrook, Mark. "The Art of Horace Isbister, E. Bosworth Deacon, and Ralph Barnby." LonM, 7 (September 1967), 76–82.

Hall, James. "The Uses of Polite Surprise." EIC, 12 (1962), 179–82.

Herring, Anthony D. "Anthony Powell: A Reaction Against Determinism." BSUF, 9 (Winter 1968), 17–21.

Hynes, Samuel. "Novelist of Society." Cweal, 70 (31 July 1959), 396–97.

Kermode, Frank. "The Interpretation of the Times (Christopher Isherwood and Anthony Powell)." ENCOUNTER, 15 (September 1960), 74–76.

Leclaire, Lucien A. "Anthony Powell: Biographie Spirituelle d'une Generation." EA, 9 (1956), 23–27.

McCall, Raymond G. "Anthony Powell's Gallery." CE, 27 (1965), 227–32.

McDowell, Frederick P.W. "'The Devious Involutions of Human Characters and Emotions': Reflections on Some Recent British Novels." WSCL, 4 (Autumn 1963), 362-65.

Mizener, Arthur. "A DANCE TO THE MUSIC OF TIME: The Novels of Anthony Powell." KR, 22 (1960), 79-92.

Quesenbery, W.D., Jr. "Anthony Powell: The Anatomy of Decay." Crit, 7 (1964), 5-26.

Radner, Sanford. "Powell's Early Novels: A Study in Point of View." Ren, 16 (1964), 194-200.

_____. "The World of Anthony Powell." ClareQ, 10 (Winter 1963), 41-47.

Ruoff, Gene W. "Social Mobility and the Artist in MANHATTAN TRANSFER and THE MUSIC OF TIME." WSCL, 5 (Winter-Spring 1964), 64-76.

Russell, John. "Quintet from the 30's: Anthony Powell." KR, 27 (1965), 698-726.

Vinson, James. "Anthony Powell's MUSIC OF TIME." Per, 10 (1958), 146-52.

Voorhees, Richard J. "Anthony Powell: The First Phase." PrS, 28 (1954), 337-44.

_____. "THE MUSIC OF TIME: Themes and Variations." DR, 42 (Autumn 1962), 213-21.

Waugh, Evelyn. "Marriage a la Mode--1936." SPECTATOR, 24 June 1960, pp. 53-54.

West, Anthony. "Wry Humor." NY, 28 (13 December 1952), 170-80.

Woodward, A.G. "The Novels of Anthony Powell." ESA, 10 (1967), 117-28.

Zigerell, James J. "Anthony Powell's MUSIC OF TIME: Chronicle of a Declining Establishment." TCL, 12 (1966), 138-46.

J[AMES]. F[ARL]. POWERS (1917-   ), AMERICAN

NOVELS

MORTE D'URBAN. Garden City, N.Y.: Doubleday, 1962.

SHORT STORIES

PRINCE OF DARKNESS AND OTHER STORIES. Garden City, N.Y.: Doubleday, 1947.

THE PRESENCE OF GRACE. Garden City, N.Y.: Doubleday, 1956.

BIBLIOGRAPHY

Wedge, George F. "Two Bibliographies. Flannery O'Connor, J.F. Powers."
Crit, 2 (1958), 59-70.

CRITICAL BOOKS

Evans, Fallon, ed. J.F. POWERS. St. Louis, Mo.: B. Herder, 1968.

Hagopian, John V. J.F. POWERS. New York: Twayne, 1967.

CRITICAL ARTICLES

Bates, Barclay W. "Flares of Special Grace: The Orthodoxy of J.F. Powers."
MQ, 11 (1969), 91-106.

Burgess, C.F. "The Case of the Hen-Pecked Priest in J.F. Powers' 'The
Valiant Woman.'" CITHARA, 9, i (1969), 67-71.

Collignon, Joseph B. "Powers' MORTE D'URBAN: A Layman's Indictment." Ren, 16 (1963), 20-21, 51-52.

Curley, Thomas. "J.F. Powers' Long Awaited First Novel." Cweal, 77 (12 October 1962), 77-78.

Degnan, James P. "J.F. Powers: Comic Satirist." ColQ, 16 (1968), 325-33.

Dolan, Paul J. "God's Crooked Line: Powers' MORTE D'URBAN." Ren, 21 (1969), 95-102.

Dupee, F.W. "In the Powers Country." PR, 30 (1963), 113-16.

Gass, William H. "Bingo Game at the Foot of the Cross." NATION, 145 (29 September 1962), 182-83.

Gilbert, Sister Mary, S.N.J.M. "MORTE D'URBAN." SR, 71 (1963), 673-75.

Hagopian, John V. "The Fathers of J.F. Powers." SSF, 5 (1968), 139-53.

_____. "Irony and Involution in J.F. Powers' MORTE D'URBAN." WSCL, 9 (1968), 151-71.

Hertzel, Leo J. "Brother Juniper, Father Urban and the Unworldly Tradition." Ren, 17 (1965), 207-10.

Hinchliffe, Arnold P. "Nightmare of Grace." BLACKFRIARS, 45 (February 1964), 61-69.

Hynes, Joseph. "Father Urban's Renewal: J.F. Powers' Difficult Precision." MLQ, 29 (1968), 450-66.

Kelly, Richard. "Father Eudex, the Judge and Judged: An Analysis of J.F. Powers' 'The Forks.'" UR, 35 (1969), 316-18.

Kristin, Sister. "The Catholic and Creativity: J.F. Powers." ABR, 15 (1964), 63-80.

O'Brien, Charles F. "MORTE D'URBAN and the Catholic Church in America." DISCOURSE, 12 (1969), 324-28.

Phelps, Donald. "Reasonable, Holy and Living." MinnR, 9 (1969), 57-62.

Poss, Stanley. "J.F. Powers: The Gin of Irony." TCL, 14 (1968), 65-74.

Rowan, Thomas, C.S.S.R. "MORTE D'URBAN: A Novel About Priests." HPR, 63 (1963), 291-94.

Sandra, Sister Mary, S.S.A. "The Priest-Hero in Modern Fiction." Person, 46 (1965), 527-42.

Steichen, Donna M. "J.F. Powers and the Noonday Devil." ABR, 20 (1969), 528-51.

Stewart, D.H. "J.F. Powers' MORTE D'URBAN as Western." WAL, 5 (1970), 31-44.

Webster, Harvey C. "Comedy and Darkness." KR, 25 (1963), 166-69.

V[ICTOR]. S[AWDON]. PRITCHETT
(1900-   ), ENGLISH

NOVELS

CLAIRE DRUMMER.   London: Benn, 1929.

SHIRLEY SANZ.   London: Gollancz, 1932.   As ELOPEMENT INTO EXILE.
Boston: Little, Brown, 1932.

NOTHING LIKE LEATHER.   London: Chatto and Windus, 1935.

DEAD MAN LEADING.   London: Chatto and Windus, 1937.

MR. BELUNCLE.   London: Chatto and Windus, 1951.

SHORT STORIES

THE SPANISH VIRGIN AND OTHER STORIES.   London: Benn, 1930.

YOU MAKE YOUR OWN LIFE.   London: Chatto and Windus, 1938.

IT MAY NEVER HAPPEN AND OTHER STORIES.   London: Chatto and Windus, 1945.

COLLECTED STORIES.   London: Chatto and Windus, 1956.

THE SAILOR, THE SENSE OF HUMOR, AND OTHER STORIES.   New York:
Knopf, 1956.

WHEN MY GIRL COMES HOME.   London: Chatto and Windus, 1961.

THE KEY TO MY HEART.   London: Chatto and Windus, 1963.

BLIND LOVE AND OTHER STORIES.   London: Chatto and Windus, 1969.

FREDERIC PROKOSCH (1908-   ), AMERICAN

NOVELS

THE ASIATICS. New York: Harper, 1935.

THE SEVEN WHO FLED. New York: Harper, 1937.

NIGHT OF THE POOR. New York: Harper, 1939.

THE SKIES OF EUROPE. New York: Harper, 1941.

THE CONSPIRATORS. New York: Harper, 1943.

AGE OF THUNDER. New York: Harper, 1945.

THE IDOLS OF THE CAVE. Garden City, N.Y.: Doubleday, 1946.

STORM AND ECHO. Garden City, N.Y.: Doubleday, 1948.

NINE DAYS TO MUKALLA. New York: Viking Press, 1953.

A TALE FOR MIDNIGHT. Boston: Little, Brown, 1955.

A BALLAD OF LOVE. New York: Farrar, Straus, 1960.

THE SEVEN SISTERS. New York: Farrar, Straus, 1962.

THE DARK DANCER. New York: Farrar, Straus, 1964.

THE WRECK OF THE CASSANDRA. New York: Farrar, Straus, 1966.

THE MISSOLONGHI MANUSCRIPT. New York: Farrar, Straus, 1968.

CRITICAL BOOKS

Squire, Radcliffe. FREDERIC PROKOSCH. New York: Twayne, 1964.

CRITICAL ARTICLES

Carpenter, Richard C. "The Novels of Frederic Prokosch." CE, 18 (1957), 261-67.

Sandra, Sister Mary, S.S.A. "The Priest-Hero in Modern Fiction." Person, 46 (1965), 527-42.

JAMES PURDY (1923-), AMERICAN

NOVELS

MALCOLM. New York: Farrar, Straus, 1959.

THE NEPHEW. New York: Farrar, Straus, 1960.

CABOT WRIGHT BEGINS. New York: Farrar, Straus, 1964.

EUSTACE CHISHOLM AND THE WORKS. New York: Farrar, Straus, 1967.

JEREMY'S VERSION: PART ONE OF SLEEPERS IN MOON-CROWNED VALLEYS. Garden City, N.Y.: Doubleday, 1970.

SHORT STORIES

DON'T CALL ME BY MY RIGHT NAME AND OTHER STORIES. New York: William Frederick Press, 1956.

63: DREAM PALACE. New York: William Frederick Press, 1956.

COLOR OF DARKNESS: 11 STORIES AND A NOVELLA. New York: New Directions, 1957.

CHILDREN IS ALL. New York: New Directions, 1962.

AN OYSTER IS A WEALTHY BEAST. Los Angeles: Black Sparrow Press, 1967.

MR. EVENING: A STORY AND NINE POEMS. Los Angeles: Black Sparrow Press, 1968.

ON THE REBOUND: A STORY AND NINE POEMS. Los Angeles: Black Sparrow Press, 1970.

CRITICAL BOOKS

Schwarzschild, Bettina. THE NOT-RIGHT HOUSE: ESSAYS ON JAMES PURDY. Columbia: University of Missouri Press, 1968.

CRITICAL ARTICLES

Baldanza, Frank. "Playing House for Keeps with James Purdy." ConL, 11 (1970), 488–510.

Burris, Shirley W. "The Emergency in Purdy's 'Daddy Wolf.'" Ren, 20 (1968), 94–98, 103.

Coffey, Warren. "The Incompleat Novelist." Com, 44 (September 1967), 98–103.

Daiches, David. "A Preface to James Purdy's MALCOLM." AR, 22 (1962), 122–30.

Denniston, Constance. "The American Romance-Parody: A Study of Purdy's MALCOLM and Heller's CATCH-22." ESRS, 14 (1965), 42–59, 63–64.

Kolve, Del. "James Purdy: An Assessment." T&T, 42 (1961), 476–77.

Krummel, Regina P. "Two Quests in Two Societies." EngR, 18 (April 1967), 28–32.

Lorch, Thomas M. "Purdy's MALCOLM: A Unique Vision of Radical Emptiness." WSCL, 6 (Summer 1965), 204–13.

McNamara, Eugene. "The Post-Modern American Novel." QQ, 69 (1962), 272–74.

Malin, Irving. "Melange a Trois." RAMPARTS, 3 (March 1965), 79–80.

Maloff, Saul. "James Purdy's Fictions: The Quality of Despair." Crit, 6 (1963), 106–12.

Morris, Robert K. "James Purdy and the Works." NATION, 205 (9 October 1967), 342–44.

Pomeranz, Regina. "The Hell of Not Loving: Purdy's Modern Tragedy." Ren, 16 (1964), 149-53.

Schott, Webster. "James Purdy: American Dreams." NATION, 198 (23 March 1964), 300-302.

Schwarzschild, Bettina. "The Forsaken: An Interpretative Essay on James Purdy's MALCOLM." TQ, 10, i (Spring 1967), 170-77.

Skerrett, Joseph T., Jr. "James Purdy and the Works: Love and Tragedy in Five Novels." TCL, 15 (1969), 25-33.

Tornquist, Elizabeth. "The New Parochialism." Com, 31 (May 1961), 449-52.

THOMAS PYNCHON (1937-), AMERICAN

NOVELS

V. Philadelphia: Lippincott, 1963.

THE CRYING OF LOT 49. Philadelphia: Lippincott, 1966.

CRITICAL ARTICLES

Alter, Robert. "The Apocalyptic Temper." Com, 41 (June 1966), 61-66.

Buckeye, Robert. "The Anatomy of the Psychic Novel." Crit, 9 (1967), 33-38, 43-44.

Davis, Robert Murray. "The Shrinking Garden and New Exits: The Comic-Satiric Novel in the Twentieth Century." KQ, 1 (1969), 5-16.

Greenberg, Alvin. "The Underground Woman: An Excursion into the V-ness of Thomas Pynchon." CHELSEA, no. 27 (1969), 58-65.

Hausdorff, Don. "Thomas Pynchon's Multiple Absurdities." WSCL, 7 (Autumn 1966), 258-69.

Tanner, Tony. "The American Novelist as Entropologist." LonM, n.s. 10 (October 1970), 5-18.

Young, James D. "The Enigma Variations of Thomas Pynchon." Crit, 10 (1968), 69-77.

FREDERIC RAPHAEL (1931-), AMERICAN

NOVELS

OBBLIGATO. London: Macmillan, 1956.

THE EARLSDON WAY. London: Cassell, 1958.

THE LIMITS OF LOVE. Philadelphia: Lippincott, 1961.

A WILD SURMISE. Philadelphia: Lippincott, 1962.

THE GRADUATE WIFE. London: Cassell, 1962.

THE TROUBLE WITH ENGLAND. London: Cassell, 1962.

LINDMANN. New York: Holt Rinehart, 1964.

DARLING. New York: New American Library, 1965.

ORCHESTRA AND BEGINNERS. New York: Viking Press, 1968.

CRITICAL ARTICLES

McDowell, Frederick P.W. "The Varied Universe of Frederic Raphael's Fiction." Crit, 8 (1965), 39-43.

_____. "World Within World: Gerda Charles, Frederick (sic) Raphael, and the Anglo-Jewish Community." Crit, 6 (1963-64), 147-50.

JOHN F[RANCISCO]. RECHY (1934-   ), AMERICAN

NOVELS

CITY OF NIGHT. New York: Grove Press, 1963.

NUMBERS. New York: Grove Press, 1967.

THIS DAY'S DEATH. New York: Grove Press, 1970.

CRITICAL ARTICLES

Heifetz, Henry. "The Anti-Social Act of Writing." StL, 4 (Spring 1964), 6-9.

Hoffman, Stanton. "The Cities of Night: John Rechy's CITY OF NIGHT and the American Literature of Homosexuality." ChiR, 17, ii-iii (1964), 195-206.

MORDECAI RICHLER (1931-), CANADIAN

NOVELS

THE ACROBATS. Toronto: Ambassador, 1954.

SON OF A SMALLER HERO. Toronto: Collins, 1955.

A CHOICE OF ENEMIES. Toronto: Collins, 1957.

THE APPRENTICESHIP OF DUDDY KRAVITZ. Toronto: Collins, 1959.

THE INCOMPARABLE ATUK. Toronto: McClelland and Stewart, 1963. As
STICK YOUR NECK OUT. New York: Simon and Schuster, 1963.

COCKSURE. Toronto: McClelland and Stewart, 1968.

SHORT STORIES

THE STREET. STORIES. Toronto: McClelland and Stewart, 1969.

CRITICAL BOOKS

Sheps, G. David. MORDECAI RICHLER. Toronto: Ryerson Press, 1970.

Woodcock, George. MORDECAI RICHLER. Toronto: McClelland and Stewart, 1970.

CRITICAL ARTICLES

Bowering, George. "And the Sun Goes Down: Richler's First Novel." CanL, no. 29 (Summer 1966), 7-17.

Cohen, Nathan. "A Conversation with Mordecai Richler." TamR, no. 1 (Winter 1957), 6-23.

_____. "Heroes of the Richler View." TamR, no. 6 (Winter 1958), 47-60.

Kattan, Naim. "Mordecai Richler: Craftsman or Artist." CanL, no. 21 (Summer 1964), 46-51.

New, William. "The Apprenticeship of Discovery." CanL, no. 29 (Summer 1966), 18-33.

Scott, Peter. "A Choice of Certainties." TamR, no. 8 (Summer 1958), 73-82.

Tallman, Warren. "Richler and the Faithless City." CanL, no. 3 (Winter 1960), 62-64.

_____. "Wolf in the Snow. Part Two: The House Repossessed." CanL, no. 6 (Autumn 1960), 463-65.

PHILIP ROTH (1933-), AMERICAN

NOVELS

LETTING GO. New York: Random House, 1962.

WHEN SHE WAS GOOD. New York: Random House, 1967.

PORTNOY'S COMPLAINT. New York: Random House, 1969.

SHORT STORIES

GOODBYE, COLUMBUS AND FIVE SHORT STORIES. Boston: Houghton Mifflin, 1959.

PENGUIN MODERN STORIES 3, with others. London: Penguin, 1969.

CRITICAL ARTICLES

Brewer, I.F. "The Anti-Hero in Contemporary Literature." IEY, 12 (1967), 55-60.

Cheuse, Alan. "A World Without Realists." StL, 4, II (Spring 1964), 68-82.

Deer, Irving, and Harriet Deer. "Philip Roth and the Crisis in American Fiction." MinnR, 6 (1966), 353-60.

Donaldson, Scott. "Philip Roth: The Meanings of LETTING GO." ConL, 11 (1970), 21-35.

Isaac, Dan. "In Defense of Philip Roth." ChiR, 17, ii-iii (1964), 84-96.

Philip Roth

Iwamoto, Iwao. "Philip Roth--Judayasei e no Hangyaku." EigoS, 115 (1969), 762-63.

Koch, Eric. "Roth's 'Goodbye Columbus.'" TamR, no. 13 (1959), 129-32.

Landis, Joseph C. "The Sadness of Philip Roth: An Interim Report." MR, 3 (1962), 259-68.

Leer, Norman. "Escape and Confrontation in the Short Stories of Philip Roth." ChS, 49 (1966), 132-46.

Mudrick, Marvin. "Who Killed Herzog? or, Three American Novelists." UDQ, 1 (1967), 61-97.

Petillon, Pierre-Yves. "Philip Roth n'est pas mort." CRITIQUE, 26 (1970), 821-38.

Roskolenko, Harry. "Portrait of the Artist as a Young Schmuck." Quadrant, 64 (1970), 25-30.

Roth, Philip. "Writing About Jews." Com, 36 (December 1963), 445-52.

Shrubb, Peter. "Portnography." Quadrant, 64 (1970), 16-24.

Solotaroff, Theodore. "Philip Roth and the Jewish Moralists. ChiR, 13 (Winter 1959), 87-99.

J[EROME]. D[AVID]. SALINGER (1919-   ), AMERICAN

NOVELS

THE CATCHER IN THE RYE. Boston: Little, Brown, 1951.

SHORT STORIES

NINE STORIES. Boston: Little, Brown, 1953.

FRANNY AND ZOOEY. Boston: Little, Brown, 1961.

RAISE HIGH THE ROOF BEAM, CARPENTERS AND SEYMOUR: AN INTRO-
DUCTION. Boston: Little, Brown, 1963.

BIBLIOGRAPHY

Beebe, Maurice, and Jennifer Sperry. "Criticism of J.D. Salinger: A Selected Checklist." MFS, 12 (1966), 377-80.

Davis, Tom. "J.D. Salinger: A Checklist." PBSA, 53 (1959), 69-71.

Fiene, Donald M. "J.D. Salinger: A Bibliography." WSCL, 4 (Winter
1963), 109-49.

CRITICAL BOOKS

Belcher, William F., and James W. Lee, eds. J.D. SALINGER AND THE
CRITICS. Belmont, Calif.: Wadsworth, 1962.

French, Warren. J.D. SALINGER: New York: Twayne, 1963.

Grunwald, Henry A., ed. SALINGER: A CRITICAL AND PERSONAL POR-
TRAIT. New York: Harper, 1962.

Gwynn, Frederick L., and Joseph L. Blotner. THE FICTION OF J.D. SAL-
INGER. Pittsburgh: University of Pittsburgh Press, 1958.

Hamilton, Kenneth. J.D. SALINGER: A CRITICAL ESSAY. Grand Rapids,
Mich.: Eerdmans, 1966.

Laser, Marvin, and Norman Fruman, eds. STUDIES IN J.D. SALINGER.
New York: Odyssey, 1963.

Marsden, Malcolm M., ed. IF YOU REALLY WANT TO KNOW: A CATCHER
CASEBOOK. Chicago: Scott, Foresman, 1963.

Miller, James E., Jr. J.D. SALINGER. Minneapolis: University of Minnesota Press, 1965.

Simonson, Harold P., and E.P. Hager, eds. SALINGER'S "CATCHER IN THE
RYE": CLAMOR VS. CRITICISM. New York: Heath, 1963.

SPECIAL ISSUES

MODERN FICTION STUDIES, 12 (1966), "J.D. Salinger Number."

WISCONSIN STUDIES IN CONTEMPORARY LITERATURE, 4 (Winter 1963),
"J.D. Salinger Issue."

CRITICAL ARTICLES

Amoruso, Vito. "La visione e il caos: Il decadentismo di Salinger." SA,
10 (1964), 317-42.

Amur, G.S. "Theme, Structure, and Symbol in THE CATCHER IN THE RYE."
IJAS, 1 (1969), 11-24.

Antonini, Giacomo. "Il successo di Salinger." FLe, 17 (28 October 1962),
1, 4.

Aronson, Harry. "J.D. Salinger--ungdomens van." VAR LOSEN, 58 (1967),
41-46.

Balke, Betty T. "Some Judeo-Christian Themes Seen Through the Eyes of J.D.

Salinger and Nathanael West." CRESSET, 31, vii (1968), 14-18.

Barr, Donald. "Saints, Pilgrims and Artists." Cweal, 67 (25 October 1957), 88-90.

Baumbach, Jonathan. "The Saint as a Young Man: A Reappraisal of THE CATCHER IN THE RYE." MLQ, 25 (1964), 461-72.

Bellman, Samuel I. "New Light on Seymour's Suicide: Salinger's 'Hapworth 16, 1924.'" SSF, 3 (1966), 348-51.

Bostwick, Sally. "Reality, Compassion and Mysticism." MidR, 5 (1963), 30-43.

Branch, Edgar M. "Mark Twain and J.D. Salinger: A Study in Literary Continuity." AQ, 9 (1957), 144-58.

Browne, Robert M. "In Defense of Esme." CE, 22 (1961), 584-85.

Bruccoli, Matthew. "States of Salinger's Book." ANTQ, 2 (1963), 21-22.

Bryan, James E. "J.D. Salinger: The Fat Lady and the Chicken Sandwich." CE, 23 (1961), 226-29.

_____. "A Reading of Salinger's 'For Esme--With Love and Squalor.'" CRITICISM, 9 (1967), 275-88.

_____. "A Reading of Salinger's 'Teddy.'" AL, 40 (1968), 352-69.

_____. "Salinger's Seymour's Suicide." CE, 24 (1962), 226-29.

Bungert, Haus. "J.D. Salingers THE CATCHER IN THE RYE: Isolation und Kommunikationsversuche des Jugendlichen." NS, (1960), 208-17.

Cagle, Charles. "THE CATCHER IN THE RYE Revisited." MQ, 4 (1963), 343-51.

Carpenter, Frederic I. "The Adolescent in American Fiction." EJ, 46 (1957), 313-19.

Cecile, Sister Marie. "J.D. Salinger's Circle of Privacy." CathW, 194 (February 1962), 296-301.

Chester, Alfred. "Salinger: How to Love Without Love." Com, 35 (June 1963), 467-74.

Chugunov, Konstantin. "Soviet Critics on J.D. Salinger's Novel THE CATCHER IN THE RYE." SovL, 5 (1962), 182-84.

Conard, Robert C. "Two Novels About Outsiders: The Kinship of J.D. Salinger's THE CATCHER IN THE RYE with Heinrich Boll's ANSICHTEN EINES CLOWNS." UDR, 5 (1968-69), 23-27.

Corbett, E.P.J. "Raise High the Barriers, Censors." AMERICA, 104 (7 January 1961), 441-43.

Costello, Donald P. "The Language of THE CATCHER IN THE RYE." AS, 34 (1959), 172-81.

_____. "Salinger and His Critics." Cweal, 79 (25 October 1963), 132-35.

Costello, Patrick. "Salinger and 'Honest Iago.'" Ren, 16 (1964), 171-74.

D'Avanzo, M.I. "Gatsby and Holden Caulfield." FITZGERALD NEWSLETTER, 38 (1967), 4-6.

Davis, Tom. "J.D. Salinger: 'Some Crazy Cliff' Indeed." WHR, 14 (1960), 97-99.

_____. "J.D. Salinger: The Identity of Sergeant X." WHR, 16 (1962), 181-83.

Deer, Irving, and John H. Randall III. "J.D. Salinger and the Reality Beyond Words." LHR, 6 (1964), 14-19.

Dodge, S.C. "The Theme of the Quest: J.D. Salinger." EngR, 8 (Winter 1957), 10-13.

Ducharme, Edward. "J.D., Sonny, Sunny, and Holden." EngR, 19 (1968), 54-58.

Fink, Guido. "Salinger, o la magia del nome propria." SA, 12 (1966), 259-76.

Fleisher, Frederic. "J.D. Salinger och hans familj." BLM, 30 (1961), 846-48.

Franconeri, Francesco. "Jerome David Salinger: Un americano in cerca d'amore." VeP, 45 (1962), 394-411.

Freese, Peter. "Jerome David Salinger: THE CATCHER IN THE RYE." LWU, 1 (1968), 123-52.

French, Warren. "Salinger's Seymour: Another Autopsy." CE, 24 (1963), 563.

_____. "An Unnoticed Salinger Story." CE, 26 (1965), 394-95.

Gale, Robert L. "Redburn and Holden--Half-Brothers One Century Removed." ForumH, 3 (Winter 1963), 32-36.

Genthe, Charles V. "Six, Sex, Sick: Seymour, Some Comments." TCL, 10 (1965), 170-71.

Giles, Barbara. "The Lonely War of J.D. Salinger." MAINSTREAM, 12 (February 1959), 2-13.

Gilman, Richard. "Salinger Considered." JUBILEE, 9 (October 1961), 38-41.

Glazier, Lyle. "The Glass Family Saga: Argument and Epiphany." CE, 27 (1965), 248-51.

Goldstein, Bernice, and Sanford Goldstein. "Bunnies and Cobras: Zen Enlightenment in Salinger." DISCOURSE, 13 (1970), 98-106.

_____. "Seymour: An Introduction--Writing as Discovery." SSF, 7 (1970), 248-56.

_____. "Zen and NINE STORIES." Ren, 22 (1970), 171-82.

Green, Martin. "Amis and Salinger: The Latitude of Private Conscience." ChiR, 11 (Winter 1957), 20-25.

Gross, Theodore. "J.D. Salinger: Suicide and Survival in the Modern World." SAQ, 68 (1969), 454-62.

Grunwald, Henry A. "He Touches Something Deep in Us." HORIZON, 4 (1962), 100-107.

Hainsworth, J.D. "J.D. Salinger." HJ, 64 (1965-66), 63-64.

_____. "Maturity in J.D. Salinger's THE CATCHER IN THE RYE." ES, 48 (1967), 426-31.

Hamada, Seijiro. "'The Laughing Man' ni tsuite." EigoS, 114 (1968), 578–79.

Hamilton, Kenneth. "Hell in New York: J.D. Salinger's 'Pretty Mouth and Green My Eyes.'" DR, 47 (Autumn 1967), 394–99.

_____. "J.D. Salinger's Happy Family." QQ, 71 (1964), 176–87.

_____. "One Way to Use the Bible: The Example of J.D. Salinger." ChS, 47 (1964), 243–51.

Hassan, Ihab. "J.D. Salinger: Rare Quixotic Gesture." WR, 21 (Summer 1957), 261–80.

Havemann, Ernest. "Search for the Mysterious J.D. Salinger." LIFE, 51 (3 November 1961), 129–30, 132–44.

Heiserman, Arthur, and James E. Miller, Jr. "J.D. Salinger: 'Some Crazy Cliff.'" WHR, 10 (1956), 129–37.

Hermann, John. "J.D. Salinger: Hello Hello Hello." CE, 22 (1960), 262–64.

Herndl, George C. "Golding and Salinger: A Clear Voice." WR, no. 502 (1964), 309–22.

Hicks, Granville. "J.D. Salinger: Search for Wisdom." SatR, 42 (25 July 1959), 13, 30.

Hinckle, Warren, et al. "A Symposium on J.D. Salinger." RAMPARTS, 1 (May 1962), 47–66.

Jacobs, Robert G. "J.D. Salinger's THE CATCHER IN THE RYE: Holden Caulfield's 'Goddam Autobiography.'" IEY, (1959), 9–14.

Jacobsen, Josephine. "The Felicity of J.D. Salinger." Cweal, 71 (26 February 1960), 589–91.

Jessey, Cornelia. "Creative Fulfillment." CEA, 22 (October–November 1963), 24–31.

Johnson, J.W. "The Adolescent Hero: A Trend in Modern Fiction." TCL, 5 (1957), 3–11.

Kanesaki, Hisao. "J.D. Salinger." JIMBUN KENKYU, 12 (June 1961), 123-34.

Kaplan, Charles. "Holden and Huck: The Odysseys of Youth." CE, 17 (1956), 76-80.

Karlstetter, Karl. "J.D. Salinger, R.W. Emerson and the Perennial Philosophy." MSpr, 63 (1969), 224-36.

Kazin, Alfred. "J.D. Salinger: 'Everybody's Favorite!'" ATLANTIC MONTHLY, 207 (August 1961), 27-31.

Kearns, Francis E. "Salinger and Golding: Conflict on the Campus." AMERICA, 108 (26 January 1963), 136-39.

Kegel, Charles H. "Incommunicability in Salinger's THE CATCHER IN THE RYE." WHR, 11 (1957), 188-90.

Kinney, Arthur F. "J.D. Salinger and the Search for Love." TSLL, 5 (1963), 111-26.

_____. "The Theme of Charity in THE CATCHER IN THE RYE." PMASAL, 48 (1963), 691-702.

Kranidas, Thomas. "Point of View in Salinger's 'Teddy.'" SSF, 2 (1964), 89-91.

Lakin, R.D. "D.W.'s: The Displaced Writer in America." MQ, 4 (1963), 295-303.

Larner, Jeremy. "Salinger's Audience: An Explanation." PR, 39 (1962), 594-98.

Laser, Marvin. "Character Names in THE CATCHER IN THE RYE." CEJ, 1 (1965), 29-40.

Leitch, David. "The Salinger Myth." TC, 168 (1960), 428-35.

Levin, Beatrice. "J.D. Salinger in Oklahoma." CJF, 19 (1961), 231-33.

Levine, Paul. "J.D. Salinger: The Development of the Misfit Hero." TCL, 4 (1958), 92-99.

Light, James F. "Salinger's THE CATCHER IN THE RYE." Expl, 18 (1960),

J[erome]. D[avid]. Salinger

Item 59.

Little, G.B. "Three Novels for Comparative Study in the Twelfth Grade."
EJ, 52 (1963), 501-5.

Luedtke, Luther S. "J.D. Salinger and Robert Burns: THE CATCHER IN THE
RYE." MFS, 16 (1970), 198-201.

Lyndenberg, John. "American Novelists in Search of a Lost World." RLV,
27 (1961), 306-21.

McCarthy, Mary. "J.D. Salinger's Closed Circuit." Harper's, 225 (October
1962), 46-48.

McIntyre, J.P. "A Preface for 'Franny and Zooey.'" CRITIC, 29 (1962),
25-28.

McNamara, Eugene. "Holden as Novelist." EJ, 54 (1965), 166-70.

Mannoni, O. "Le masque et la parole." TM, 20 (1964), 930-42.

Marcus, Fred H. "THE CATCHER IN THE RYE: A Live Circuit." EJ, 52
(1963), 1-8.

Margolis, John D. "Salinger's THE CATCHER IN THE RYE." Expl, 21
(1963), Item 23.

Meral, Jean. "The Ambiguous Mr. Antolini in Salinger's CATCHER IN THE
RYE." CALIBAN, 7 (1970), 55-58.

Mizener, Arthur. "Defining 'the Good American': J.D. Salinger and the
Glass Family." LISTENER, 68 (16 August 1962), 241-42.

_____. "The Love Song of J.D. Salinger." Harper's, 218 (February 1959),
83-90.

Moore, R.P. "The World of Holden." EJ, 54 (1965), 159-65.

Nathan, Monique. "J.D. Salinger et le reve americain." CRITIQUE, 179
(1962), 229-305.

Noland, Richard W. "The Novel of Personal Formula: J.D. Salinger."
UKCR, 33 (1966), 19-24.

Noon, William T. "Three Young Men in Rebellion." THOUGHT, 38 (Winter 1963), 559-77.

O'Hara, J.D. "No Catcher in the Rye." MFS, 9 (1963), 370-76.

Oldsey, Bernard S. "The Movies in the Rye." CE, 23 (1961), 209-15.

Peavy, Charles D. "'Did You Ever Have a Sister?' Holden, Quentin, and Sexual Innocence." FQ, 1, iii (1968), 82-95.

_____. "Holden's Courage Again." CEA, 28 (October 1965), 1, 6, 9.

Perrine, Laurence. "Teddy? Booper? Or Blooper?" SSF, 4 (1967), 217-24.

Phillips, Paul. "Salinger's FRANNY AND ZOOEY." MAINSTREAM, 15 (1962), 32-39.

Pilkington, John. "About This Madman Stuff." UMSE, 7 (1966), 65-75.

Reiman, Donald H. "Salinger's THE CATCHER IN THE RYE." Expl, 22 (1963), Item 58.

Ross, Theodore J. "Notes on J.D. Salinger." CJF, 22 (1963), 149-53.

Sakamoto, Masayuki. "Salinger ni okeru 'Sezuku' to 'Chozoku.'" EigoS, 115 (1969), 692-93.

Sato, Hiroko. "The World of J.D. Salinger. E&S, 10 (1962), 42-53.

Schulz, Max F. "Epilogue to SEYMOUR: AN INTRODUCTION: Salinger and the Crisis of Consciousness." SSF, 5 (1968), 128-38.

Seltzman, Daniel. "Therapy and Antitherapy in Salinger's 'Zooey.'" AI, 25 (1968), 140-62.

Seng, Peter J. "The Fallen Idol: The Immature World of Holden Caulfield." CE, 23 (1961), 203-209.

Sethom, Mohamed. "La societe dans l'oeuvre de J.D. Salinger." EA, 22 (1969), 270-78.

_____. "L'Univers verbal de J.D. Salinger." EA, 21 (1968), 57-64.

Slabey, Robert M. "THE CATCHER IN THE RYE: Christian Theme and Symbol." CLAJ, 6 (1963), 170-83.

_____. "Salinger's Casino': Wayfarers and Spiritual Acrobats." EngR, 14 (February 1964), 16-20.

_____. "Sergeant X and Seymour Glass." WHR, 16 (1962), 376-77.

Steiner, George. "The Salinger Industry." NATION, 189 (14 November 1959), 360-63.

Stevenson, David L. "J.D. Salinger: The Mirror of Crisis." NATION, 184 (9 March 1957), 215-17.

Stone, Edward. "Salinger's Carrousel." MFS, 13 (1967), 520-23.

Strauch, Carl F. "Kings in the Back Row: Meaning Through Structure--A Reading of Salinger's THE CATCHER IN THE RYE." WSCL, 2 (Winter 1961), 5-30.

Takenaka, Toyoko. "On Seymour's Suicide." KAL, 12 (1970), 54-61.

Tirmalai, C.K. "Salinger's THE CATCHER IN THE RYE." Expl, 22 (1964), Item 56.

Tosta, Michael R. "'Will the Real Sergeant X Please Stand Up.'" WHR, 16 (1962), 376.

Travis, Mildred K. "Salinger's THE CATCHER IN THE RYE." Expl, 21 (1962), Item 36.

Trowbridge, Clinton W. "Salinger's Symbolic Use of Character and Detail in THE CATCHER IN THE RYE." CimR, 4 (1968), 5-11.

_____. "The Symbolic Structure of THE CATCHER IN THE RYE." SR, 74 (Summer 1966), 681-93.

Vanderbilt, Kermit. "Symbolic Resolution in THE CATCHER IN THE RYE: The Cap, The Carrousel, and the American West." WHR, 17 (1963), 271-77.

Veza, Laurette. "J.D. Salinger--L'attrape-coeur ou Holden Resartus." LanM, 61 (1967), 56-65.

Way, Brian. "'Franny and Zooey' and J.D. Salinger." NEW LEFT REVIEW,

15 (May-June 1962), 72-82.

Wells, A.R.   "Huck Finn and Holden Caulfield: The Situation of the Hero."
OUR, 2 (1960), 31-44.

Wiebe, D.E.   "Salinger's 'A Perfect Day for Bananafish.'"   Expl, 23 (1964),
Item 3.

Wiegand, William.   "J.D. Salinger's Seventy-eight Bananas."   ChiR, 11, iv
(Winter 1958), 3-19.

_____.   "The Knighthood of J.D. Salinger."   NRep, 141 (19 October 1959),
19-22.

_____.   "Salinger and Kierkegaard."   MinnR, 5 (1965), 137-56.

Yamaya, Saburo.   "J.D. Salinger's Quest of 'The Valley of the Sick.'"
SELit, 40 (1964), 215-43.

WILLIAM SANSOM (1912-), ENGLISH

NOVELS

THE BODY. London: Hogarth Press, 1949.

THE FACE OF INNOCENCE. London: Hogarth Press, 1951.

A BED OF ROSES. London: Hogarth Press, 1954.

THE LOVING EYE. London: Hogarth Press, 1956.

THE CAUTIOUS HEART. London: Hogarth Press, 1958.

THE LAST HOURS OF SANDRA LEE. London: Hogarth Press, 1961.

GOODBYE. London: Hogarth Press, 1966.

SHORT STORIES

FIREMAN FLOWER. London: Hogarth Press, 1944.

THREE. London: Hogarth Press, 1946.

SOUTH: ASPECTS AND IMAGES FROM CORSICA, ITALY AND SOUTHERN FRANCE. London: Hodder and Stoughton, 1948.

THE EQUILIBRIAD. London: Hogarth Press, 1948.

SOMETHING TERRIBLE, SOMETHING LOVELY. London: Hogarth Press, 1948.

THE PASSIONATE NORTH: SHORT STORIES. London: Hogarth Press, 1950.

A TOUCH OF THE SUN. London: Hogarth Press, 1952.

LORD LOVE US. London: Hogarth Press, 1954.

A CONTEST OF LADIES. London: Hogarth Press, 1956.

AMONG THE DAHLIAS. London: Hogarth Press, 1957.

THE STORIES OF WILLIAM SANSOM. London: Hogarth Press, 1963.

THE ULCERATED MILKMAN. London: Hogarth Press, 1966.

THE VERTICAL LADDER AND OTHER STORIES. London: Chatto and Windus, 1969.

CRITICAL ARTICLES

Vickery, John B. "William Sansom and Logical Empiricism." THOUGHT, 36 (Summer 1961), 231-45.

IRWIN SHAW (1913-), AMERICAN

NOVELS

THE YOUNG LIONS. New York: Random House, 1948.

THE TROUBLED AIR. New York: Random House, 1950.

LUCY CROWN. New York: Random House, 1956.

TWO WEEKS IN ANOTHER TOWN. New York: Random House, 1960.

VOICES OF A SUMMER DAY. New York: Delacorte Press, 1965.

RICH MAN, POOR MAN. New York: Delacorte Press, 1970.

SHORT STORIES

SAILOR OFF THE BREMEN AND OTHER STORIES. New York: Random House, 1939.

WELCOME TO THE CITY AND OTHER STORIES. New York: Random House, 1942.

ACT OF FAITH AND OTHER STORIES. New York: Random House, 1946.

MIXED COMPANY: COLLECTED STORIES. New York: Random House, 1950.

TIP ON A DEAD JOCKEY AND OTHER STORIES. New York: Random House, 1957.

LOVE ON A DARK STREET AND OTHER STORIES. New York: Delacorte Press, 1965.

RETREAT AND OTHER STORIES. London: New English Library, 1970.

CRITICAL ARTICLES

Evans, Bergen. "Irwin Shaw." EJ, 60 (1951), 485-91. Also in CE, 13 (1951), 71-77.

Fiedler, Leslie. "Irwin Shaw: Adultery, the Last Politics." Com, 22 (July 1956), 71-74.

Startt, William. "Irwin Shaw: An Extended Talent." MQ, 2 (1961), 325-37.

ROBERT SHAW (1927-), ENGLISH

NOVELS

THE HIDING PLACE. London: Chatto and Windus, 1959.

THE SUN DOCTOR. London: Chatto and Windus, 1961.

THE CURE OF SOULS:
> THE FLAG. London: Chatto and Windus, 1965.
>
> THE MAN IN THE GLASS BOOTH. London: Chatto and Windus, 1967.
>
> A CARD FROM MOROCCO. London: Chatto and Windus, 1969.

CRITICAI ARTICLES

Neumeyer, Peter F. "Arcadia Revisited: Arthur Goldman and Nicholas Poussin." UR, 36 (1970), 263-67.

WILFRID SHEED (1930-), AMERICAN

NOVELS

A MIDDLE CLASS EDUCATION. Boston: Houghton Mifflin, 1960.

THE HACK. New York: Macmillan, 1963.

SQUARE'S PROGRESS. New York: Farrar, Straus, 1965.

OFFICE POLITICS. New York: Farrar, Straus, 1966.

MAX JAMISON. New York: Farrar, Straus, 1970. As THE CRITIC. London: Weidenfeld and Nicolson, 1970.

SHORT STORIES

THE BLACKING FACTORY AND PENNSYLVANIA GOTHIC: A SHORT NOVEL AND A LONG STORY. New York: Farrar, Straus, 1968.

ALAN SILLITOE (1928-), ENGLISH

NOVELS

SATURDAY NIGHT AND SUNDAY MORNING. London: W.H. Allen, 1958.

THE GENERAL. London: W.H. Allen, 1960.

KEY TO THE DOOR. London: Macmillan, 1961.

THE DEATH OF WILLIAM POSTERS. London: Macmillan, 1965.

A TREE ON FIRE. London: Macmillan, 1967.

A START IN LIFE. London: W.H. Allen, 1970.

SHORT STORIES

THE LONELINESS OF THE LONG-DISTANCE RUNNER. London: W.H. Allen, 1959.

THE RAGMAN'S DAUGHTER. London: W.H. Allen, 1963.

GUZMAN GO HOME AND OTHER STORIES. London: Macmillan, 1968.

CRITICAL ARTICLES

Atherton, Stanley S. "Alan Sillitoe's Battleground." DR, 48 (Autumn 1968), 324-31.

Denny, N. "The Achievement of the Long-distance Runner." THEORIA, no. 24 (1965), 1-12.

Gindin, James. "Alan Sillitoe's Jungle." TSLL, 4 (1962), 35-48.

Hurrell, John D. "Alan Sillitoe and the Serious Novel." Crit, 4 (1960-61), 3-16.

Isaacs, Neil D. "No Man in His Humour: A Note on Sillitoe." SSF, 4 (1967), 350-51.

Kermode, Frank. "Rammel." NStat, 69 (15 May 1965), 587-94.

Klotz, Gunther. "Naturalistiche Zuge in Alan Sillitoes Roman SATURDAY NIGHT AND SUNDAY MORNING." ZAA, 10 (1962), 153-61.

Levine, Paul. "Some Middle-Aged Fiction." HudR, 18 (1965-66), 587-94.

McDowell, Frederick P.W. "Self and Society: Alan Sillitoe's KEY TO THE DOOR." Crit, 6 (1963), 116-23.

Penner, Allen R. "Dantesque Allegory in Sillitoe's KEY TO THE DOOR." Ren, 20 (1968), 79-85, 103.

_____. "THE GENERAL: Exceptional Proof of a Critical Rule." SHR, 4 (1970), 135-43.

_____. "Human Dignity and Social Anarchy: Alan Sillitoe's 'The Loneliness of the Long-distance Runner.'" WSCL, 10 (Spring 1969), 253-65.

_____, "Illusory Deluge: Alan Sillitoe's 'Noah's Art.'" CLAJ, 12 (1968), 134-41.

_____. "The Political Prologue and Two Parts of a Trilogy: THE DEATH OF WILLIAM POSTERS and A TREE ON FIRE, A Liturgy for Revolution." UR, 35 (1968), 11-20.

_____. "'What Are Yo' Looking So Bleddy Black For?': Survival and Bitters in 'On Saturday Afternoon.'" SSF, 4 (1967), 300-307.

Roselli, John. "A Cry from the Brick Streets." REPORTER, (10 November 1960), 37-42.

Staples, Hugh B. "SATURDAY NIGHT AND SUNDAY MORNING: Alan Sillitoe and the White Goddess." MFS, 10 (1964), 171-81.

Stephane, Nelly. "Alan Sillitoe." EUROPE, no. 417-18 (1964), 289-93.

Sterne, Richard Clark. "GUZMAN GO HOME AND OTHER STORIES."
SatR, 52 (22 November 1969), 86.

West, Anthony. "On the Inside Looking In." NY, 35 (5 September 1959),
103.

C[HARLES]. P[ERCY]. SNOW (1905-   ), ENGLISH

NOVELS

DEATH UNDER SAIL. London: Heinemann, 1932.

NEW LIVES FOR OLD (published anonymously). London: Gollancz, 1933.

THE SEARCH. London: Gollancz, 1934.

STRANGERS AND BROTHERS:
>   STRANGERS AND BROTHERS. London: Faber, 1940.
>   THE LIGHT AND THE DARK. London: Faber, 1947.
>   TIME OF HOPE. London: Faber, 1949.
>   THE MASTERS. London: Macmillan, 1951.
>   THE NEW MEN. London: Macmillan, 1954.
>   HOMECOMINGS. London: Macmillan, 1956. As HOMECOM-
>   ING. New York: Scribner, 1956.
>   THE CONSCIENCE OF THE RICH. London: Macmillan, 1958.
>   THE AFFAIR. London: Macmillan, 1960.
>   CORRIDORS OF POWER. London: Macmillan, 1964.
>   THE SLEEP OF REASON. London: Macmillan, 1968.
>   LAST THINGS. London: Macmillan, 1970.

CRITICAL BOOKS

Cooper, William. C.P. SNOW. London: Longmans, Green, 1959.

Davis, Robert Gorham. C.P. SNOW. New York: Columbia University Press, 1965.

Greacen, Robert. THE WORLD OF C.P. SNOW. New York: London House and Maxwell, 1963.

Karl, Frederick R. THE POLITICS OF CONSCIENCE: THE NOVELS OF C. P. SNOW. Carbondale: Southern Illinois University Press, 1963.

Leavis, F.R. THE TWO CULTURES: THE SIGNIFICANCE OF C.P. SNOW. New York: Random House, 1963.

Thale, Jerome. C.P. SNOW. Edinburgh: Oliver and Boyd, 1964.

CRITICAL ARTICLES

Adams, Robert. "Pomp and Circumstance: C.P. Snow." ATLANTIC MONTHLY, 214 (November 1964), 95-98.

Bergonzi, Bernard. "The World of Lewis Eliot." TC, 167 (1960), 214-25.

Bernard, Kenneth. "C.P. Snow and Modern Literature." UR, 31 (1965), 231-33.

Burgess, Anthony. "Powers That Be." ENCOUNTER, 24 (January 1965), 71-76.

Cooper, William. "The World of C.P. Snow." NATION, 184 (2 February 1957), 104-5.

Dobree, Bonamy. "The Novels of C.P. Snow." LHY, 2 (July 1961), 28-34.

Finkelstein, Sidney. "The Art and Science of C.P. Snow." MAINSTREAM, 14 (September 1961), 31-57.

Fison, Peter. "A Reply to Bernard Bergonzi's 'The World of Lewis Eliot.'" TC, 167 (1960), 568-71.

Gardner, Helen. "The World of C.P. Snow." NStat, 55 (29 March 1958), 409-10.

Greacen, Robert. "The World of C.P. Snow." TQ, 4 (1961), 266-74.

Green, Martin. "Lionel Trilling and the Two Cultures." EIC, 13 (1963), 375-85.

_____. "A Literary Defence of THE TWO CULTURES." CritQ, 4 (1962), 155–62.

Halio, Jay L. "C.P. Snow's Literary Limitations." NWR, 5 (1962), 97–102.

Hall, William. "The Humanism of C.P. Snow." WSCL, 4 (Spring–Summer 1963), 199–208.

Hamilton, Kenneth. "C.P. Snow and Political Man." QQ, 69 (1962), 416–27.

Jaffa, Herbert C. "C.P. Snow, Portrait of Man as an Adult." HUMANIST, 24 (September–October 1964), 148–50.

Johnson, Pamela Hansford. "Three Novelists and the Drawing of Character." E&S, 3 (1950), 82–89.

Kazin, Alfred. "A Gifted Boy from the Midlands." REPORTER, 20 (5 February 1959), 37–39.

Ketals, Violet B. "Shaw, Snow, and the New Man." Person, 47 (1966), 520–31.

Leavis, F.R. "Two Cultures? The Significance of C.P. Snow." MCR, 5 (1962), 90–101.

MacDonald, Alastair. "Imagery in C.P. Snow." UR, 32 (June 1966), 303–6; (October 1966), 33–38.

Mandel, E.W. "Anarchy and Organization." QQ, 70 (1963), 131–41.

_____. "C.P. Snow's Fantasy of Politics." QQ, 69 (1962), 24–37.

Mayne, Richard. "The Club Armchair." ENCOUNTER, 21 (November 1963), 76–82.

Millgate, Michael. "Structure and Style in the Novels of C.P. Snow." REL, 1 (April 1960), 34–41.

Miner, Earl. "C.P. Snow and the Realistic Novel." NATION, 190 (25 June 1960), 555–56.

Muggeridge, Malcolm. "Oh No, Lord Snow." NRep, 151 (28 November 1964), 27–29.

Murray, Bryon O. "C.P. Snow: Grounds for Reappraisal." Person, 47 (1966), 91–101.

Nott, Kathleen. "The Type to Which the Whole Creation Moves?" EN-COUNTER, 18 (February 1962), 87–88, 94–97.

Rabinovitz, Rubin. "C.P. Snow vs. the Experimental Novel." CuF, 10, iii (1967), 37–41.

Shestakov, Dmitri. "What C.P. Snow Means to Us." SovL, 1 (1966), 174–79.

Smith, LeRoy W. "C.P. Snow as Novelist: A Delimitation." SAQ, 64 (1965), 316–31.

Stanford, Derek. "C.P. Snow: The Novelist as Fox." Meanjin, 19 (1960), 236–51.

_____. "A Disputed Master: C.P. Snow and His Critics." MONTH, 29 (February 1963), 91–94.

_____. "Sir Charles and the Two Cultures." CRITIC, 21 (1962), 17–21.

Stanford, Raney. "The Achievement of C.P. Snow." WHR, 16 (1962), 43–52.

_____. "Personal Politics in the Novels of C.P. Snow." Crit, 2 (1958), 16–28.

Thale, Jerome. "C.P. Snow: The Art of Worldliness." KR, 22 (1960), 621–34.

Turner, Ian. "Above the Snow-Line: The Sociology of C.P. Snow." OVER-LAND, 18 (Winter-Spring 1960), 42–43.

Vogel, Albert W. "The Academic World of C.P. Snow." TCL, 9 (1963), 143–52.

Wagner, Geoffrey. "Writer in the Welfare State." Cweal, 65 (12 October 1956), 49–50.

Wall, Stephen. "The Novels of C.P. Snow." LonM, n.s. 4 (April 1964), 68–74.

Watson, Kenneth. "C.P. Snow and THE NEW MEN." ENGLISH, 15 (1965), 134–39.

Webster, Harvey C. "The Sacrifices of Success." SatR, 41 (12 July 1958), 8–10.

SUSAN SONTAG (1933-), AMERICAN

NOVELS

THE BENEFACTOR. New York: Farrar, Straus, 1963.

DEATH KIT. New York: Farrar, Straus, 1967.

CRITICAL ARTICLES

Holbrook, David. "What New Sensibility?" CQ, 3 (1968), 153-63.

TERRY SOUTHERN (1924-), AMERICAN

NOVELS

FLASH AND FILIGREE. New York: Coward-McCann, 1958.

CANDY, with Mason Hoffenberg (as Maxwell Kenton). Paris: Olympia Press, 1958. By Terry Southern and Mason Hoffenberg. New York: Putnam, 1964.

THE MAGIC CHRISTIAN. New York: Random House, 1960.

BLUE MOVIE. Cleveland: World, 1970.

SHORT STORIES

RED-DIRT MARIJUANA AND OTHER TASTES. New York: New American Library, 1967.

CRITICAL ARTICLES

Algren, Nelson. "The Donkeyman by Twilight." NATION, 198 (18 May 1964), 509-12.

McLaughlin, John J. "Satirical Comical Pornographical CANDY." KanQ, 1 (1969), 98-103.

MURIEL SPARK (1918-), ENGLISH

NOVELS

THE COMFORTERS. London: Macmillan, 1957.

ROBINSON. London: Macmillan, 1958.

MEMENTO MORI. London: Macmillan, 1959.

THE BALLAD OF PECKHAM RYE. London: Macmillan, 1960.

THE BACHELORS. London: Macmillan, 1960.

THE PRIME OF MISS JEAN BRODIE. London: Macmillan, 1961.

THE GIRLS OF SLENDER MEANS. London: Macmillan, 1963.

THE MANDELBAUM GATE. London: Macmillan, 1965.

THE PUBLIC IMAGE. London: Macmillan, 1968.

THE DRIVER'S SEAT. London: Macmillan, 1970.

SHORT STORIES

THE GO-AWAY BIRD AND OTHER STORIES. London: Macmillan, 1958.

VOICES AT PLAY (includes four plays and six stories). London: Macmillan, 1961.

COLLECTED STORIES I. London: Macmillan, 1967.

CRITICAL BOOKS

Malkoff, Karl. MURIEL SPARK. New York: Columbia University Press, 1968.

Stanford, Derek. MURIEL SPARK: A BIOGRAPHICAL AND CRITICAL STUDY. Fontwell, Engl.: Centaur Press, 1963.

CRITICAL ARTICLES

Baldanza, Frank. "Muriel Spark and the Occult." WSCL, 6 (Summer 1965), 190–203.

Berthoff, Warner. "Fortunes of the Novel: Muriel Spark and Iris Murdoch." MR, 8 (1967), 304–13.

Casson, Alan. "Muriel Spark's THE GIRLS OF SLENDER MEANS." Crit, 7 (1965), 94–96.

Cohen, Gerda L. "Tilting the Balance." MIDSTREAM, 12 (January 1966), 68–70.

Davison, Peter. "The Miracles of Muriel Spark." ATLANTIC MONTHLY, 222 (October 1968), 139–42.

Dierickx, J. "A Devil-figure in a Contemporary Setting: Muriel Spark's THE BALLAD OF PECKHAM RYE." RLV, 33 (1967), 576–87.

Dobie, Ann B. "Muriel Spark's Definition of Reality." Crit, 12 (1970), 20–27.

_____. "THE PRIME OF MISS JEAN BRODIE: Muriel Spark Bridges the Credibility Gap." ArQ, 25 (1970), 217–28.

Fay, Bernard. "Muriel Spark en sa fleur." NRF, 14 (1966), 307–15.

Gable, Sister Mariella. "Prose Satire and the Modern Christian Temper." ABR, 11 (1960), 29–30, 33.

Greene, George. "A Reading of Muriel Spark." THOUGHT, 43 (Autumn 1968), 393–407.

Grosskurth, Phyllis. "The World of Muriel Spark: Spirits or Spooks?" TamR, no. 39 (1966), 65–67.

Hynes, Samuel. "The Prime of Muriel Spark." Cweal, 75 (23 February 1962), 562-68.

Jacobsen, Josephine. "A Catholic Quartet." ChS, 47 (1964), 140-43.

Kermode, Frank. "The Novel as Jerusalem: Muriel Spark's MANDELBAUM GATE." ATLANTIC MONTHLY, 216 (October 1965), 92-98.

_____. "The Prime of Miss Muriel Spark." NStat, 66 (27 September 1963), 397-98.

Lanning, George. "Silver Fish in the Plumbing." KR, 23 (1961), 173-75, 177-78.

Lodge, David. "The Uses and Abuses of Omniscience: Method and Meaning in Muriel Spark's THE PRIME OF MISS JEAN BRODIE." CritQ, 12 (1970), 235-57.

Mayne, Richard. "Fiery Particle: On Muriel Spark." ENCOUNTER, 25 (December 1965), 61-68.

Murphy, Carol. "A Spark of the Supernatural." APPROACH, no. 60 (Summer 1966), 26-30.

Ohmann, Carol B. "Muriel Spark's ROBINSON." Crit, 8 (1965), 70-84.

Potter, Nancy A.J. "Muriel Spark: Transformer of the Commonplace." Ren, 17 (1965), 115-20.

Ricks, Christopher. "Extreme Distances." NYRB, 11 (19 December 1968), 30-32.

Romijn Meijer, Henk. "Het satirische talent van Muriel Spark." TIRADE, 6 (1962), 157-69.

Schneider, Harold W. "A Writer in Her Prime: The Fiction of Muriel Spark." Crit, 5 (1962), 28-45.

Soule, George. "Must a Novelist Be an Artist?" CM, 5 (Spring 1964), 92-98.

Stanford, Derek. "The Work of Muriel Spark: An Essay on Her Fictional Method." MONTH, 28 (August 1962), 92-99.

Updike, John. "Creatures of the Air." NY, 37 (30 September 1967), 161-67.

ELIZABETH SPENCER (1921-), AMERICAN

NOVELS

FIRE IN THE MORNING. New York: Dodd, Mead, 1948.

THIS CROOKED WAY. New York: Dodd, Mead, 1952.

THE VOICE AT THE BACK DOOR. New York: McGraw-Hill, 1956.

THE LIGHT IN THE PIAZZA. New York: McGraw-Hill, 1960.

KNIGHTS AND DRAGONS. New York: McGraw-Hill, 1965.

NO PLACE FOR AN ANGEL. New York: McGraw-Hill, 1967.

SHORT STORIES

SHIP ISLAND AND OTHER STORIES. New York: McGraw-Hill, 1968.

CRITICAL ARTICLES

Burger, Nash K. "Elizabeth Spencer's Three Mississippi Novels." SAQ, 63 (1964), 351-54.

Haley, Josephine. "An Interview with Elizabeth Spencer." NMW, 1 (1968), 42-53.

Kauffmann, Stanley. "Sense and Sensibility." NRep, 152 (26 June 1965), 27-28.

Miller, Nolan. "Three of the 'Best.'" AR, 21 (1961), 123-25.

DAVID DEREK STACTON (1923-68), AMERICAN

NOVELS

DOLORES. London: Faber & Faber, 1954.

A FOX INSIDE. London: Faber & Faber, 1955.

THE SELF-ENCHANTED. London: Faber & Faber, 1956.

REMEMBER ME. London: Faber & Faber, 1957.

ON A BALCONY. London: Faber & Faber, 1958.

SEGAKI. London: Faber & Faber, 1958.

A SIGNAL VICTORY. London: Faber & Faber, 1960.

A DANCER IN DARKNESS. London: Faber & Faber, 1960.

THE JUDGES OF THE SECRET COURT. London: Faber & Faber, 1961.

TOM FOOL. London: Faber & Faber, 1962.

OLD ACQUAINTANCE. London: Faber & Faber, 1962.

SIR WILLIAM. London: Faber & Faber, 1963.

KALIYUGA. London: Faber & Faber, 1965.

PEOPLE OF THE BOOK. New York: Putnam, 1965.

CRITICAL BOOKS

Reiss, Malcolm. DAVID DEREK STACTON, 1923–1968. Berkeley: University of California Library, 1968.

Library pamphlet.

JEAN STAFFORD (1915-), AMERICAN

NOVELS

BOSTON ADVENTURE. New York: Harcourt, Brace, 1944.

THE MOUNTAIN LION. New York: Harcourt, Brace, 1947.

THE CATHERINE WHEEL. New York: Harcourt, Brace, 1952.

SHORT STORIES

CHILDREN ARE BORED ON SUNDAY. New York: Harcourt, Brace, 1953.

BAD CHARACTERS. New York: Farrar, Straus, 1964.

COLLECTED STORIES. New York: Farrar, Straus, 1969.

CRITICAL ARTICLES

Burns, Stuart L. "Counterpoint in Jean Stafford's THE MOUNTAIN LION."
Crit, 9 (1967), 20-32.

Hassan, Ihab. "Jean Stafford: The Expense of Style and the Scope of Sensibility." WR, 19 (Spring 1955), 185-203.

Liberman, M.M. "THE COLLECTED STORIES." SR, 77 (1969), 516-29.

Vickery, Olga W. "Jean Stafford and the Ironic Vision." SAQ, 61 (1962), 484-91.

_____. "The Novels of Jean Stafford." Crit, 5 (1962), 14-26.

WALLACE STEGNER (1909-), AMERICAN

NOVELS

REMEMBERING LAUGHTER. Boston: Little, Brown, 1937.

THE POTTER'S HOUSE. Muscatine, Iowa: Prairie Press, 1938.

ON A DARKLING PLAIN. New York: Harcourt, Brace, 1940.

FIRE AND ICE. New York: Duell, Sloan, 1941.

THE BIG ROCK CANDY MOUNTAIN. New York: Duell, Sloan, 1943.

SECOND GROWTH. Boston: Houghton Mifflin, 1947.

THE PREACHER AND THE SLAVE. Boston: Houghton Mifflin, 1950. As JOE
HILL: A BIOGRAPHICAL NOVEL. New York: Doubleday, 1969.

A SHOOTING STAR. New York: Viking Press, 1961.

ALL THE LITTLE LIVE THINGS. New York: Viking Press, 1967.

SHORT STORIES

THE WOMEN ON THE WALL. Boston: Houghton Mifflin, 1950.

THE CITY OF THE LIVING. Boston: Houghton Mifflin, 1956.

CRITICAL ARTICLES

Burke, Hatton. "The Ninth Circle." SR, 70 (1962), 172–75.

Eisenger, Chester E. "Twenty Years of Wallace Stegner." CE, 20 (1958), 110–16.

Flora, Joseph M. "Vardis Fisher and Wallace Stegner: Teacher and Student." WAL, 5 (1970), 121–28.

Harlow, Robert. "Whitmud Revisited." CanL, no. 16 (1963), 63–66.

Saporta, Marc. "Wallace Stegner." INFORMATIONS ET DOCUMENTS, no. 187 (1963), 23–26.

Tyler, R.L. "The I.W.W. and the West." AQ, 12 (1960), 175–87.

RICHARD G[USTAVE]. STERN (1928-   ), AMERICAN

NOVELS

GOLK. New York: Criterion Books, 1960.

EUROPE; OR, UP AND DOWN WITH SCHREIBER AND BAGGISH. New York: McGraw-Hill, 1961.

IN ANY CASE. New York: McGraw-Hill, 1962.

STITCH. New York: Harper, 1965.

SHORT STORIES

TEETH, DYING, AND OTHER MATTERS. New York: Harper, 1964.

1968: A SHORT NOVEL, AN URBAN IDYLL. FIVE STORIES AND TWO TRADE NOTES. New York: Holt Rinehart, 1970.

CRITICAL ARTICLES

Raeder, Robert L. "An Interview with Richard G. Stern." ChiR, 18 (Autumn-Winter 1965-66), 170-75.

DAVID STOREY (1933-), ENGLISH

NOVELS

THIS SPORTING LIFE. London: Longmans, Green, 1960.

FLIGHT INTO CAMDEN. London: Longmans, Green, 1960.

RADCLIFFE. London: Longmans, Green, 1963.

CRITICAL ARTICLES

Churchill, Thomas. "Waterhouse, Storey, and Fowles: Which Way Out of the Room?" Crit, 10 (1968), 72-87.

Gindin, James. "The Fable Begins to Break Down." WSCL, 8 (Winter 1967), 5-8.

McGuiness, Frank. "The Novels of David Storey." LonM, 3 (March 1964), 79-93.

Storey, David. "Writers on Themselves: Journey Through a Tunnel." LISTENER, 70 (1 August 1963), 159-61.

WILLIAM STYRON (1925-), AMERICAN

NOVELS

LIE DOWN IN DARKNESS. Indianapolis: Bobbs-Merrill, 1951.

THE LONG MARCH. New York: Random House, 1956.

SET THIS HOUSE ON FIRE. New York: Random House, 1960.

THE CONFESSIONS OF NAT TURNER. New York: Random House, 1967.

BIBLIOGRAPHY

Schneider, Harold W. "Two Bibliographies: Saul Bellow, William Styron." Crit, 3 (1960), 71-91.

CRITICAL BOOKS

Clarke, John H., ed. WILLIAM STYRON'S "NAT TURNER": TEN BLACK WRITERS RESPOND. Boston: Beacon Press, 1968.

Fossum, Robert H. WILLIAM STYRON. Grand Rapids, Mich.: Eerdmans, 1968.

Friedman, Melvin J., and Irving Malin, eds. WILLIAM STYRON'S "THE CONFESSIONS OF NAT TURNER": A CRITICAL HANDBOOK. Belmont, Calif.: Wadsworth, 1970.

Mackin, Cooper R. WILLIAM STYRON. Austin, Tex.: Steck-Vaughn, 1969.

CRITICAL ARTICLES

Baumbach, Jonathan. "Paradise Lost: The Novels of William Styron." SAQ, 63 (1964), 207-17.

Bell, Bernard W. "The Confessions of Styron." AmD, 5, i (1968), 3-7.

Benson, Alice R. "Techniques in the Twentieth-Century Novel for Relating the Particular to the Universal: SET THIS HOUSE ON FIRE." PMASAL, 48 (1962), 587-94.

Bryant, Jerry H. "The Hopeful Stoicism of William Styron." SAQ, 62 (1963), 539-50.

Core, George. "THE CONFESSIONS OF NAT TURNER and the Burden of the Past." SLJ, 2 (1970), 117-34.

_____. "NAT TURNER and the Final Reckoning of Things." SoR, 4 (1968), 745-51.

Davis, Robert Gorham. "Styron and the Students." Crit, 3 (1960), 37-46.

Durden, Robert F. "William Styron and His Black Critics." SAQ, 68 (1969), 181-87.

Emmanuel, Pierre. "L'histoire d'une solitude." PREUVES, 217 (1969), 17-20.

Fenton, Charles A. "William Styron and the Age of the Slob." SAQ, 59 (1960), 469-76.

Foster, Richard. "An Orgy of Commerce: William Styron's SET THIS HOUSE ON FIRE." Crit, 3 (1960), 59-70.

Friedman, Melvin J. "THE CONFESSIONS OF NAT TURNER: The Convergence of 'Nonfiction Novel' and 'Meditation on History.'" JPC, 1 (1967), 166-75.

_____. "William Styron: An Interim Appraisal." EJ, 50 (1961), 149-58, 192.

Galloway, David D. "The Absurd Man as a Tragic Hero: The Novels of William Styron." TSLL, 6 (1965), 512-34.

Gresset, Michel. "LES CONFESSIONS DE NAT TURNER: L'histoire reele et le roman. Un sociodrame americain." PREUVES, 217 (1969), 3-5.

Hays, Peter L. "The Nature of Rebellion in THE LONG MARCH." Crit, 8 (1966), 70-74.

Holder, Alan. "Styron's Slave: THE CONFESSIONS OF NAT TURNER." SAQ, 68 (1969), 167-80.

Klotz, Marvin. "The Triumph Over Time: Narrative Form in William Faulkner and William Styron." MissQ, 17 (Winter 1963-64), 9-20.

Lawson, John H. "Styron: Darkness and Fire in the Modern Novel." MAIN-STREAM, 13 (October 1960), 9-18.

Lawson, Lewis A. "Cass Kinsolving: Kierkegaardian Man of Despair." WSCL, 3 (Fall 1962), 54-66.

McNamara, Eugene. "William Styron's LONG MARCH: Absurdity and Authority." WHR, 15 (1961), 267-72.

Matthiessen, Peter, and George Plimpton. "The Art of Fiction, V: An Interview with William Styron." ParisR, no. 5 (1954), 42-57.

Moore, L. Hugh. "Robert Penn Warren, William Styron, and the Use of Greek Myth." Crit, 8 (1966), 75-87.

Morse, J. Mitchell. "Social Relevance, Literary Judgment, and the New Right: Or, The Inadvertent Confessions of William Styron." CE, 30 (1969), 605-16.

Mudrick, Marvin. "Mailer and Styron: Guests of the Establishment." HudR, 17 (1964), 346-66.

Neri, Judith. "On the CONFESSIONS of Nat Turner." UMANESIMO, 2 (1968), 135-38.

Newcomb, Horace. "William Styron and the Act of Memory: THE CONFESSIONS OF NAT TURNER." ChiR, 20, i (1968), 86-94.

O'Connell, Shaun. "Expense of Spirit: The Vision of William Styron." Crit, 8 (1966), 20-33.

Ratner, Marc L. "The Rebel Purged: Styron's THE LONG MARCH." ArlQ, 2, ii (1969), 27-42.

_____. "Styron's Rebel." AQ, 21 (1969), 595–608.

Robb, Kenneth A. "William Styron's Don Juan." Crit, 8 (1966), 34–46.

Rubin, Louis D. "William Styron and Human Bondage: THE CONFESSIONS OF NAT TURNER." HC, 4, v (1967), 1–12.

Stevenson, David L. "Styron and the Fiction of the Fifties." Crit, 3 (1960), 47–58.

Swanson, William J. "Religious Implications in THE CONFESSIONS OF NAT TURNER." CimR, 12 (1970), 57–66.

Thompson, John. "Rise and Slay." Com, 44 (November 1967), 81–85.

Tragle, Henry I. "Styron and His Sources." MR, 11 (1970), 134–53.

Urang, Gunnar. "The Broader Vision: William Styron's SET THIS HOUSE ON FIRE." Crit, 8 (1966), 47–69.

Wiemann, Renate. "William Styron: LIE DOWN IN DARKNESS." NS, 19 (1970), 321–32.

HARVEY SWADOS (1920-), AMERICAN

NOVELS

OUT WENT THE CANDLE. New York: Viking Press, 1955.

FALSE COIN. Boston: Little, Brown, 1959.

THE WILL. Cleveland: World, 1963.

STANDING FAST. Garden City, N.Y.: Doubleday, 1970.

SHORT STORIES

ON THE LINE. Boston: Little, Brown, 1957.

NIGHTS IN THE GARDENS OF BROOKLYN. Boston: Little, Brown, 1961.

A STORY FOR TEDDY--AND OTHERS. New York: Simon and Schuster, 1965.

CRITICAL ARTICLES

Feinstein, Herbert. "Contemporary American Fiction: Harvey Swados and Leslie Fiedler." WSCL, 2 (Winter 1961), 79-98.

Mizener, Arthur. "Some Kinds of Modern Novel." SR, 69 (1961), 155-56.

Siegelman, Ellen. "A Battle of Wills: Swados' New Novel." Crit, 7 (1964), 125-28.

ELIZABETH TAYLOR (1912-), ENGLISH

NOVELS

AT MRS. LIPPINCOTE'S. London: Davies, 1945.

PALLADIAN. London: Davies, 1946.

A VIEW OF THE HARBOUR. London: Davies, 1947.

A WREATH OF ROSES. London: Davies, 1949.

A GAME OF HIDE-AND-SEEK. London: Davies, 1951.

THE SLEEPING BEAUTY. London: Davies, 1953.

ANGEL. London: Davies, 1957.

IN A SUMMER SEASON. London: Davies, 1961.

THE SOUL OF KINDNESS. London: Chatto and Windus, 1964.

THE WEDDING GROUP. London: Chatto and Windus, 1968.

SHORT STORIES

HESTER LILLY AND OTHER STORIES. London: Davies, 1954.

THE BLUSH AND OTHER STORIES. London: Davies, 1958.

A DEDICATED MAN AND OTHER STORIES. London: Chatto and Windus, 1965.

CRITICAL ARTICLES

Austin, Richard. "The Novels of Elizabeth Taylor." Cweal, 62 (10 June 1955), 258-59.

Boll, Ernest. "AT MRS. LIPPINCOTE'S and TRISTRAM SHANDY." MLN, 65 (1950), 119-21.

Liddell, Robert. "The Novels of Elizabeth Taylor." REL, 1, ii (April 1960), 54-61.

PETER H[ILLSMAN]. TAYLOR (1919-   ), AMERICAN

NOVELS

A WOMAN OF MEANS. New York: Harcourt, Brace, 1950.

SHORT STORIES

A LONG FOURTH AND OTHER STORIES. New York: Harcourt, Brace, 1948.

THE WIDOWS OF THORNTON. New York: Harcourt, Brace, 1954.

HAPPY FAMILIES ARE ALL ALIKE: A COLLECTION OF STORIES. New York: McDowell, Obolensky, 1959.

MISS LEONORA WHEN LAST SEEN AND FIFTEEN OTHER STORIES. New York. Obolensky, 1963

THE COLLECTED STORIES OF PETER TAYLOR. New York: Farrar, Straus, 1969.

BIBLIOGRAPHY

Smith, James P.   "A Peter Taylor Checklist."   Crit, 9 (1967), 31-36.

CRITICAL ARTICLES

Brown, Ashley.   "The Early Fiction of Peter Taylor."   SR, 70 (1962), 599-602.

Cathey, Kenneth C.   "Peter Taylor: An Evaluation."   WR, 28 (Autumn 1953),

15-17.

Smith, James P. "Narration and Theme in Taylor's A WOMAN OF MEANS." Crit, 9 (1967), 19-30.

Wilcox, Thomas. "A Novelist of Means." SR, 59 (1951), 151-54.

PAUL THEROUX (1941-), AMERICAN

NOVELS

WALDO. Boston: Houghton Mifflin, 1967.

FONG AND THE INDIANS. Boston: Houghton Mifflin, 1968.

GIRLS AT PLAY. Boston: Houghton Mifflin, 1969.

MURDER IN MOUNT HOLLY. London: Alan Ross, 1969.

J[OHN]. R[ONALD]. R[EVEL]. TOLKIEN
(1892-   ), ENGLISH

NOVELS

THE HOBBIT; OR, THERE AND BACK AGAIN. London: Allen and Unwin, 1937.

FARMER GILES OF HAM. London: Allen and Unwin, 1949.

THE LORD OF THE RINGS:

   THE FELLOWSHIP OF THE RING. London: Allen and Unwin, 1954.

   THE TWO TOWERS. London: Allen and Unwin, 1955.

   THE RETURN OF THE KING. London: Allen and Unwin, 1955.

SMITH OF WOOTTON MANOR. London: Allen and Unwin, 1967.

BIBLIOGRAPHY

West, Richard C. "An Annotated Bibliography of Tolkien Criticism." EXTRA-POLATION, 10 (1968), 17-45.

_____. "An Annotated Bibliography of Tolkien Criticism." Orcrist, 1 (1966-67), 32-55; 2 (1967-68), 40-54; 3 (1969), 22-23.

CRITICAL BOOKS

Carter, Lin. TOLKIEN: A LOOK BEHIND "THE LORD OF THE RINGS." New York: Ballantine, 1969.

Ellwood, Gracia F. GOOD NEWS FROM TOLKIEN'S MIDDLE EARTH. Grand Rapids, Mich.: Eerdmans, 1969.

Hillegas, Mark R., ed. SHADOWS OF THE IMAGINATION: THE FAN-
TASIES OF C.S. LEWIS, J.R.R. TOLKIEN, AND CHARLES WILLIAMS.
Carbondale: Southern Illinois University Press, 1969.

Isaacs, Neil D., and Rose A. Zimbardo, eds. TOLKIEN AND THE CRITICS:
ESSAYS ON J.R.R. TOLKIEN'S THE LORD OF THE RINGS. Notre Dame,
Ind.: University of Notre Dame Press, 1968.

Ready, William. THE TOLKIEN RELATION: A PERSONAL INQUIRY. Chicago: Regnery, 1968.

_____. UNDERSTANDING TOLKIEN AND THE LORD OF THE RINGS.
New York: Paperback Library, 1969.

Stimpson, Catharine R. J.R.R. TOLKIEN. New York: Columbia University
Press, 1969.

SPECIAL ISSUES

MANKATO STATE COLLEGE STUDIES, 2 (1967), "The Tolkien Papers."

CRITICAL ARTICLES

Auden, W.H. "At the End of the Quest, Victory." NYTBR, 2 January 1956,
p. 5.

_____. "Good and Evil in THE LORD OF THE RINGS." CritQ, 10 (1968),
138-42.

_____. "The Hero is a Hobbit." NYTBR, 31 October 1954, p. 37.

_____. "The Quest Hero." TQ, 4 (1962), 81-93.

_____. "A World Imaginary, But Real." ENCOUNTER, 3 (November 1954),
59-62.

Ballif, Sandra. "A Sindarin-Quenya Dictionary, More or Less, Listing All
Elvish Words Found in THE LORD OF THE RINGS, THE HOBBIT, and THE
ROAD GOES EVER ON by J.R.R. Tolkien." MYTHLORE, 1, i (1969), 41-
44; ii (1969), 33-36; iv (1969), 23-26.

Beagle, Peter S. "Tolkien's Magic Ring." HOLIDAY, 39 (June 1966), 128,
130, 133-34.

Blissett, William. "The Despots of the Rings." SAQ, 58 (1959), 448–56.

Boswell, George W. "Proverbs and Phraseology in Tolkien's LORD OF THE RINGS Complex." UMSE, 10 (1969), 59–65.

Bradley, Marion Z. "Men, Halfling and Hero Worship." NIEKAS, 16 (30 June 1966), 25–44.

Braude, Nan. "Sion and Parnassus: Three Approaches to Myth." MYTHLORE, 1, i (1969), 6–8.

_____. "Tolkien and Spenser." MYTHLORE, 1, iii (1969), 8–13.

Castell, Daphne. "The Realms of Tolkien." NEW WORLDS, 50 (November 1966), 143–54.

Christensen, Bonniejean M. "Report from the West: Exploitation of THE HOBBIT." Orcrist, 4 (1969), 15–16.

Cox, C.B. "The World of the Hobbits." SPECTATOR, 30 December 1966, p. 844.

Duriez, Colin. "Leonardo, Tolkien, and Mr. Baggins." MYTHLORE, 1, ii (1969), 18–28.

Ellwood, Robert. "The Japanese HOBBIT." MYTHLORE, 1, iii (1969), 14–17.

Epstein, E.L. "The Novels of J.R.R. Tolkien and the Ethnology of Medieval Christendom." PQ, 48 (1969), 517–25.

Evans, W.D. Emrys. "THE LORD OF THE RINGS." THE SCHOOL LIBRARIAN, 16 (December 1968), 284–88.

Fifield, Merle. "Fantasy in the Sixties." EJ, 55 (1966), 841–44.

GoodKnight, Glen. "A Comparison of Cosmological Geography in the Works of J.R.R. Tolkien, C.S. Lewis, and Charles Williams." MYTHLORE, 1, iii (1969), 18–22.

Halle, Louis J. "History Through the Mind's Eye." SatR, 39 (28 January 1956), 11–12.

Hayes, Noreen, and Robert Renshaw. "Of Hobbits: THE LORD OF THE RINGS." Crit, 9 (1967), 58–66.

Hope, Francis. "Welcome to Middle Earth." NStat, 72 (11 November 1966), 701-2.

Huxley, Francis. "The Endless Worm." NStat, 50 (1 November 1955), 587-89.

Irwin, W.R. "There and Back Again: The Romances of Williams, Lewis, and Tolkien." SR, 69 (1961), 566-78.

Juhren, Marcella. "The Ecology of Middle Earth." MYTHLORE, 2, i (1970), 4-6, 9.

Kilby, Clyde S. "The Lost Myth." ASoc, 6 (1969), 155-63.

_____. "Tolkien and Coleridge." Orcrist, 3 (1969), 16-19.

_____. "Tolkien as Scholar and Artist." TJ, 3 (Spring 1967), 9-11.

Leaud, F. "L'Epopee religieuse de J.R.R. Tolkien." EA, 20 (1968), 265-81.

Levitin, Alexis. "The Genre of THE LORD OF THE RINGS." Orcrist, 3 (1969), 4-8, 23.

_____. "Power in THE LORD OF THE RINGS." Orcrist, 4 (1969), 11-14.

Lewis, C.S. "The Dethronement of Power." T&T, 43 (1955), 1373-74.

_____. "The Gods Return to Earth." T&T, 35 (1954), 1082-83.

Lobdell, James C. "Words That Sound Like Castles." NatR, 19 (5 September 1967), 972-74.

Matthewson, Joseph. "The Hobbit Habit." ESQUIRE, 66 (September 1966), 130-31, 221-22.

Menen, Aubrey. "Learning to Love the Hobbits." DIPLOMAT, 18 (October 1966), 32-34, 37-38.

Mesibov, Bob. "Tolkien and Spiders." Orcrist, 4 (1969), 3-5.

Miesel, Sandra L. "Some Motifs and Sources for LORD OF THE RINGS." RQ, 3 (1968), 125-28.

_____. "Some Religious Aspects of LORD OF THE RINGS." RQ, 3 (1968), 209-13.

Miller, David M. "Hobbits: Common Lens for Heroic Experience." Orcrist, 3 (1969), 11-15.

Monsman, Gerald. "The Imaginative World of J.R.R. Tolkien." SAQ, 69 (1970), 264-78.

Norman, Philip. "The Prevalence of Hobbits." NYTMag, 15 January 1967, pp. 30-31, 97, 100, 102.

Ottevaere-van Praag, Ganna. "Retour a l'epopee mythologique: LE MAITRE DES ANNEAUX de J.R.R. Tolkien." RLV, 33 (1967), 237-45.

Parker, Douglass. "Hwaet We Holbytla...." HudR, 9 (1956-57), 598-609.

Pfotenhauer, Paul. "Christian Themes in Tolkien." CRESSET, 32, iii (1969), 13-15.

Ratliff, William E., and Charles G. Flinn. "The Hobbit and the Hippie." ModA, 12 (Spring 1968), 142-46.

Ready, William. "The Tolkien Relation." CANADIAN LIBRARY, 25 (September 1968), 128-36.

Reilly, R.J. "Tolkien and the Fairy Story." THOUGHT, 38 (Spring 1963), 89-103.

Reinken, Donald L. "J.R.R. Tolkien's THE LORD OF THE RINGS: A Christian Refounding of the Political Order." ChrPer, Winter 1966, pp. 16-23.

Roberts, Mark. "Adventure in English." EIC, 6 (1956), 450-59.

Robinson, James. "The Wizard and History: Saruman's Vision of a New Order." Orcrist, 1 (1966-67), 13-17.

Ryan, J.S. "German Mythology Applied--The Extension of the Literary Folk Memory." FOLKLORE, 77 (Spring 1966), 45-59.

Sale, Roger. "England's Parnassus: C.S. Lewis, Charles Williams, and J.R.R. Tolkien." HudR, 17 (1964), 215-25.

Spacks, Patricia M. "'Ethical Patterns' in THE LORD OF THE RINGS." Crit, 3 (1959), 30–42.

Stein, Ruth M. "The Changing Style in Dragons." Elem Eng, 45 (February 1968), 181–83.

Stevens, Cj. "Sound Systems of the Third Age of Middle Earth." QJS, 54 (October 1968), 232–40.

Stewart, Douglas J. "The Hobbit War." NATION, 205 (9 October 1967), 332–35.

Straight, Michael. "Fantastic World of Professor Tolkien." NRep, 134 (16 January 1956), 24–26.

Taylor, William R. "Frodo Lives: J.R. Tolkien's THE LORD OF THE RINGS." EJ, 56 (1967), 818–21.

Thomson, George H. "THE LORD OF THE RINGS: The Novel as Traditional Romance." WSCL, 8 (Winter 1967), 43–59.

Tolkien, J.R.R. "Tolkien on Tolkien." DIPLOMAT, 18 (October 1966), 39.

Traversi, Derek. "The Realm of Gondor." MONTH, 15 (June 1956), 370–71.

Webster, Deborah C. "Good Guys, Bad Guys: A Clarification on Tolkien." Orcrist, 2 (1967–68), 18–23.

West, Richard C. "Contemporary Medieval Authors." Orcrist, 3 (1969), 9–10, 15.

_____. "The Interlace and Professor Tolkien: Medieval Narrative Technique in THE LORD OF THE RINGS." Orcrist, 1 (1966–67), 19–31.

_____. "Tolkien in the Letters of C.S. Lewis." Orcrist, 1 (1966–67), 3–13.

_____. "The Tolkienians: Some Introductory Reflections on Alan Garner, Carol Kendall, and Lloyd Alexander." Orcrist, 2 (1967–68), 4–15.

Wilson, Edmund. "Oo Those Awful Orcs!" NATION, 182 (14 April 1956), 312–14.

Winter, Karen C. "Grendel, Gollum, and the Unman." Orcrist, 2 (1967–68), 28–37.

Wojcik, Jan, S.J. "Tolkien and Coleridge: Remaking of the 'Green Earth.'" Ren, 20 (1968), 134–39, 146.

Woods, Samuel H., Jr. "J.R.R. Tolkien and the Hobbits." CimR, 1 (September 1967), 44–52.

HONOR TRACY [LILBUSH WINGFIELD]
(1915-), ENGLISH

NOVELS

THE DESERTERS. London: Methuen, 1954.

THE STRAIGHT AND NARROW PATH. London: Methuen, 1956.

THE PROSPECTS ARE PLEASING. London: Methuen, 1958.

A NUMBER OF THINGS. London: Methuen, 1960.

A SEASON OF MISTS. London: Methuen, 1961.

THE FIRST DAY OF FRIDAY. London: Methuen, 1963.

MEN AT WORK. London: Methuen, 1966.

THE BEAUTY OF THE WORLD. London: Methuen, 1967. As SETTLED IN
CHAMBERS. New York: Random House, 1968.

THE BUTTERFLIES OF THE PROVINCE. London: Methuen, 1970.

JOHN UPDIKE (1932-   ), AMERICAN

NOVELS

THE POORHOUSE FAIR. New York: Knopf, 1959.

RABBIT, RUN. New York: Knopf, 1960.

THE CENTAUR. New York: Knopf, 1963.

OF THE FARM. New York: Knopf, 1965.

COUPLES. New York: Knopf, 1968.

SHORT STORIES

THE SAME DOOR. New York: Knopf, 1959.

PIGEON FEATHERS AND OTHER STORIES. New York: Knopf, 1962.

THE MUSIC SCHOOL. New York: Knopf, 1966.

BECH: A BOOK. New York: Knopf, 1970.

BIBLIOGRAPHY

Taylor, C. Clarke. JOHN UPDIKE: A BIBLIOGRAPHY. Kent, Ohio: Kent State University Press, 1969.

CRITICAL BOOKS

Hamilton, Alice, and Kenneth, Hamilton. THE ELEMENTS OF JOHN UPDIKE. Grand Rapids, Mich.: Eerdmans, 1969.

Hamilton, Kenneth. JOHN UPDIKE: A CRITICAL ESSAY. Grand Rapids, Mich.: Eerdmans, 1967.

Samuels, Charles T. JOHN UPDIKE. Minneapolis: University of Minnesota Press, 1969.

CRITICAL ARTICLES

Alley, Alvin D. "THE CENTAUR: Transcendental Imagination and Metamorphic Death." EJ, 56 (1967), 982-85.

Brenner, Gerry. "RABBIT, RUN: John Updike's Criticism of the 'Return to Nature.'" TCL, 12 (1966), 3-14.

Burgess, Anthony. "Language, and Myth, and Mr. Updike." Cweal, 88 (11 February 1966), 557-59.

Cimatti, Pietro. "Burroughs e Updike." FLe, 17 (29 August 1962), 3.

DeLogu, Pietro. "La narrativa di John Updike." SA, 10 (1964), 343-68.

Doyle, P.A. "Updike's Fiction: Motifs and Techniques." CathW, 199 (September 1964), 356-62.

Duncan, G.H. "The Thing Itself in 'Rabbit, Run.'" EngR, 13 (April 1963), 36-37.

Fisher, Richard E. "John Updike: Theme and Form in the Garden of Epiphanies." MSpr, 56 (Fall 1962), 255-60.

Flint, Joyce. "John Updike and COUPLES: The WASP's Dilemma." RS, 36 (1968), 340-47.

Galloway, David D. "The Absurd Man as Saint: The Novels of John Updike." MFS, 10 (1964), 111-27.

Guyol, Hazel Sample. "The Lord Loves a Cheerful Corpse." EJ, 55 (1966), 863-66.

Hamilton, Alice. "Between Innocence and Experience: From Joyce to Updike." DR, 49 (1969), 102-9.

Hamilton, Alice, and Kenneth Hamilton. "Theme and Technique in John Updike's MIDPOINT." Mosaic, 4 (1970), 79-106.

Hill, John S. "Quest for Belief: Theme in the Novels of John Updike." SHR, 3 (1969), 166-75.

La Course, Guerin. "The Innocence of John Updike." Cweal, 77 (8 February 1963), 512-14.

Le Vot, Andre. "Le petit monde de John Updike." LanM, 63 (1969), 66-73.

_____. "Updike, ou le mythe d'Antee." LanM, 59 (1965), 50-55.

Muradian, Thaddeus. "The World of Updike." EJ, 54 (1965), 577-84.

Murphy, R.W. "John Updike." HORIZON, 4 (1962), 84-85.

Novak, Michael. "Updike's Quest for Liturgy." Cweal, 78 (10 May 1963), 192-95.

Petillon, Pierre-Yves. "Le desespoir de John Updike." CRITIQUE, 25 (1969), 972-77.

Petter, H. "John Updike's Metaphoric Novels." ES, 50 (1969), 197-206.

Popescu, Petru. "CENTAURUL de John Updike." RoLit, (3 April 1969), 19.

Reising, R.W. "Updike's 'A Sense of Shelter.'" SSF, 7 (1970), 651-52.

Rupp, Richard H. "John Updike: Style In Search of A Center." SR, 75 (1967), 693-709.

Seelbach, Wilhelm. "Die antike Mythologie in John Updikes Roman THE CENTAUR." ARCADIA, 5 (1970), 176-94.

Standley, Fred L. "RABBIT, RUN: An Image of Life." MQ, 8 (1967), 371-81.

Stubbs, John C. "The Search for Perfection in RABBIT, RUN." Crit, 10 (1968), 94-101.

Suderman, Elmer F.   "The Right Way and the Good Way in RABBIT RUN."
UR, 36 (1969), 13-21.

Tate, Sister Judith M.   "John Updike: Of Rabbits and Centaurs."   CEA, 22
(February-March 1964), 44-51.

Ward, J.A.   "John Updike's Fiction."   Crit, 5 (1962), 27-40.

Wyatt, Bryant N.   "John Updike: The Psychological Novel in Search of
Structure."   TCL, 13 (1967), 89-96.

Yates, Norris W.   "The Doubt and Faith of John Updike."   CE, 26 (1965),
469-74.

GORE VIDAL (1925-   ), AMERICAN

NOVELS

WILLIWAW. New York: Dutton, 1946.

IN A YELLOW WOOD. New York: Dutton, 1947.

THE CITY AND THE PILLAR. New York: Dutton, 1948.

THE SEASON OF COMFORT. New York: Dutton, 1949.

A SEARCH FOR THE KING: A 12TH CENTURY LEGEND. New York: Dutton, 1950.

DARK GREEN, BRIGHT RED. New York: Dutton, 1950.

THE JUDGMENT OF PARIS. New York: Dutton, 1952.

DEATH IN THE FIFTH POSITION (as Edgar Box). New York: Dutton, 1952.

DEATH BEFORE BEDTIME (as Edgar Box). New York: Dutton, 1953.

MESSIAH. New York: Dutton, 1954.

DEATH LIKES IT HOT (as Edgar Box). New York: Dutton, 1954.

THREE: WILLIWAW, A THIRSTY EVIL, JULIAN THE APOSTATE. New York: New American Library, 1962.

JULIAN. Boston: Little, Brown, 1964.

WASHINGTON, D.C. Boston: Little, Brown, 1967.

MYRA BRECKINRIDGE. Boston: Little, Brown, 1968.

TWO SISTERS: A MEMOIR IN THE FORM OF A NOVEL. Boston: Little, Brown, 1970.

SHORT STORIES

A THIRSTY EVIL: SEVEN SHORT STORIES. New York: Zero Press, 1956.

CRITICAL BOOKS

White, Ray Lewis. GORE VIDAL. New York: Twayne, 1968.

CRITICAL ARTICLES

Hoffman, Stanton. "The Cities of Night: John Rechy's CITY OF NIGHT and the American Literature of Homosexuality." ChiR, 17, ii-iii (1964-65), 197-98.

Walter, Eugene. "Conversations with Gore Vidal." TRANSATLANTIC REVIEW, no. 4 (Summer 1960), 5-17.

KURT VONNEGUT, JR. (1922-), AMERICAN

NOVELS

PLAYER PIANO. New York: Scribner, 1952.

THE SIRENS OF TITAN. New York: Dell, 1959.

MOTHER NIGHT. New York: Fawcett, 1962.

CAT'S CRADLE. New York: Holt Rinehart, 1963.

GOD BLESS YOU, MR. ROSEWATER; OR, PEARLS BEFORE SWINE. New
York: Holt Rinehart, 1965.

SLAUGHTERHOUSE-FIVE; OR, THE CHILDREN'S CRUSADE. New York:
Delacorte Press, 1969.

SHORT STORIES

CANARY IN A CATHOUSE. New York: Fawcett, 1961.

WELCOME TO THE MONKEY HOUSE: A COLLECTION OF SHORT WORKS.
New York: Delacorte Press, 1968.

CRITICAL ARTICLES

Bryan, C.D.B. "Kurt Vonnegut on Target." NRep, 155 (8 October 1966),
21-26.

Pagetti, Carlo. "Kurt Vonnegut, tra fanta scienza e utopia." SA, 12 (1966),
301-22.

Palmer, Raymond C. "Vonnegut's Major Concerns." IEY, 14 (1969), 3-10.

Scholes, Robert. "'Mithridates, he died old': Black Humor and Kurt Vonnegut, Jr." HC, 3 (October 1966), 1-12.

Tanner, Tony. "The Uncertain Messenger: A Study of the Novels of Kurt Vonnegut, Jr." CritQ, 11 (1969), 297-315.

DAVID R[USSELL]. WAGONER (1926-), AMERICAN

NOVELS

THE MAN IN THE MIDDLE. New York: Harcourt, Brace, 1954.

MONEY MONEY MONEY. New York: Harcourt, Brace, 1955.

ROCK. New York: Viking Press, 1958.

THE ESCAPE ARTIST. New York: Farrar, Straus, 1965.

BABY, COME ON INSIDE. New York: Farrar, Straus, 1968.

WHERE IS MY WANDERING BOY TONIGHT? New York: Farrar, Straus, 1970.

CRITICAL ARTICLES

Schafer, William J. "David Wagoner's Fiction: In the Mills of Satan." Crit, 9 (1967), 71-89.

JOHN WAIN (1925-), ENGLISH

NOVELS

HURRY ON DOWN. London: Secker and Warburg, 1953. As BORN IN CAPTIVITY. New York: Knopf, 1954.

LIVING IN THE PRESENT. London: Secker and Warburg, 1955.

THE CONTENDERS. London: Macmillan, 1958.

A TRAVELLING WOMAN. London: Macmillan, 1959.

STRIKE THE FATHER DEAD. London: Macmillan, 1962.

THE YOUNG VISITORS. London: Macmillan, 1965.

THE SMALLER SKY. London: Macmillan, 1967.

A WINTER IN THE HILLS. London: Macmillan, 1970.

SHORT STORIES

NUNCLE AND OTHER STORIES. London: Macmillan, 1960.

DEATH OF THE HIND LEGS AND OTHER STORIES. London: Macmillan, 1966.

CRITICAL ARTICLES

Bluestone, George. "John Wain and John Barth: The Angry and the Accurate." MR, 1 (1960), 582-89.

Lehmann, J. "The Wain-Larkin Myth." SR, 66 (1958), 578–87.

McDowell, Frederick P.W. "'The Devious Involutions of Human Character and Emotions': Reflections on Some Recent British Novels." WSCL, 4 (Autumn 1963), 342–44.

Mellown, Elgin W. "Steps Toward Vision: The Development of Technique in John Wain's First Seven Novels." SAQ, 68 (1969), 330–42.

O'Connor, William Van. "John Wain: The Will to Write." WSCL, 1 (Winter 1960), 35–49.

Ross, Theodore J. "A Good Girl is Hard to Find." NRep, 141 (21 September 1959), 17–19.

Walzer, Michael. "John Wain: The Hero in Limbo." Per, 10 (1958), 137–45.

Yvard, P. "John Wain: Revolte et neutralite." EA, 23 (1970), 380–94.

REX WARNER (1905-), ENGLISH

NOVELS

THE WILD GOOSE CHASE. London: Boriswood, 1937.

THE PROFESSOR. London: Boriswood, 1938.

THE AERODROME. London: Lane, 1941.

WHY WAS I KILLED? A DRAMATIC DIALOGUE. London: Lane, 1943.
As RETURN OF THE TRAVELLER. Philadelphia: Lippincott, 1944.

MEN OF STONES: A MELODRAMA. London: Lane, 1949.

ESCAPADE: A TALE OF AVERAGE. London: Lane, 1953.

THE YOUNG CAESAR. London: Collins, 1958.

IMPERIAL CAESAR. London: Collins, 1960.

PERICLES THE ATHENIAN. London: Collins, 1963.

THE CONVERTS. London: Bodley Head, 1967.

CRITICAL BOOKS

McLeod, A.L., ed. THE ACHIEVEMENT OF REX WARNER. Sydney: Wentworth, 1965.

_____. REX WARNER: WRITER. Sydney: Wentworth, 1960.

Rajan, B., and Andrew Pearse, eds. FOCUS ONE: KAFKA AND REX WARNER. London: Dobson, 1945.

CRITICAL ARTICLES

Churchill, Thomas. "Rex Warner: Homage to Necessity." Crit, 10 (1968), 30–44.

Davenport, John. "Re-assessment: The Air Marshall's Story." SPECTATOR, 24 June 1966, p. 796.

DeVitis, A.A. "Rex Warner and the Cult of Power." TCL, 6 (1960), 107–16.

Drenner, Don V.R. "Kafka, Warner, and the Cult of Power." KM, 1952, pp. 62–64.

Gorlier, Claudio. "Rex Warner." PARAGONE, 2 (April 1951), 76–80.

Harris, Henry. "The Symbol of the Frontier in the Social Allegory of the 'Thirties.'" ZAA, 14 (1966), 127–40.

Howarth, Herbert. "Pieces of History." Crit, 2 (1956), 54–64.

Maini, Darshan Singh. "Rex Warner's Political Novels: An Allegorical Crusade Against Fascism." IJES, 2 (1961), 91–107.

ROBERT PENN WARREN (1905-), AMERICAN

NOVELS

NIGHT RIDER. Boston: Houghton Mifflin, 1939.

AT HEAVEN'S GATE. New York: Harcourt, Brace, 1943.

ALL THE KING'S MEN. New York: Harcourt, Brace, 1946.

WORLD ENOUGH AND TIME: A ROMANTIC NOVEL. New York: Random House, 1950.

BAND OF ANGELS. New York: Random House, 1955.

THE CAVE. New York: Random House, 1959.

WILDERNESS: A TALE OF THE CIVIL WAR. New York: Random House, 1961.

FLOOD: A ROMANCE OF OUR TIMES. New York: Random House, 1964.

SHORT STORIES

BLACKBERRY WINTER. Cummington, Mass.: Cummington Press, 1946.

THE CIRCUS IN THE ATTIC AND OTHER STORIES. New York: Harcourt, Brace, 1947.

BIBLIOGRAPHY

Beebe, Maurice, and Erin Marcus. "Criticism of Robert Penn Warren: A

Selected Checklist." MFS, 6 (1960), 83-88.

Huff, Mary N. ROBERT PENN WARREN: A BIBLIOGRAPHY. New York: David Lewis, 1968.

CRITICAL BOOKS

Beebe, Maurice, and Leslie Field, eds. ROBERT PENN WARREN'S "ALL THE KING'S MEN": A CRITICAL HANDBOOK. Belmont, Calif.: Wadsworth, 1966.

Bohner, Charles H. ROBERT PENN WARREN. New York: Twayne, 1964.

Casper, Leonard. ROBERT PENN WARREN: THE DARK AND BLOODY GROUND. Seattle: University of Washington Press, 1960.

Longley, John L[ewis]. ROBERT PENN WARREN. Austin, Tex.: Steck-Vaughn, 1969.

_____. ROBERT PENN WARREN: A COLLECTION OF CRITICAL ESSAYS. New York: New York University Press, 1965.

Moore, L. Hugh. ROBERT PENN WARREN AND HISTORY: "THE BIG MYTH WE LIVE." The Hague: Mouton, 1970.

Poenicke, Klaus. ROBERT PENN WARREN: KUNSTWERK UND KRITISCHE THEORIE. Heidelberg: Carl Winter, 1959.

Sochatoff, A. Fred, et al. "ALL THE KING'S MEN": A SYMPOSIUM. Pittsburgh: Carnegie Institute of Technology, 1957.

West, Paul. ROBERT PENN WARREN. Minneapolis: University of Minnesota Press, 1964.

SPECIAL ISSUES

MODERN FICTION STUDIES, 6 (1960), "Special Robert Penn Warren Number."

CRITICAL ARTICLES

Allen, Charles A. "Robert Penn Warren: The Psychology of Self-Knowledge." L&P, 8 (Spring 1958), 21-25.

Anderson, Charles Roberts. "Violence and Order in the Novels of Robert Penn Warren." HoR, 6 (1953), 88–105.

Antonini, Giacomo. "Il Mito della dignita umana. Penn Warren: Nostalgia per il vecchio Sud." FLe, 4 (22 January 1956), 1–2.

_____. "Penn Warren e il primato dello stile." FLe, 1 (12 January 1955), 5–6.

Arnavon, Cyrille. "Robert Penn Warren: Interprete de l'histoire americaine." EUROPE, 494 (1970), 205–26.

Blum, Morgan. "Promises as Fulfillment." KR, 21 (1959), 97–120.

Bradbury, John M. "Robert Penn Warren's Novels: The Symbolic and Textural Patterns." ACCENT, 13 (Spring 1953), 77–89.

Burt, David J., and Annette C. Burt. "Robert Penn Warren's Debt to Ibsen in NIGHT RIDER." MissQ, 22 (1969), 359–61.

Campbell, Harry Modean. "Warren as Philosopher in WORLD ENOUGH AND TIME." HoR, 6 (1953), 106–16.

Casper, Leonard. "Trial By Wilderness: Warren's Exemplum." WSCL, 3 (Fall 1962), 45–53.

_____. "Warren and the Unsuspecting Ancestor." WSCL, 2 (Summer 1961), 43–49.

Clark, Marden J. "Religious Implications in the Novels of Robert Penn Warren." BYUS, 4 (1961), 67–79.

Clements, A.L. "Theme and Reality in AT HEAVEN'S GATE and ALL THE KING'S MEN." CRITICISM, 5 (1963), 27–44.

Davison, Richard A. "Physical Imagery in Robert Penn Warren's 'Blackberry Winter.'" GaR, 22 (1968), 482–88.

_____. "Robert Penn Warren's 'Dialectical Configuration' and THE CAVE." CLAJ, 10 (1967), 349–57.

Douglas, Wallace W. "Drug Store Gothic: The Style of Robert Penn Warren." CE, 15 (1954), 265–72.

Flint, F. Cudworth. "Mr. Warren and the Reviewers." SR, 64 (1956), 632-45.

Frank, Joseph. "Romanticism and Reality in Robert Penn Warren." HudR, 4 (1951), 248-58.

Frank, William. "Warren's Achievement." CE, 19 (1958), 365-66.

Frohock, W.M. "Mr. Warren's Albatross." SWR, 26 (1952), 48-59.

Garrett, George. "The Function of the Pasiphae Myth in BROTHER TO DRAGONS." MLN, 74 (1959), 311-13.

Gerard, Albert. "Robert Penn Warren, romancier de la responsabilite." RGB, 96 (1960), 27-39.

Girault, N.R. "The Narrator's Mind as Symbol: An Analysis of ALL THE KING'S MEN." ACCENT, 7 (Summer 1947), 220-34.

Goldfarb, Russell M. "Robert P. Warren's Tollivers and George Eliot's Tullivers." UR, 36 (1970), 209-13.

Gross, Seymour L. "The Achievement of Robert Penn Warren." CE, 19 (1958), 361-65.

_____. "Conrad and ALL THE KING'S MEN." TCL, 3 (1957), 27-32.

Hardy, John Edward. "Robert Penn Warren's Double Hero." VQR, 36 (1960), 583-97.

Havard, William C. "The Burden of the Literary Mind: Some Meditations on Robert Penn Warren as Historian." SAQ, 62 (1963), 516-31.

Hicks, John. "Exploration of Value: Warren's Criticism." SAQ, 62 (1963), 508-15.

Hynes, Samuel. "Robert Penn Warren: The Symbolic Journey." UKCR, 17 (1951), 279-85.

Inge, M. Thomas. "An American Novel of Ideas." UCQ, 12, iv (1967), 35-40.

Jones, Madison. "The Novels of Robert Penn Warren." SAQ, 62 (1963), 488-98.

Justus, James H. "The Mariner and Robert Penn Warren." TSLL, 7 (1966), 117-28.

_____. "A Note on John Crowe Ransom and Robert Penn Warren." AL, 41 (1969), 425-30.

_____. "The Uses of Gesture in Warren's THE CAVE." MLQ, 26 (1965), 448-61.

_____. "Warren's WORLD ENOUGH AND TIME and Beauchamp's CON-FESSION." AL, 33 (1962), 500-11.

Kaplan, Charles. "Jack Burden: Modern Ishmael." CE, 22 (1966), 19-24.

Kazin, Alfred. "The Seriousness of Robert Penn Warren." PR, 26 (1959), 312-16.

Kelvin, Norman. "The Failure of Robert Penn Warren." CE, 18 (1957), 355-64.

King, Roma A., Jr. "Time and Structure in the Early Novels of Robert Penn Warren." SAQ, 56 (1957), 486-93.

Letargeez, J. "Robert Penn Warren's View of History." RLV, 22 (1956), 533-43.

Longley, John I. "Robert Penn Warren: American Man of Letters." A&S, (Spring 1965), 16-22.

McCarthy, Paul. "Sports and Recreation in ALL THE KING'S MEN." MissQ, 22 (1969), 113-30.

McDowell, Frederick P.W. "Robert Penn Warren's Criticism." ACCENT, 15 (Summer 1955), 173-96.

_____. "The Romantic Tragedy of Self in WORLD ENOUGH AND TIME." Crit, 1 (1957), 34-48.

Martin, Terence. "BAND OF ANGELS: The Definition of Self-definition." FOLIO, 21 (Winter 1955), 31-37.

Meckier, Jerome. "Burden's Complaint: The Disintegrated Personality as Theme and Style in Robert Penn Warren's ALL THE KING'S MEN." SNNTS, 2, i (1970), 7-21.

Mizener, Arthur. "Robert Penn Warren: ALL THE KING'S MEN." SoR, 3 (1967), 874–94.

_____. "The Uncorrupted Consciousness." SR, 72 (Autumn 1964), 690–98.

Mohrt, Michel. "Robert Penn Warren and the Myth of the Outlaw." YFS, no. 10 (1953), 70–84.

Moore, John R. "Robert Penn Warren: You Must Go Home Again." SoR, 4 (1968), 320–32.

Moore, L. Hugh. "Robert Penn Warren and the Terror of Answered Prayer." MissQ, 21 (1968), 29–36.

_____. "Robert Penn Warren, William Styron, and the Use of Greek Myth." Crit, 8 (1966), 75–87.

Payne, Ladell. "Willie Stark and Huey Long: Atmosphere, Myth, or Suggestion?" AQ, 20 (1968), 580–95.

Ray, Robert J. and Ann. "Time in ALL THE KING'S MEN: A Stylistic Analysis." TSLL, 5 (1963), 452–57.

Rubin, Louis D. "All the King's Meanings." GaR, 8 (1954), 422–34.

_____. "'Theories of Human Nature': Kazin or Warren?" SR, 69 (July–September 1961), 500–506.

Ruoff, James. "Humpty Dumpty and ALL THE KING'S MEN: A Note on Robert Penn Warren's Teleology." TCL, 3 (1957), 128–34.

Ryan, Alvan S. "Robert Penn Warren's NIGHT RIDER: The Nihilism of the Isolated Temperament." MFS, 7 (1961), 338–46.

Sale, Roger. "Having It Both Ways in ALL THE KING'S MEN." HudR, 14 (1961), 68–76.

Samuels, Charles T. "In the Wilderness." Crit, 5 (1962), 46–57.

Scott, James B. "The Theme of Betrayal in Robert Penn Warren's Stories." THOTH, 5 (1964), 74–84.

Shepherd, Allen. "Character and Theme in R.P. Warren's FLOOD." Crit, 9 (1967), 95–102.

_____ . "Robert Penn Warren as a Philosophical Novelist." WHR, 24 (1970), 157-68.

_____ . "Robert Penn Warren's 'Prime Leaf' as Prototype of NIGHT RIDER." SSF, 7 (1970), 469-71.

Sillars, Malcolm O. "Warren's ALL THE KING'S MEN: A Study in Populism." AQ, 9 (1957), 345-53.

Stewart, John L. "Robert Penn Warren and the Knot of History." ELH, 26 (1959), 102-36.

Strout, Cushing. "ALL THE KING'S MEN and the Shadow of William James." SoR, 6 (1970), 920-34.

Strugnell, John R. "Robert Penn Warren and the Uses of the Past." REL, 4, iv (October 1963), 93-102.

Sullivan, Walter. "The Historical Novelist and the Existential Peril: Robert Penn Warren's BAND OF ANGELS." SLJ, 2 (1970), 104-16.

Warren, Robert Penn. "ALL THE KING'S MEN: The Matrix of Experience." YR, 53 (1964), 161-67.

_____ . "Writer at Work: How a Story Was Born and How, Bit by Bit, It Grew." NYTBR, (1 March 1959), 4-5, 36.

Wasserstrom, William. "Robert Penn Warren: From Paleface to Redskin." PrS, 31 (1957), 323-33.

Watkins, Floyd C. "Billie Potts at the Fall of Time." MissQ, 11 (1958), 19-28.

Weathers, Winston. "'Blackberry Winter' and the Use of Archetypes." SSF, 1 (1964), 45-51.

Weissbuch, Ted N. "Jack Burden: Call Me Carraway." CE, 22 (1961), 361.

White, Robert. "Robert Penn Warren and the Myth of the Garden." FaS, 3 (Winter 1954), 59-67.

Whittington, Curtis, Jr. "The 'Burden' of Narration: Democratic Perspective and First-Person Point of View in the American Novel." SHR, 2, (1968), 236-45.

Wilcox, Earl. "Warren's ALL THE KING'S MEN, Epigraph." Expl, 26 (1967), Item 29.

KEITH [SPENCER] WATERHOUSE (1929-   ), ENGLISH

NOVELS

THERE IS A HAPPY LAND. London: Joseph, 1957.

BILLY LIAR. London: Joseph, 1959.

JUBB. London: Joseph, 1963.

THE BUCKET SHOP. London: Joseph, 1968. As EVERYTHING MUST GO.
New York: Putnam, 1969.

CRITICAL ARTICLES

Churchill, Thomas. "Waterhouse, Storey, and Fowles: Which Way Out of
the Room?" Crit, 10 (1968), 72-07.

JEROME WEIDMAN (1913-), AMERICAN

NOVELS

I CAN GET IT FOR YOU WHOLESALE. New York: Simon and Schuster, 1937.

WHAT'S IN IT FOR ME? New York: Simon and Schuster, 1938.

I'LL NEVER GO THERE ANYMORE. New York: Simon and Schuster, 1941.

THE LIGHTS AROUND THE SHORE. New York: Simon and Schuster, 1943.

TOO EARLY TO TELL. New York: Reynal, 1946.

THE PRICE IS RIGHT. New York: Harcourt, Brace, 1949.

THE HAND OF THE HUNTER. New York: Harcourt, Brace, 1951.

GIVE ME YOUR LOVE. New York: Eton, 1952.

THE THIRD ANGEL. Garden City, N.Y.: Doubleday, 1953.

YOUR DAUGHTER IRIS. Garden City, N.Y.: Doubleday, 1955.

THE ENEMY CAMP. New York: Random House, 1958.

BEFORE YOU GO. New York: Random House, 1960.

THE SOUND OF BOW BELLS. New York: Random House, 1962.

WORD OF MOUTH. New York: Random House, 1964.

413

OTHER PEOPLE'S MONEY. New York: Random House, 1967.

THE CENTER OF THE ACTION. New York: Random House, 1969.

FOURTH STREET EAST. New York: Random House, 1970.

SHORT STORIES

THE HORSE THAT COULD WHISTLE "DIXIE" AND OTHER STORIES. New York: Simon and Schuster, 1939.

THE CAPTAIN'S TIGER. New York: Reynal, 1947.

A DIME A THROW. Garden City, N.Y.: Doubleday, 1957.

MY FATHER SITS IN THE DARK AND OTHER SELECTED STORIES. New York: Random House, 1961. As WHERE THE SUN NEVER SETS AND OTHER STORIES. London: Heinemann, 1964.

THE DEATH OF DICKIE DRAPER AND NINE OTHER STORIES. New York: Random House, 1965.

CRITICAL ARTICLES

Rosenthal, Raymond. "What's In It for Weidman?" Com, 27 (February 1959), 171-73.

EUDORA WELTY (1909-), AMERICAN

NOVELS

THE ROBBER BRIDEGROOM. Garden City, N.Y.: Doubleday, 1942.

DELTA WEDDING. New York: Harcourt, Brace, 1946.

THE PONDER HEART. New York: Harcourt, Brace, 1954.

LOSING BATTLES. New York: Random House, 1970.

SHORT STORIES

A CURTAIN OF GREEN. Garden City, N.Y.: Doubleday, 1941.

THE WIDE NET AND OTHER STORIES. New York: Harcourt, Brace, 1943.

THE GOLDEN APPLES. New York: Harcourt, Brace, 1949.

SELECTED STORIES. New York: Modern Library, 1954.

THE BRIDE OF THE INNISFALLEN AND OTHER STORIES. New York: Harcourt, Brace, 1955.

THIRTEEN STORIES. New York: Harcourt, Brace, 1965.

BIBLIOGRAPHY

Gross, Seymour L. "Eudora Welty: A Bibliography of Criticism and Comment." SECRETARY'S NEWS SHEET, BIBLIOGRAPHICAL SOCIETY, UNIVERSITY OF VIRGINIA, no. 45 (1960), 1-32.

Jordan, Leona. "Eudora Welty: Selected Criticism." BB, 23 (1960), 14–15.

McDonald, W.U., Jr. "Eudora Welty Manuscripts: An Annotated Finding List." BB, 24 (1963), 44–46.

Smythe, Katherine H. "Eudora Welty: A Checklist." BB, 26 (1956), 207-8.

CRITICAL BOOKS

Appel, Alfred, Jr. A SEASON OF DREAMS: THE FICTION OF EUDORA WELTY. Baton Rouge: Louisiana State University Press, 1965.

Bryant, J.A., Jr. EUDORA WELTY. Minneapolis: University of Minnesota Press, 1964.

Isaacs, Neil D. EUDORA WELTY. Austin, Tex.: Steck-Vaughn, 1969.

Kieft, Ruth M. Vande. EUDORA WELTY. New York: Twayne, 1962.

SPECIAL ISSUES

SHENANDOAH, 20, iii (1969), "Special Eudora Welty Number."

CRITICAL ARTICLES

Appel, Alfred, Jr. "Powerhouse's Blues." SSF, 2 (1966), 221-34.

Blackwell, Louise. "Eudora Welty: Proverbs and Proverbial Phrases in THE GOLDEN APPLES." SFQ, 30 (1966), 332-41.

Bradham, Jo Allen. "'A Visit of Charity': Menippean Satire." SSF, 1 (1964), 258-63.

Buswell, Mary Catherine. "The Love Relationships of Women in the Fiction of Eudora Welty." WVUPP, 13 (1962), 94-106.

Cochran, Robert W. "Welty's 'Petrified Man.'" Expl, 27 (1968), Item 25.

Curley, Daniel. "Eudora Welty and the Quondam Obstruction." SSF, 5 (1968), 209-24.

Daly, Saralyn R. "'A Worn Path' Retrod." SSF, 1 (1964), 133-39.

Daniel, Robert. "The World of Eudora Welty." HoR, 6 (1953), 49-58.

Drake, Robert. "Comments on Two Eudora Welty Stories." MissQ, 13 (1960), 123-31.

_____. "The Reasons of the Heart." GaR, 11 (1957), 420-26.

French, Warren. "A Note on Eudora Welty's THE PONDER HEART." CE, 15 (1954), 474.

Galli, Lorenza. "La narrativa di Eudora Welty." SA, 5 (1959), 281-300.

Gorlier, Claudio. "Tre Esperienze Narrative." GALLERIA, 4 (December 1954), 349-59.

Gossett, Louise Y. "Eudora Welty's New Novel: The Comedy of Loss." SLJ, 3 (1969), 122-37.

Graham, Kenneth. "La double vision d'Eudora Welty." NRF, (17 November 1969), 744-53.

Griffith, Albert J. "The Numinous Vision: Eudora Welty's 'Clytie.'" SSF, 4 (1966), 80-82.

_____. "Welty's 'Death of a Traveling Salesman.'" Expl, 20 (1962), Item 38.

Griffith, Benjamin W. "'Powerhouse' as a Showcase of Eudora Welty's Methods and Themes." MissQ, 19 (1966), 79-84.

Hardy, John Edward. "The Achievement of Eudora Welty." SHR, 2 (1968), 269-78.

_____. "DELTA WEDDING as Region and Symbol." SR, 60 (1952), 397-418.

Harris, Wendell V. "The Thematic Unity of Welty's THE GOLDEN APPLES." TSLL, 6 (1964), 92-95.

_____. "Welty's 'The Key.'" Expl, 17 (1958), Item 61.

Hartley, Lodwick. "Proserpina and the Old Ladies." MFS, 3 (1957), 350-54.

Henley, Elton F. "Confinement-Escape Symbolism in Eudora Welty's 'Livvie.'" IEY, 10 (1965), 60-63.

Hicks, Granville. "Eudora Welty." CE, 14 (1952), 69-76.

Hodgins, Audrey. "The Narrator as Ironic Device in a Short Story of Eudora Welty." TCL, 1 (1956), 215-19.

Holland, Robert B. "Dialogue as a Reflection of Place in THE PONDER HEART." AL, 35 (1963), 352-58.

Howell, Elmo. "Eudora Welty's Comedy of Manners." SAQ, 69 (1970), 469-79.

_____. "Eudora Welty's Negroes: A Note on 'A Worn Path.'" XUS, 9 (1970), 28-32.

Isaacs, Neil D. "Four Notes on Eudora Welty." NMW, 2 (1969), 42-54.

_____. "Life for Phoenix." SR, 61 (January-March 1963), 75-81.

Jones, William M. "Eudora Welty's Use of Myth in 'Death of a Traveling Salesman.'" JAF, 73 (1960), 18-23.

_____. "Growth of a Symbol: The Sun in Lawrence and Eudora Welty." UKCR, 26 (1959), 68-73.

_____. "Name and Symbol in the Prose of Eudora Welty." SFQ, 22 (1958), 173-85.

_____. "The Plot as Search." SSF, 5 (1967), 37-43.

_____. "Welty's 'A Worn Path.'" Expl, 15 (1957), Item 57.

_____. "Welty's 'Petrified Man.'" Expl, 15 (1957), Item 21.

Kieft, Ruth M. Vande. "The Mysteries of Eudora Welty." GaR, 15 (1961), 343-57.

Kirkpatrick, Smith. "The Annotated Powerhouse." SR, (1969), 94-108.

Lief, Ruth Ann. "A Progression of Answers." SSF, 2 (1965), 343-50.

McBurney, William H. "Welty's 'The Burning.'" Expl, 16 (1957), Item 9.

McDonald, W.U., Jr. "Eudora Welty's Revisions of 'A Piece of News.'" SSF, 7 (1970), 232-47.

_____. "Welty's 'Kella': Irony, Ambiguity, and the Ancient Mariner." SSF, 1 (1964), 59-61.

_____. "Welty's 'Social Consciousness': Revisions of 'The Whistle.'" MFS, 16 (1970), 193-98.

May, Charles E. "The Difficulty of Loving in 'A Visit of Charity.'" SSF, 6 (1969), 338-41.

Morris, Harry C. "Eudora Welty's Use of Mythology." SHENANDOAH, 6 (Spring 1955), 34-40.

_____. "Zeus and the Golden Apples: Eudora Welty." PERSPECTIVES USA, 5 (1953), 190-99.

Opitz, Kurt. "Eudora Welty: The Order of a Captive Soul." Crit, 7 (1965), 79-91.

Palmer, Melvin Delmar. "Welty's 'A Visit of Charity.'" Expl, 22 (1964), Item 69.

Ringe, Donald A. "Welty's 'Petrified Man.'" Expl, 18 (1960), Item 32.

Rubin, Louis D. "Two Ladies of the South." SR, 63 (August 1955), 671-81.

Toole, William B. III. "The Texture of 'A Visit of Charity.'" MissQ, 20 (1967), 43-46.

Trefman, Sara. "Welty's 'A Worn Path.'" Expl, 24 (1966), Item 56.

Vickery, John B. "William Blake and Eudora Welty's 'Death of a Salesman.'" MLN, 76 (1961), 625-32.

Welty, Eudora. "The Eye of the Story." YR, 55 (1966), 265-74.

_____. "How I Write." VQR, 31 (1955), 240-55.

_____. "Must the Novelist Crusade?" ATLANTIC REVIEW, 216 (1965), 104-8.

_____. "Place in Fiction." SAQ, 55 (1956), 57-72.

_____. "Words into Fiction." SoR, 1 (1965), 543-53.

West, Ray B., Jr. "Three Methods of Modern Fiction: Ernest Hemingway, Thomas Mann, Eudora Welty." CE, 12 (1951), 193-203.

ANTHONY [PANTHER] WEST (1914-   ), ENGLISH

NOVELS

ON A DARK NIGHT. London: Eyre and Spottiswoode, 1949. As THE VIN-
TAGE. Boston: Houghton Mifflin, 1950.

ANOTHER KIND. London: Eyre and Spottiswoode, 1951.

HERITAGE. New York: Random House, 1955.

THE TREND IS UP. London: Hamish Hamilton, 1961.

DAVID REES AMONG OTHERS. London: Hamish Hamilton, 1970.

JOHN [ALFRED] WILLIAMS (1925-   ), AMERICAN

NOVELS

THE ANGRY ONES. New York: Ace, 1960.

NIGHT SONG. New York: Farrar, Straus, 1961.

SISSIE. New York: Farrar, Straus, 1963. As JOURNEY OUT OF ANGER.
London: Eyre and Spottiswoode, 1965.

THE MAN WHO CRIED I AM. Boston: Little, Brown, 1967.

SONS OF DARKNESS, SONS OF LIGHT. Boston: Little, Brown, 1969.

ANGUS WILSON (1913-), ENGLISH

NOVELS

HEMLOCK AND AFTER. London: Secker and Warburg, 1952.

ANGLO-SAXON ATTITUDES. London: Secker and Warburg, 1956.

THE MIDDLE AGE OF MRS. ELIOT. London: Secker and Warburg, 1958.

THE OLD MEN AT THE ZOO. London: Secker and Warburg, 1961.

LATE CALL. London: Secker and Warburg, 1964.

NO LAUGHING MATTER. London: Secker and Warburg, 1967.

SHORT STORIES

THE WRONG SET AND OTHER STORIES. London: Secker and Warburg, 1949.

SUCH DARLING DODOS AND OTHER STORIES. London: Secker and War-burg, 1950.

A BIT OFF THE MAP AND OTHER STORIES. London: Secker and Warburg, 1957.

DEATH DANCE: TWENTY-FIVE STORIES. New York: Viking Press, 1969.

CRITICAL BOOKS

Gransden, K.W. ANGUS WILSON. London: Longmans, Green, 1969.

Halio, Jay L. ANGUS WILSON. Edinburgh: Oliver & Boyd, 1964.

CRITICAL ARTICLES

Biles, Jack I. "A STUDIES IN THE NOVEL Interview: An Interview in London with Angus Wilson." SNNTS, 2, i (1970), 76-87.

Bradbury, Malcolm. "The Short Stories of Angus Wilson." SSF, 3 (1966), 117-25.

Burgess, Anthony. "Powers That Be." ENCOUNTER, 24 (January 1965), 71-76.

Cockshut, A.O.J. "Favoured Sons: The Moral World of Angus Wilson." EIC, 9 (1959), 50-60.

Cox, C.B. "The Humanism of Angus Wilson: A Study of HEMLOCK AND AFTER." CritQ, 3 (1961), 227-37.

Drescher, Horst W. "Angus Wilson: An Interview." NS, 17 (1968), 351-56.

Engelborghs, Maurits. "Kroniek: Engelse letteren: Werk van Angus Wilson." DWB, 102 (1957), 181-89.

Gindin, James. "The Fable Breaks Down." WSCL, 8 (Winter 1967), 10-17.

_____. "The Reassertion of the Personal." TQ, 1 (1958), 126-34.

Halio, Jay L. "The Novels of Angus Wilson." MFS, 8 (1962), 171-81.

Katona, Anna. "Angus Wilson's Fiction and its Relation to the English Tradition." ALitASH, 10 (1968), 111-27.

Kermode, Frank. "Mr. Wilson's People." SPECTATOR, 21 November 1958, pp. 705-6.

Lindberg, Margaret. "Angus Wilson: THE OLD MEN AT THE ZOO as Allegory." IEY, 14 (1969), 44-48.

Millgate, Michael. "Angus Wilson." ParisR, no. 17 (1958), 89-105.

Narita, Seiju. "A Reformer, not a Revolutionary." EigoS, 115 (1969), 752-59.

Poston, Lawrence. "A Conversation with Angus Wilson." BA, 40 (1966), 29-31.

Scott-Kilvert, Ian. "Angus Wilson." REL, 1, ii (1960), 42-53.

Servotte, Herman. "Experiment en traditie: Angus Wilson's NO LAUGHING MATTER." DWB, 113 (1968), 324-35.

Shaw, Valerie A. "THE MIDDLE AGE OF MRS. ELIOT and LATE CALL: Angus Wilson's Traditionalism." CritQ, 12 (1970), 9-27.

Smith, William J. "Angus Wilson's England." Cweal, 82 (26 March 1965), 18-21.

Trickett, Rachel. "Recent Novels: Craftsmanship in Violence and Sex." YR, 57 (1968), 446-48.

Vallette, J. "Angus Wilson un peu par lui-meme." MdF, 334, no. 1142 (1958), 313-16.

COLIN WILSON (1931-), ENGLISH

NOVELS

RITUAL IN THE DARK. London: Gollancz, 1960.

ADRIFT IN SOHO. London: Gollancz, 1961.

THE WORLD OF VIOLENCE. London: Gollancz, 1963. As THE VIOLENT WORLD OF HUGH GREEN. Boston: Houghton Mifflin, 1963.

MAN WITHOUT A SHADOW: THE DIARY OF AN EXISTENTIALIST. London: Barker, 1963. As THE SEX DIARY OF GERARD SORME. New York: Dial Press, 1963.

NECESSARY DOUBT. London: Barker, 1964.

THE GLASS CAGE: AN UNCONVENTIONAL DETECTIVE STORY. London: Barker, 1966.

THE MIND PARASITES. London: Barker, 1967.

THE PHILOSOPHER'S STONE. London: Barker, 1969.

THE KILLERS. London: New English Library, 1970. As LINGARD. New York: Crown, 1970.

THE GOD OF THE LABYRINTH. London: Hart-Davis, 1970.

CRITICAL BOOKS

Campion, Sidney. THE WORLD OF COLIN WILSON. London: Muller, 1963.

CRITICAL ARTICLES

Dillard, R.H. "Toward an Existential Realism: The Novels of Colin Wilson."
HC, 4, iv (October 1967), 1-12.

HERMAN WOUK (1915-), AMERICAN

NOVELS

AURORA DAWN. New York: Simon and Schuster, 1947.

THE CITY BOY. New York: Simon and Schuster, 1948.

THE CAINE MUTINY. Garden City, N.Y.: Doubleday, 1951.

MARJORIE MORNINGSTAR. Garden City, N.Y.: Doubleday, 1955.

YOUNGBLOOD HAWKE. Garden City, N.Y.: Doubleday, 1962.

DON'T STOP THE CARNIVAL. Garden City, N.Y.: Doubleday, 1965.

CRITICAL ARTICLES

Browne, James R. "Distortion in THE CAINE MUTINY." CE, 17 (1956), 216–18.

Carpenter, Frederic I. "Herman Wouk." CE, 17 (1956), 211–15.

———. "Herman Wouk and the Wisdom of Disillusion." EJ, 45 (1956), 1–6, 32.

Fitch, Robert E. "The Bourgeois and the Bohemian." AR, 16 (1956), 131–45.

Geismar, Maxwell. "The Age of Wouk." NATION, 181 (5 November 1955), 399–400.

Gordis, Robert. "Religion and One Dimension: The Judaism of Herman Wouk." MIDSTREAM, 6 (Winter 1960), 82-90.

McElderry, B.R. "The Conservative as Novelist." ArQ, 15 (1959), 128-36.

Swados, Harvey. "Popular Taste in THE CAINE MUTINY." PR, 20 (1953), 248-56.

Wouk, Herman. "On Being Put under Glass." CLC, 5 (1956), 3-9.

AUTHOR AND CRITIC INDEX

AUTHOR AND CRITIC INDEX

This index is alphabetized letter-by-letter and numbers refer to page numbers. The name of each writer of fiction considered in the text is capitalized and inclusive page numbers are given for his/her section. When multiple articles by one critic appear on a page, the number of articles appears in parentheses following the page number, e.g., Aldridge, John W. 8 (2), 107.

Bondy, Francois 48
Bone, Robert A. 9, 48, 142
Bonosky, Philip 48
Booth, Wayne C. 246
Bork, Alfred M. 129
Bosano, J. 197
Bosquet, Alain 129
Bostwick, Sally 319
Boswell, George W. 381
BOURJAILY, VANCE 85
Bowden, Edwin T. 124
BOWEN, JOHN 87
Bowen, Robert O. 275
Bowering, George 313
Bowers, Frederick 149
Bowles, Patrick 67
BOWLES, PAUL 89-90
Boyle, Alexander 181 (2)
BOYLE, KAY 91-92
Boyle, Ted E. 34, 163
Bracher, Frederick 112 (2)
Bradbury, John M. 3, 405
Bradbury, Malcolm 75 (3), 253, 426
Bradford, M. E. 48
Bradham, Jo Allen 416
Bradley, Marion Z. 381
Brady, Charles A. 243
BRAINE, JOHN 93-94
Branch, Edgar M. 319
Braude, Nan 381 (2)
Braybrook, Neville 163 (2), 181 (3)
Bree, Germaine 68
Breit, Harvey 28
Brenner, Conrad 259
Brenner, Gerry 390
Brewer, J. E. 193, 216, 315
Brewster, Dorothy 216
Brick, Allan 68, 259
Brierre, Annie 203
Brittain, Joan T. 273 (2), 275 (2)
Brockway, James 163
Bromberg, Jan 203
Brooke, Jocelyn 292
BROOKE-ROSE, CHRISTINE 95
Brooke-Rose, Christine 68
Brooks, Van Wyck 4
BROPHY, BRIGID 97
Broughton, George 28
Broughton, Panthea R. 28

Brower, Brock 220
Brown, Ashley 289, 375
Brown, Clayton M. 200
Brown, Daniel R. 197
Brown, Terence 34
Browne, James R. 431
Browne, Robert M. 319
Browning, Preston, Jr. 275
Bruell, Edwin 287
Bruccoli, Matthew 319
Bryan, C. D. B. 395
Bryan, James E. 319 (4)
Bryant, J. A., Jr. 416
Bryant, Jerry H. 368
Bryden, Ronald 181
Bryer, Jackson R. 55, 66, 191, 258
Bucco, Martin 108 (2)
Buckeye, Robert 307
BUECHNER, FREDERICK 99
Bufkin, E. C. 7, 163 (2), 270
Bungert, Haus 319
Burger, Nash K. 28, 355
BURGESS, ANTHONY 101-2
Burgess, Anthony 5, 181, 342, 390, 426
Burgess, C. F. 295
Burke, Hatton 362
Burke, John J., Jr., S.J. 275
Burkom, Selma R. 216 (2)
Burns, Stuart L. 275 (4), 359
Burress, L. A. 203
Burris, Shirley W. 304
BURROUGHS, WILLIAM 103-4
Burt, Annette C. 405
Burt, David J. 405
Burton, Arthur 196
Buswell, Mary Catherine 416
Byatt, A. S. 252
Byrd, Scott 56

C

Cagle, Charles 319
Calder, John 66
Calder-Marshall, Arthur 181
CALISHER, HORTENSE 105
Callan, Edward 287
Cambon, Glauco 75
Campbell, Felicia F. 259

Author and Critic Index

Author and Critic Index